Problems in European Politics

Problems in European Politics

Kenneth Christie

National University of Singapore

Nelson-Hall Publishers / Chicago

Project editor: Dorothy Anderson
Copy editor: Carol Albright
Typesetter: Precision Typographers
Printer: Capital City Press
Cover Painting: "Sea of Dreams" by Paula Bain

Library of Congress Cataloging-in-Publication Data

Christie, Kenneth.
  Problems in European politics / Kenneth Christie.
    p.   cm.
  Includes bibliographical references and index.
  ISBN 0-8304-1323-5
    1. Europe—Politics and science—1989–   I. Title.
D2009.C47   1995
320.94—dc20   94-27604
                                                                               CIP

Manufactured in the United States of America

10 9 8 7 6 5 4 3 2 1

 The paper used in this book meets the minimum requirements of American National Standard for Information Sciences—Permanence of Paper for Printed Library Materials, ANSI Z39.48-1984.

For my daughter,
Jacqueline Hope Christie

Contents

Acknowledgments

I would like to acknowledge the insights and suggestions of my undergraduate students over the years. At Florida State University and the National University of Singapore, I learned that many students were and are increasingly interested in the "undercurrents" of European (and other) politics rather than informative but descriptive accounts of different institutions. To a large extent they prompted and stimulated me to write a text on topics and issues that made them (and me) think more about some of the underlying problems and agendas in Western Europe.

On a personal note I would like to thank my best friend, Jim Shedden, who was always there to encourage and support me in my professional and personal life despite the long distances involved. And finally, I would like to thank Richard Meade and Dorothy Anderson of Nelson-Hall, and Carol Albright, editor, for their support and useful suggestions in the production of this text.

When I had re-read the text I thought that the following quote would be a suitable introduction to the problems facing Western Europe today.

> We are often told that the present age is an age of cynicism and despair, of crumbling values and the dissolution of fixed standards and landmarks of Western civilization. But this is neither true nor even plausible. So far from showing the loose texture of a collapsing order, the world is today stiff with rigid rules and codes and ardent, irrational religions. So far from evincing the toleration which springs from the cynical disregard of the ancient sanctions, it treats heterodoxy as the supreme danger.
> —Sir Isaiah Berlin,
> *Political Ideas in the Twentieth Century* (1950)

ix

1
Introduction: Patterns and Trends in Western European Politics

The New Europe. It's a curiously old-fashioned and American, even Wilsonian, concept: the dream that a jaded old continent, so drenched in blood, so haunted by the ghosts of dead ideologies, can be renewed overnight born again as a peaceful consumer society. The Gaul will lie down with the Teuton, the Russian with the Pole. Abkhazian and Georgian will live in harmony and none shall have a dark, chauvinist, violent thought. . . . Welcome to the oldest of Europes, seethingly dangerous beneath the New.[1]

A Framework for Studying European Politics

In his excellent travel book *Europe, Europe*, the German poet and author Hans Enzensberger poses the question, "What else is Europe but a conglomeration of mistakes?"[2] The decade of the nineties will be a period of major political and social change in Europe, and it seems an appropriate time to examine some of these "mistakes" and problems in European political systems.

The startling changes in Eastern Europe, the movement towards European integration, German reunification, and all the implications of these occurred simultaneously at the end of the 1980s and the beginning of the 1990s. Together, they point to significant dislocations in the Europe of the post–Second World War period. And these dislocations are worth examining because they will have an enormous impact on the shape of the new Europe that is emerging. The events of 1989 not only changed the rules of the political game for

1

Eastern Europe but also meant major systemic changes and related political implications for Western Europe. The waning of Cold War tensions has produced a Europe that will increasingly focus on other problems, which were to some extent present before but were casually ignored in view of perceived higher, more important **political problems**. Now these issues will come to occupy a much greater role in the political strategies of Western European nations. In other words, agendas that existed in the past, though mainly hidden, may now appear at the heart of the new European politics. They are old agendas because they have always been there; they are new agendas because they won't go away. In fact they take on more importance with the cataclysmic changes at the end of the 1980s.

Rather than focusing on such traditional aspects of European politics as institutions, parties, and bureaucracies, this book will analyze from a comparative perspective many of the **undercurrents** in each of four major systems. These areas are problematic because they are often controversial and difficult to define in terms of black and white. Many cause difficulties for the smooth operation of the political system because they don't seem to fit in with the traditional political agenda. But despite the unwillingness of political establishments to firmly locate these problems within the agenda, they in fact represent some of the most pressing and important issues of advanced industrial nations.

They are difficult to deal with because many politicians see them as irresolvable; they don't fit neatly into the political structure. Rather they represent dark underlying forces and currents threatening to disrupt and perhaps dismember the political status quo.

Therefore the task is to look at these problem areas (or at least what I think are the most important ones) in a comparative sense. One example is the sensitive issue for British politics of writer Salman Rushdie, under Iranian sentence of death as a religious heretic. How does government in a liberal democratic society deal (or not deal) with the several issues at stake here—freedom of speech, civil liberties, the problems of managing a multiracial society, protection of minority rights, etc.? How can a government appear to accommodate beliefs that appear contradictory to some of its basic tenets? And of course the contextual implications of this as a case study will help the reader move from the specific to the general and vice versa.

Themes in European Politics

Just as there is a rationale for organizing this book in an analytical sense, so also is there a thematic explanation for the framework developed to examine European politics.

The major theme argued throughout the book is that European politics has shown and still exhibits a series of **continuities** and **discontinuities** that can be seen quite clearly by examining certain patterns and trends in contemporary political life.

What do we mean by the terms *continuity* and *discontinuity*? *Continuity*, as defined by the *Oxford Advanced Learners Dictionary* (1988), refers basically to "the state of being continuous." But this is problematic because of the complexity of the word's meaning. Turning to the thesaurus, we find that the term is synonymous with several words, including *cohesion, flow, progression, sequence,* and *succession.* For our purposes some elaboration is in order. Here the term *continuity* basically refers to the idea that political systems develop and change in a fairly smooth, peaceful, and unbroken tradition; that there are reasonably smooth transitions in politics and no real major difficulties in accommodating the changes that accompany such transitions. Continuity in this respect would seem to represent an almost linear view of politics, which may be seen to proceed in a straight line from one happy stage to the next. This is not the argument. Politics is rarely if ever linear in this sense, but it can be continuous. There may be minor disruptions, but they don't affect the basic underpinnings of the system; such disruptions can be part of politics and societal forces, but they fail to undermine in a radical way the very nature of the system.

On the other hand, the word *discontinuity* is usually associated with a "break" or interruption in the process. Here it refers to the idea that politics is rarely a smooth progression but rather a constant process of struggle and conflict, which absorbs the system constantly and in moments of crisis threatens the very nature of the system. The concept of discontinuity assumes society's susceptibility to major and minor disruption, its difficulty in accommodating change and accepting it. It embodies the notion that there have been sharp and frequent altercations in the political system in the past and that these may resurface to pose a threat or grave problem to the system. This is not to say that the political system is inherently unstable or constantly in crisis. Obviously when one assesses the post-1945 history of Western Europe and the stability of France, Germany, and Italy, one would have to conclude that overall they have been to a large extent stable and predictable, exhibiting continuity in political institutions and the relationships of these to society. Here the idea of discontinuity would refer to the changes and instabilities of previous regimes that have an influence or could potentially have an influence on the future welfare and stability of the current system. It refers to underlying currents that threaten the social fabric, not always visible but there just the same and rising to the surface materially from time to time in one form or another: race riots, poll tax clashes, and book burning in the United Kingdom; anti-Semitic violence and the ability of an extreme right party to garner 15 percent of the popular vote in France. It refers to political violence and terrorism in Italy vis-à-vis the Red Brigades, and the development of an environmentally conscious political group in Germany.

In other words, there are elements of discontinuity in continuity, and these are as important to study as the basic elements of continuity. In the most basic terms, both bear upon the survival of the idea and the practice of liberal democracy.

Emerging Patterns and Problems: Crises in European Politics

The fact that the liberal democracies of Western Europe appear to be consensus based does not preclude significant challenges to their political systems and social stability. Such challenges have been constantly in evidence throughout the development of Western democracies. Historically, France, Italy, and Germany have experienced the most discontinuity in this respect and Britain the most continuity. But it is important to note that no system is immune to these problems; starting in the mid 1960s, the illusion of complete stability based on prosperity and modernization was quickly eroded as the advanced industrial democracies faced new forms of crises that had their roots in previously unresolved political agendas.

One way of characterizing the development of European politics from early historical stages to the present is in terms of a series of crises.[3] This is useful for our purposes, because such a framework finds expression in the ideas of continuity and discontinuity.

Some historians and political scientists have distinguished five major crises to explain how nations develop (or how nations become nation-states). The idea of a sequence of crises implies that one follows from the other in some sort of chronological order. So nations, it is argued, go through the **five crises of nation building** in this order:

1. Identity
2. Legitimacy
3. Penetration
4. Participation
5. Distribution

The first crisis postulated is one of **identity**. To constitute a nation, it is argued, people have to develop a sense of national identity

4

over, above, and beyond their tribal, local, and regional affiliations. Recently we have seen that this is not occurring in parts of Europe. The Serbian and Croatians do not necessarily offer undying loyalty to Yugoslavia, and in 1991 this once unified nation was on the verge of disintegration. The Lithuanians and other Baltic peoples were interested in secession from the overarching Soviet Union. Erstwhile nations are coming apart at the seams, while other regional groupings such as the European Community were attempting to integrate even further. In 1993, Czechoslovakia split into two states. Identity appeared in crisis even in the United Kingdom, with its long history of nation building and stability. The people of Northern Ireland, for instance, are confused over the question of identity and loyalty. Are they British, Irish, Northern Irish, from Ulster, or something else? And what does their identity mean for their political allegiance?

Establishing an identity appears to be an ongoing process in politics that affects not only the Third World but also the so-called developed nations of Western Europe. Throughout the text we will be attempting to deal with some of the difficulties this problem poses for the liberal democracies of Western Europe.

A second crisis nations must face in their development is one of **legitimacy**. That is the feeling that their government, their political arrangements and regime, indeed their overall system is legitimate and should be obeyed. If citizens do not feel their system is legitimate, then it is possible they will get rid of it, perhaps by staging a revolution as the Nicaraguans did in 1979 against the dictatorship of Somoza and as the Rumanians did in 1989 when they overthrew the illegitimate government of Nicolas Ceaucescu. If a system is perceived as illegitimate, it requires a great deal of coercion to maintain it. Iraq under Saddam Hussein, for instance, relied and relies on such coercion, as did Haiti under the Duvaliers and Chile under General Pinochet.

For most of the countries in Western Europe this is no longer a major problem; few could claim with any credibility that these states rely on coercion and intimidation to maintain the systems that we see operating. But legitimacy may be undermined from time to time in certain sections of society. In Northern Ireland, for instance, a substantial portion of the community still appears to find unacceptable the proclaimed legitimacy of the governing arrangements. In the United Kingdom the electoral system regularly brings governments to power who are not elected by a majority of the eligible electorate, and there are substantial numbers of Scots who would like to see themselves as an independent nation.

Throughout the text the questions "Legitimate to whom?" and "Why?" will recur often.

5

A third crisis consists of the notion of **penetration**. As nations begin to develop and governments expand their rule over larger sections of the community, gathering taxes and revenues, they may encounter resistance (a recent example might be the poll tax controversy in the U.K.). Government as the main form of centralized authority has to penetrate these areas successfully if the process of nation building is to work. If penetration fails or breaks down, then problems are created for the central authorities as in the rebellions in the Baltic states.

England, for instance, managed to penetrate its peripheries and hinterland fairly successfully from early days, while the rest of Europe appeared to take longer. France established a highly centralized system under the auspices of Napoleon. Although this question is largely settled in contemporary Europe, certain signs of rebellion and disobedience raise doubts that penetration will ever be achieved completely.

The fourth crisis is **participation**. Once most of the crises are resolved, people begin to seek ways to participate in their society's affairs. They might, for example, struggle to expand the electoral franchise. A party system develops, and parliaments play a role in dealing with the new demands placed on the system. Mass participation may evolve slowly, but once granted by elites and institutionalized, the system usually becomes cohesive and less prone to violence and instability. If mass participation is not granted, however, and citizens are constantly denied participatory rights, then rebellion, protest, and even civil war may result. Again in Western Europe this is not a major threat to the system, since all the countries we will deal with have established elections and competitive party systems which allow the citizens some freedom of choice and the feeling that they can participate in selecting their rulers and government. Despite the view of some writers that this is a very superficial and often meaningless form of participation, it does allow citizens at the very least an outlet to vent their opposition to government policy and therefore to try and change it.

The last major crisis in this ideal world is a permanent feature of even the most advanced industrial societies: the crisis or problem of **distribution**, or who gets what. Once we have many interests taking part in politics, the struggle turns to distribution of wealth and resources within the political community. It appears very unlikely that any state will ever solve this problem adequately, mainly because to a large extent "equality" is an almost undefinable ideal. Western Europe has been somewhat successful in this, although France, for example, displays vast inequalities in its economic system.

Even though I discuss the five crises, I do not adhere to the simplistic use of a scheme that suggests that each state proceeds logically from one stage to another. Rather the sequence may be mixed up, and some crises may not occur so dramatically. And of course some crises may be ongoing within and across the political system one is dealing with. In sum, this is not a rigid model that fits all societies equally well, but it at least provides us with a framework for comparison. It is a framework that should be used loosely and not exclusively to portray the development of European nations; it can be useful in suggesting where the continuities and discontinuities can be located.

Why Compare?

Why do we compare when we think and write about politics? In several ways, comparisons create a rationale for the study of different societies' politics.

First, to compare is a very natural way of thinking. It is natural to study people, their ideas, behavior, and institutions in reference to others. Such curiosity is part of human nature and we may even gain a deeper and more objective understanding in the process of comparison. One could take the famous dictum of René Descartes, *Cogito, ergo sum*, one step further and say, "I think therefore I am comparing."[4]

Second, we compare so as to avoid **ethnocentrism**, the belief that the universe centers around you or your particular political, social, and economic system. By stepping outside of the particular and narrow context in which we find ourselves, we can avoid a short-sighted and sometimes tunnel-visioned way of looking at politics and gain a wider worldview.

Comparison allows us reference points for judgments and measurements of where we stand in relation to other societies. The poet John Donne once said that "No man is an island." One of the crucial political lessons for nation-states of the twentieth century is precisely that: that we live in a global system of **interdependence**. Our economies and social systems are linked and interact with one another to such an extent that we would find it difficult to live without one another. Thus no nation is an island either; we must compare in order to gain information and knowledge about how we relate to each other.

When we argue that the Soviet Empire is crumbling, it is important to ask ourselves, "Crumbling in comparison to what? Is it disintegrating compared to the Russian state of 1917, or the far-flung

British Empire after the Second World War? Can we compare the views of the French Front National leader, Jean-Marie Le Pen, to those of Germany's Adolf Hitler? Just what is the difference? Is Italy's North-South divide similar to the gulf in Britain between North and South?

Finally, comparing nations allows us the chance to develop analytical tools and use the knowledge we have gained. For instance, it provides us with the ability to gain more valuable insights from the general media—newspapers, magazines, books, and television. We begin to understand what is similar and what is different (the basis of comparison), what is unique and what is common in each system. When we read about other governments and societies, we are able to assess how well (or how badly) one mode of explanation for one society can help us to understand another. So we apply these frameworks in order to see if the same rules apply across the board. In other words comparative politics allows us to uncover specific and similar kinds of phenomena in light of different historical and social backgrounds.

In a nutshell, the function or purpose of comparative study is to identify uniformities and differences between countries and explain them.

Choosing Nations

Four major European actors have been chosen for purposes of comparison. These are the United Kingdom, France, Germany, and Italy. Why choose them? For several reasons. First, they constitute the "core" of Western European politics: they have had an important impact on Europe's development historically, politically, and economically. They have the largest populations of Western Europe and, in the case of the UK and France, have attained widespread influence through transference of democratic ideals and institutions to previous colonies. All of them have had an impact on the political development of Europe in one way or another. They constitute important forces in the development of a united (or, alternatively, disunited) Europe. They cannot be ignored.

Second, it would be hard to understand the events of the twentieth century on the Continent without regard to the two major wars fought on European soil and thus almost impossible to understand without reference to Germany and Italy (and the development of fascism) and to Great Britain and France in these historical events. To argue that Europe has been shaped by its past is a cliche that approximates the truth. As the philosopher George Santayana put it, "Those who do not remember the past are condemned to repeat it."[5]

Third and finally, all four countries are representative of "liberal democracy" and advanced industrial societies, and yet clearly they have not solved most of the problems that we will be dealing with.

During the period of the 1970s and 1980s, many scholars were arguing that postindustrial democracies in Western Europe were in crisis. That liberal democracies could no longer cope with the demands and requirements of their citizenries was a repeated view in much of the literature, and the question whether these systems could survive was an often debated proposition. To a large extent, the four countries studied here have responded well to the challenges facing them. Their constitutions and political arrangements have not cracked in the face of pressure. This does not mean that they have been let off the hook, however. Clearly, as we have seen, new challenges and problems face the Continent. Ethnic rivalries, immigration, racism, unemployment, and assimilating diverse cultures constitute immense problems for the new Europe. If Western Europe cannot accommodate these changes and remain politically stable, can we realistically expect less stable nations in the Third World to succeed?

Does democracy have a future? What are the implications of the developing European superstate for liberal democracy in Western Europe? As Aleksandr Solzhenitsyn wrote, "Democracies are islands lost in an immense river of history. The water is always rising." Part of the task of this book is to assess how the "water" is rising for these important European liberal democracies and the political implications of the situation.

Plan of the Text

Each chapter will deal with the four societies respectively, and a final chapter will focus on the European Community. To help develop an analytical framework, each chapter will include a historical overview pointing briefly to the main events and the continuities, discontinuities, and problems these societies have faced in their development.

Each chapter will also include a section on political culture and change, providing an overall view of the political beliefs, attitudes, and values that appear to predominate in each nation and how these particular aspects have changed over time. This section of each chapter will include a case study that seeks to highlight the general "picture" in that society while inviting comparison. For instance, in the case of France we will deal with the ambivalence of French attitudes

9

towards politics and politicians and examine how this affects the wider context of politics. Some political scientists have argued that the French cannot make up their mind whether they want freedom or authority. Is this split personality a sign of continuity or discontinuity? In the case of Germany, I will examine the development of "green" consciousness in politics and its effect on the larger spectrum of German politics vis-à-vis changes in the value structure.

A third section in each chapter deals with the problem of "internal wounds"—events or developments that have caused strife and conflict in these societies and that have not been fully resolved (or even partially resolved in some instances). They may resurface in the form of terrorism or other acts of violence and bitterness.

In the case of British politics, for instance, one might classify Northern Ireland not only as an internal wound but also as a permanent tumor on the body politic. It appears in this light as the most difficult problem to solve facing any European government, in part because we can trace the conflict back at least four hundred years. Within the case study framework, these roots as well as major factors in the conflict will be discussed.

With regard to Italy we will deal with the problem of political violence that recurs periodically. A great deal of the literature on Italian politics discusses the "crisis" syndrome that seems to mark that political system. The titles themselves signify doubt regarding the stability of the republic: *Does Government Exist in Italy?* or *Surviving without Governing*, or even *Italy: An Uncertain Republic*. How then does Italy's system manage to survive? This section will try to provide some answers.

Fourth, I will deal with issues of race, religion, and immigration and the difficulties these pose in multiracial societies. In France, for instance, the rise of a major extreme-right party in the 1980s under the tutelage of Jean-Marie Le Pen has been the cause of a great deal of controversy and difficulty. Here the emphasis will be on explaining the Le Pen phenomenon and the strategies of his racist-based party. Why has it been successful? In the case of Germany, the problem of *Gastarbeiter* ("guest workers" from Turkey, for instance) has also provoked some neo-Nazi reactions, and we will be examining the role of immigrants in Germany and what this means for the political system.

Section five will focus on a recurring problem that differentiates each society in a fairly distinctive but not unique manner. For example, France's current efforts to manage problems in its empire echo former actions of Britain. In Italy the North-South divide continues, as does Germany's uncertainty over whether it wants a major political role in international affairs (as witnessed during the Gulf War). The idea is to present a contemporary problem for each society and illustrate how there are similarities with other nations despite the apparent uniqueness of each. Is the British malaise unique? During the 1970s and 1980s it was common to characterize Britain's decline with such terms as "sickness" and "disease." However, unemployment and rising inflation were common in several Western European countries and usually combined into "stagflation" as a result of the Continent's economic problems. Is Britain then really so unusual in comparison to other societies? Is France alone in having problems managing the remnants of its African empire, or is the U.K. comparable in attempting to hold on to its last vestiges of an imperial past? Again the point is to detect exactly what is different and what is similar in these problem areas, what is continuous and what is discontinuous.

At the end of each chapter a conclusion will be offered attempting to draw together the various strands of the argument for each society, along with a brief glossary of the key terms and concepts found in each chapter.

The final chapter, on the European Community, will deal with the EC's problems and prospects along similar lines as the country chapters. What are the main problems in the movement and achievement of European union, political and economic? Will Europe emerge as the federal system envisioned by Jacques Delors, or will the community more closely correspond to the Thatcher version of a "Europe des patries"? In assessing the tricky problem of European defense after the end of the Cold War, our attention is drawn to the role of Europe in the Gulf crisis in 1990–91. Finally I will examine the dilemma that immigration poses to Europe and its impact on "new" versions of what security constitutes.

The concluding chapter will bring together the strands and present suggestions for future study and research.

Summary

This book is an attempt to introduce students to comparative European politics from a different and original perspective. Rather than focusing on the institutions or "normal" politics in Western Europe, which have been covered in great detail elsewhere, it looks at Europe from a problem-oriented perspective. What disturbs the normal workings of the systems of Britain, France, Germany, and Italy? What types of crisis scenario pervade politics, and are these crises continuous or discontinuous in nature?

It uses the comparative method in order to filter out points of reference such as race and internal divisions. It does not ignore areas of controversy because the view presented here argues that such controversy is the very stuff of politics. These areas of constant and heated debate are very much worth examining and at least as important as the details of how government structures work.

The hope is that such an approach will stimulate and encourage students of comparative politics to participate in lively discussions regarding the very nature of politics and society.

Key Terms and Concepts

Each term appears in the text in boldface type.

Continuities	Interdependence
Discontinuities	Legitimacy
Distribution	Participation
Ethnocentrism	Penetration
Five crises of nation building	Political problems
Identity	Undercurrents

2

The United Kingdom

Historical Overview

To many people, the United Kingdom represents the one country that is distinguished by a long tradition of continuous democratic rule, stemming from the end of the English Civil War in the seventeenth century. Parliamentary sovereignty, accepted then as a constitutional principle, continues to the present day, when politicians and keen observers of the constitution argue over changing many of the principles and institutions that permeate British society. The British Isles were last invaded in the eleventh century and experienced their last major internal conflict in the late seventeenth century, with the exception of the Irish troubles. For at least three hundred years the British have enjoyed uninterrupted tradition, continuity in political development, and the absence of major political crises that threatened to overthrow the state and cause turmoil.

This was not always the case. Until the eleventh century, Britain was plagued by repeated invasions by such European groups as the Celts, Gaels, and Romans. The last succeeded in making mainland Britain one of the major centers of their civilization. In A.D. 400, the Romans were finally obliged to return home to try to salvage a declining empire, leaving Britain undefended. Subsequently, such Teutonic tribes as the Angles, Saxons, Jutes, and thereafter the Danes established primitive state structures there, effectively driving the Celtic tribes to the northern and western peripheries of the island, where they formed a Celtic fringe. "Core areas start to form, centered around Wessex and the Danelaw, and the final invasion of Britain, led by William the Conqueror in 1066, established Norman rule.

At this stage the beginning of political unification in Britain started to become a reality. The Normans moved into Ireland and Wales, bringing an organized system of taxation and administration and establishing a primitive form of population counting with the *Domesday Book*, which allowed them to have census statistics. The beginning of the centralized state dating from this period was to have a crucial role in the political development of Britain.

The natural protection that an island afforded meant that Britain was free from conquest from this period on and therefore to a large extent free to develop its own political institutions and mold its own form of government without outside intervention and interference. This important fact was to shape British history and the island's political development for the next 900 years and to establish its uniqueness among Western European nations. And in turn its insularity ensured a long period of continuous political development and indigenous institution building, free of the major social revolutions that swept the Continent in the eighteenth and nineteenth centuries.

Having borders that could not be invaded by land meant that Britain could forego the expense of a large army and concentrate on developing its sea power, which would not only provide necessary defense but also establish the country as a major industrial and imperial power by the nineteenth century.

Evolution and continuity are two terms that characterize Britain's development. Its progress toward a liberal democracy occurred in several stages and coincided with its development as a centralized rather than fragmented state. In order to examine this development, it is necessary to understand how the final version, the United Kingdom of Great Britain and Northern Ireland, came about.

It was a tradition of centralized authority and national integration that brought about the United Kingdom, and this, as mentioned, was initiated with the arrival of the Normans in the eleventh century and furthered by the English Tudor monarchs in the sixteenth century. It was under the Tudors, for instance, that Wales (a collection of Gaelic communities annexed in 1284 by Edward I) was incorporated officially into the English state by the 1536 Act of Union. Despite the fact that Wales constituted a Celtic community, the English, with their penetration of the periphery, carried out a process of Anglicization, bringing the Welsh increasingly under the control of the core areas. Thus the easiest part of achieving a United Kingdom was attained: Wales never had a unified political system of its own or indigenous institutions, it had never fully reached the status of nationhood, and so the English could quite easily incorporate it into their own political system.

The 1603 Union of the Crowns (integrating the monarchies of Scotland and England) was a further stage in uniting Britain. It led in turn to the securing of England's northern boundary in 1707, with the Act of Union between Scotland and England. By the beginning of the eighteenth century, the centralized English state included all three countries that constituted the island of Great Britain. The securing of recognizable borders was a crucial development which enabled the British state to concentrate on matters other than defending its boundaries.

The English in comparison to the rest of Europe made an early start in grappling with the major problems of political development. By the seventeenth century, they had achieved most of the crucial elements of the modern nation state.

First, a national consciousness had been established in the Middle Ages. The common language of English provided the basis for the development of a homogeneous culture, particularly in England, and it was England that constituted the largest, most heavily populated, and richest (in terms of resources) area of Britain.

Second was the resolution of conflict between church and state: the former was relegated to a minor role in the country's political life, and the latter was elevated to the major political role. England adopted the Anglican form of Christianity as opposed to the Roman model. In 1534 King Henry VIII declared himself head of the church in England, and today this role is assumed by Queen Elizabeth II. The "political reformation" of 1534 was a rebellion against Rome's external interference and Henry VIII's enduring contribution to the modern British state. Henry wanted the Roman Catholic pope to grant him a divorce because his wife, Catherine of Aragon, had not produced a male heir to the throne. The pope refused, and Henry set about getting the Catholic church out of England and England out of the Catholic church. The new Anglican church gave Henry his divorce in 1534, leaving him free to marry five other wives in succession after his divorce, two of whom he had beheaded. Intrinsically, the English Reformation was an act of resistance against external interference, but at the same time it was an important assertion of a newfound national identity. It ensured that from the sixteenth century onwards Britain would be outside the mainstream of European political development and thus more capable of producing its own indigenous institutions and constitutional arrangements.

Third, a set of political institutions were established by the seventeenth century. They were the outgrowth of a bloody civil war fought between two alternative views of the question Who rules? From this revolutionary period the framework of parliamentary government developed. It helped to promote the flourishing of commercial interests within the system with the realization that a nation's political power is dependent on its economic power.

It was in this period that the crucial principle of the **"Sovereignty of Parliament"** was established, allowing Parliament to make and pass laws. This arrangement provided the basis for the establishment of democracy in the United Kingdom.

Finally, the securing of recognizable and defensible borders, so crucial to the security of the English state, occurred in stages, beginning in the thirteenth century, when Wales was annexed, and continuing until 1707, when the Act of Union with Scotland sealed the northern border.

By the end of the seventeenth century, England was a nation-state in the modern sense of the word and had acquired all the characteristics of the nation-state including a distinctive language, art, religion, political institutions, and the capability of defining territorial boundaries.

It had gained a sense of political identity necessary to its development and had managed to penetrate the peripheries to provide for secure borders. These crises were solved much earlier than their counterparts on the mainland of Europe. Since the period of the seventeenth century and the so-called Great Revolution, Britain has developed more or less uninterrupted by outside influences. The legitimacy of the political system, for instance, was achieved through the gradual extension of the right to vote at various stages in the nineteenth and twentieth centuries. After the first major reform of the constituencies in 1832, other acts in 1867 and 1884 extended the franchise to increasing numbers of adult males. Two acts, in 1918 and 1928, offered the vote to all men and women. Voting also became a more legitimate procedure in 1872, when polls were made secret in an effort to reduce bribery and political corruption in the system.

By the end of the First World War, the Labour party had successfully replaced the main rival of the Conservatives, the Liberal party, in part because Labour had benefited by the extension of the vote to the poorer, working classes.

The final stages in the development of what we now know as the United Kingdom were still to be completed, however. And it was these final stages that constituted a major problem for the English state and provided a consistent source of strain and disunity in an otherwise United Kingdom. The difficulty or problem, of course, is the case of Ireland. (This will be explored in further detail in the Internal Wounds section.)

Ireland was colonized and subjugated to English rule from the eleventh century onwards. At the beginning of the seventeenth century the northern part of the island and nine of its thirty-six counties received some 170,000 settlers from Scotland and England. They remained unintegrated with the natives of the region, who were mainly Roman Catholic. The majority of the settlers were Calvinistic Scottish Protestants, who introduced their own different customs and agricultural techniques.

The final version of the United Kingdom, the political arrangement we have today, was not to appear until more than 120 years later, when the partition of Ireland into North and South became a political and social reality and the United Kingdom of Great Britain and Northern Ireland emerged in its present territorial form. Civil strife throughout the nineteenth and early twentieth century had forced a reconsideration of the Irish problem. When independence was granted to the new Irish Republic in 1921, the six predominantly Protestant counties in the North refused to join and remained in the United Kingdom with their own parliament at Stormont.

Challenges to the United Kingdom

Despite the fact that by the early 1920s the final version of what we now know as the United Kingdom of Great Britain and Northern Ireland had been established, challenges to the structure and existence of the unitary state continued to be important features of political life in the United Kingdom. In fact tendencies towards disintegration were all the more apparent after several centuries of increasing political integration.

Peripheral Nationalism. The main challenges to the United Kingdom came from the peripheries in the form of nationalism as a political force among their subjects. Apparently sections of the peripheral communities were unhappy with their position within the United Kingdom. The most obvious challenge came from Northern Ireland where a substantial minority—the one-third of the population who were Roman Catholic—did not fully accept their governing arrangements as legitimate but desired political and social change. Despite the fact that the U.K. appeared to be prone to disintegration in this part of its territory, in fact it held together remarkably well. National unity was fostered by two world wars, and questions of

peripheral nationalism were shelved; they could attract little support when the British state was experiencing such a major crisis.

To a large extent, the challenge of the peripheries to the unitary structure of the United Kingdom did not really appear until the mid 1970s. The Scottish National party (SNP), which wanted independence for Scotland, and the Welsh party, the Plaid Cymru, which wanted some powers devolved but not full independence, had made a limited impact on British politics in the preceding decades. Certainly, they had benefited from economic and social discontent, and the feeling that their affairs had been managed incompetently by London was fairly acute. However, from an electoral viewpoint their support still remained a fairly small minority. But in the late 1960s and early 1970s, people in the peripheries started to express more openly their dissatisfaction with the dominance of the two-party system at Westminster and its apparent failure to meet the needs of the peripheries. In 1969 the government established a Royal Commission on the Constitution, partly as a response to these developments. It reported in 1973 but was superseded the following year, when the 1974 general election boosted the fortunes of the nationalist parties dramatically. The SNP was also boosted by an "eruptive" factor, the discovery of North Sea oil, which allowed the Scottish nationalists to make the case that they could survive economically without England.[1]

In the October 1974 general election the SNP increased its representation dramatically, to eleven out of seventy-one Scottish seats (or 2.9 percent of the total votes cast in the U.K.). Perhaps more importantly, the SNP received the second-largest number of votes cast in Scotland. At the same time, Plaid Cymru obtained three of the thirty-six seats available in Wales. Threatened, the Labour party (which has traditionally been strong in Scotland in particular and the peripheries in general) devised new proposals for the **devolution** of government in Scotland and Wales. The Scotland and Wales Acts of 1978 would in theory have produced something quite different from the familiar unitary state. Authority would have been delegated to regional assemblies in the respective countries with shared powers; in essence there would have been a quasi-federal arrangement with certain powers retained at a U.K. level (such as overall national defense and taxation) and certain other powers delegated to a regional level.

To test the depth of feeling for the implementation of these proposals, the Government decided to hold referendums in Scotland and Wales on the first of March, 1979. The results indicated that Wales decisively rejected devolution by four to one, whereas Scotland was in favor by a narrow margin. However, this vote did not meet the threshold requirement imposed by the government. Over 40 percent of the total eligible electorate would have had to vote positively for devolution before it would have been enacted.[2] Plans for devolution were shelved and the nationalist members of Parliament withdrew their support from the Labour government. The result was that Labour lost the confidence of Parliament and was forced to call a general election in 1979, which returned a Conservative government. If Labour had been lukewarm about devolution, the Conservatives positively despised the idea and immediately repealed both acts.

Peripheral nationalism had failed to disturb the unitary state. The state had successfully staved off the challenge of discontinuity and managed to preserve itself.

This was not the end of the story, however. Demands for independence and devolution may have died down and virtually disappeared in the 1980s, but by the beginning of the 1990s they were making some recovery. This resulted in part from more than a decade of Conservative rule from 1979 (the Conservatives were and are generally unpopular in Scotland), in part from the movement towards closer integration with Europe. Many Scots would prefer to negotiate with Europe from an independent basis rather than from within the context of the United Kingdom. There has also been an increase in all party support for a Scottish assembly, including the development of a pressure group to further these demands. Perhaps more important, many opinion polls in the 1990s have indicated that around 80 percent of the Scottish public supports some form of devolution. Their hopes were almost certainly dashed with the 1992 election victory of the Conservative party, which achieved a fourth consecutive term to the chagrin of the Scottish nationalists and the Labour party. The SNP in fact only managed to secure three seats in the new Parliament (one less than the Welsh Plaid Cymru). In the wake of the election, however, a group that claimed cross-party support, Scotland United, came forward as a voice of protest and dissent to Tory hegemony in the northern periphery. The stage is set for the 1990s to witness increasing nationalism in the peripheral areas, particularly given the examples of Eastern Europe and other major political changes set in motion towards the end of the 1980s.

An Unwritten Constitution.

Like a well established garden, the major features of the British Constitution today reflect the plantings of many different proprietors. . . . The Constitution can only be understood as the product of historical inertia.[3]

Underlying much of the development of British political stability, indeed creating the conditions for development, is the British constitution. In this section we will clarify some of the debate concerning the British constitution and what this means. Some theorists continually talk of constitutional crises; others refuse to accept that Britain has a constitution. What exactly constitutes a constitution?

> The word is used in at least two senses, only one of which is to describe a single document which sets out the rules of political authority in a state. Constitution can also be used more broadly to refer to the rules and principles themselves, whatever the form in which they are found. In this latter sense, we do have a constitution. Indeed under this definition every state must have one.[4]

One of their constitution's most admirable aspects, in fact, to Britons is the perception that it reflects the knowledge and wisdom of the past. It works because it is an unwritten constitution, not engraved in stone; there is no one major, single document which encapsulates the significance of the constitution. It is derived from several sources including **convention, statute law, common law**, and other works. Whereas the United States has a written document, the United Kingdom's "constitution" is mainly uncodified in nature; therein lies a flexibility unmatched in most other nations' political credos. It is an evolving body of political rules; the main provisions date back to the seventeenth century—for example, the sovereignty of parliament, the rule of law, a unitary form of government, and **constitutional monarchy**.

The sovereignty of Parliament and constitutional monarchy questions were resolved as early as the seventeenth century when Parliament after a long civil war became supreme and other bodies in the polity subordinate to its wishes. Today the queen of England occupies a purely symbolic role as head of state, approving the decisions of others but remaining outside the real process of politics. Parliamentary supremacy refers to the position that acts of Parliament are higher than any other law, and courts cannot overturn any law made by Parliament. It is only recently that controversy over this sovereignty has been raised, because of Britain's membership in a supranational body, the European Economic Community (EEC) (an issue to be discussed in the final chapter). Even the German leader Adolf Hitler greatly admired the British Parliament, referring to it as "the temple of the nation's glory." The idea of the unitary state extends parliamentary supremacy throughout the length and breadth of the United Kingdom (meaning England, Scotland, Wales, and Northern Ireland). Federalism as it exists in the United States and

---

Examples of Constitutional Sources

1. *Statute law: Acts of Parliament and subordinate legislation.* Much of the constitution is in fact written in this form.
   a. Magna Carta, 1215. Limited the power of the king over the Barons.
   b. Habeas Corpus, 1679. Prevents incarceration in prison for unspecified amount of time.
   c. European Communities Act, 1972. Ensured Britain's entry into the EEC.

Statutes are important because they override all other kinds of constitutional sources. In practice these are no more than the ordinary laws passed by Parliament.

2. *Common Law.* Customs and precedents. Judicial decisions and interpretations, royal prerogatives (including power to declare war). With the gradual erosion of the political power of the monarchy, the royal prerogative has been effectively transferred to the cabinet and prime minister.
3. *Conventions.* These are important but informal rules of behavior; they are not enforced by the judicial system or by Parliament.
4. *Binding Rules.* Collective responsibility, ministerial responsibility, the monarch's assent to passage of legislation. The resignation of government after losing a vote of confidence in the House of Commons.
5. *Authoritative Works.* These offer important guidance and intellectually persuasive works on aspects of the constitution. For example, Sir Edward Coke, *Institutes of the Law of England* (1628–44); A. V. Dicey, *An Introduction to the Study of the Law of the Constitution* (1885); Walter Bagehot, *The English Constitution* (1867).

Germany does not exist in this context. Rather, government is centralized and distributes various powers to the different local and regional units. France and Italy are similar to the United Kingdom in this respect, also displaying a unitary form of constitution.

It is not quite accurate to describe the British constitution as unwritten; it would be more accurate to see it as *uncodified*. That is, parts of it are written, but they are not available in one concise document. There are several different sources of the constitution.

In recent years the "efficient" and "dignified" aspects of the constitution that Walter Bagehot described in the nineteenth century have come under attack from several fronts. There appears to no longer exist a consensus that the constitution is a trusted and time-honored mechanism that can adequately deal with the problems and developments in contemporary British society. And because it has played such a large part in the development and stability of the United Kingdom's political process throughout the centuries, the problems that the constitution now faces are worth examining briefly.

Problems with the Constitution. Despite its unwritten form and the fact that it has several disparate sources, the constitution represents a long line of continuous development in English philoso-phy and tradition building. The "rules of the game" have in effect been well established over centuries of evolution. The constitution is also described by many sources as exceptionally flexible primarily because of its unwritten form. This makes it easy to produce amend-ments; during the two world wars the respective lives of each Parlia-ment in power at the time were simply extended until the end of the war. In a society with constitutionally declared fixed elections this would not have been possible. Most political science textbooks on the subject would consent to the view that the constitution is a "happy," dignified, efficient, and workable foundation.

However, the constitution and British political development have also had their fair share of difficulties and discontinuities from a historical perspective. They have included a violent civil war in the seventeenth century, the difficulties and crises attendant in ex-tending participation to the masses vis-à-vis the reform acts of 1832 to 1918, the endemic strife over home rule for Ireland prior to 1914, and the continuing levels of violence after 1918 to the present day. It would be deceiving to present British political development as one smooth passage from beginning to end. On the other hand, one should remember that the constitution has adapted fairly well (certainly in comparison to other European states) in weathering these various storms.

While some would argue that its unwritten nature provides a unique flexibility to adapt to contemporary circumstances, others would point out that it is flawed by ambiguity and may be misapplied in many situations. It is significant that increasingly in contemporary British politics in the last twenty years alternative views that would like to see parts of this constitutional "wisdom" amended have been trying to make their impact felt. Debate concerns various issues, but all are concerned with the role of the constitution and the changes that many think should take place regarding it.

Recent challenges to the often praised constitution took the form of nationalism in Scotland and Wales (both peripheral areas) under the rubric of devolution proposals, the troubles in Northern Ireland, and changes in the party system, to mention a few. When the SDP/Liberal Alliance party managed to do so well in the elections in the 1980s, the Queen was in communication with all sorts of constitutional lawyers who were advising her on the various implications of a hung Parliament, where no one party had an outright majority. Similar fears were present before the 1992 general election. The introduction of a written constitution and a bill of rights to the agenda was widely argued for, along with electoral reform to replace the "first past the post" system (in which a candidate needs only a plurality of the vote to win a seat), and the reform or abolition of the archaic House of Lords. In 1982, one political scientist, Philip Norton, delineated six different approaches to reforming the constitution in a book entitled *The Constitution in Flux*,[5] a title that obviously had some bearing on the problem at hand.

In December 1988 a group of concerned citizens, writers, and political activists signed the document **Charter 88**, requiring a bill of rights, electoral reform, open government, the rule of law, reform for the House of Lords, more control over the executive, and the reform of the judiciary, who would be ensured independence—among other demands for constitutional change. The interesting thing about the document is that it represented people from every part of the political spectrum who were fed up with one of the great "continuities" in British politics and clearly desired to introduce some "discontinuities."

It is partly myth that the constitution is unwritten, but it is true that it is uncodified. The virtue of the present system is that it is flexible. In such a situation the rules can change; however, it would perhaps be more beneficial to British citizens to know that they had certain rights not subject to the whims of the times.

Politics in Postwar Britain

At the end of the Second World War, Britain was in complete economic disarray. If one were to compare the victors and the losers of the war today, one would have to argue that in part the victors lost and the losers won. The economic positions of the United Kingdom and Germany in the postwar period were radically different than before the war. Germany emerged as an economic giant in Europe, Britain as a third-rate industrial nation. In part this was to be expected. If we accept Paul Kennedy's thesis of **relative decline**—that nations rise and fall in comparison to one another—then we can see that Britain was already in decline from the late nineteenth century onwards, the fall being presaged by the rise of the United States. Two world wars left the United Kingdom financially exhausted; the country was forced to sell most of its overseas assets to pay for these wars. It was a classical case of "imperial overstretch." By 1945 Britain could no longer afford its empire and had no alternative but to withdraw. India and Pakistan were given independence in 1947; Palestine was given up and the state of Israel established in 1948. In the Suez crisis of 1954–56, the British were humiliated and forced to withdraw when they could not gain American support for their actions in Egypt. This served to highlight to the world just how far Britain had fallen in terms of influence at the level of international affairs. Subsequently, other British colonial possessions claimed independence around the globe. In 1962 Dean Acheson, the American secretary of state, bluntly pointed out that "Britain has lost an empire and not yet found a role." And as a result the United Kingdom was reduced to a medium-sized European power, a country that could not in the postwar period keep pace economically with the other major Western European states. The cliché that Britain had won the war but lost the peace was borne out by the abysmal economic performance of British industry throughout the decades following the end of the war.

Britain was consumed by what has been called the "**British disease.**" Low economic growth, constant strike activity from the trade unions, poor levels of productivity, and mediocre economic management supported a thesis and demonstrated a reality of malaise at all levels throughout British society.[6]

The Seventies and Beyond

To a large extent we have seen that the United Kingdom has been the product of many centuries of continuous political development. The modern British state has not been subject to a major political revolution as the other European states have. It has thus been able to experience an evolutionary process of political development whose reforms have not abolished medieval institutions but managed to adapt and integrate them into the fabric of society. Political and social change has come about gradually despite the fact that in the post-1945 period Britain's world role has changed dramatically and witnessed discontinuity as a result.

There is little doubt that the United Kingdom had difficulty adapting to its new status in light of the global political and economic changes that took place in this period. This can be seen in the efforts of Britain (after considerable reluctance) to join the European Economic

Community (EEC) in 1961. The difficult relationship of Britain to continental Europe was highlighted by its inability to gain membership in the community until Conservative Prime Minister Edward Heath finally gained access in 1972, with full membership coming in 1973.

Despite economic difficulties and stagnation, the political system in the United Kingdom has experienced a great deal of continuity even in the postwar period. Military dictatorship, emergency governments, new constitutions, and internal strife (discounting Northern Ireland) have not been an integral part of the British political scene. The Conservative party maintained political power from 1979 into the 1990s and clearly represented the continuity of a certain brand of party politics if nothing else. The political leadership of Margaret Thatcher throughout the 1980s and Tory continuation in the leadership of John Major with the general election victory of 1992 illustrate that changing governments and leaders does not come easily to the British electorate for one reason or another. This was despite the predictions of most polls, surveys, and analysts, who were convinced that Labour would secure victory in the 1992 election. Ultimately the British public decided to remain with the continuity of a party that had managed thirteen years in office, winning three consecutive general elections. With a fourth election victory it seems unlikely that the Conservatives will be seriously challenged in the 1990s by a Labour Party in complete disarray.

John Major's Term in Office

Iron entered my soul. You need a touch of steel. Otherwise you become like India rubber.
> Margaret Thatcher, March 30, 1980, quoted in the
> *Guardian Weekly*, Dec. 2, 1990.

It should be a compassionate society. Genuinely compassionate—because some people do need a special helping hand to help them enjoy a full life.
> John Major, Conservative party campaign letter, July 1991

On November 22, 1990, Margaret Thatcher, who had been the longest-running British prime minister in postwar British history, accepted the advice of her cabinet to resign from the premier's office. She had won three consecutive elections for the Conservatives in 1979, 1983, and 1987, ending an era of consensus politics and forging a new set of policies based on ideology and confrontation. More than anyone else, she transformed the image of the prime minister into a presidential figure and attempted with partial success to change the shape of British politics. The last days of **Thatcherism**, plagued by a troubled economy and cabinet disaffection, were her worst. The two major issues that brought her down were the poll tax and the division of the Conservatives over European integration; in effect these sounded the death knell of office for the "Iron Lady." The question remained, How would her successor fare, given her record and impact on British politics? How could anyone fit into Thatcher's shoes? The answer was a surprising one.

John Major was elected as Conservative leader and therefore prime minister on November 27, 1990; at forty-seven, he became the youngest prime minister in British history. He was elected for three main reasons. First, he was Thatcher's choice, and this gave him a tremendous head start over his nearest opponents. In just five days of intraparty campaigning he had overtaken far better known figures such as Michael Heseltine (who had been campaigning for the job for the previous five years) and Douglas Hurd. It was in effect a political coup d'etat and left many shocked.

Second, he was chosen because he was seen as someone who could unite the Conservative Party and heal the divisions caused by Thatcher's policies. Major was chosen because he was viewed as a man of moderation, someone who would bring compromise, consensus, and dialogue back to Conservative policy, which had for so long been dominated by Thatcher's confrontational style. The choice was to some extent for the sake of party unity.

Finally, Major defeated his opponents because they represented styles and ideas unacceptable not only to the Conservative party elite but also to the average conservative voter. Heseltine was seen as too uncompromising and controversial; Hurd as too patrician and establishment oriented (the establishment had already come under heavy attack from Thatcher). In the end Major was seen as closer in reality to the average Tory voter and the man more likely than his nearest opponents to win the general election for the Tories.[7] In defeat Heseltine was compensated by the unenviable position of Secretary of State for the Environment in charge of reforming the poll tax.

Major was not faced with an easy task in the aftermath of Thatcher. Uniting the Conservatives over Europe and solving the poll tax issue also created problems for him. The new prime minister's background was also the cause of some contempt from contemporaries and the public alike. Born in 1943, he was the son of a circus trapeze artist and a singer and as such was one of the few British P.M.'s to have experienced "downward mobility." He left school at sixteen in the early 1960s and lived for eight months on the unemployment queue, collecting two pounds and eighty-seven pence a week in "dole money." One of his peers actually commented that "he stood out simply because he was so hopeless!" Major, however, astutely developed his political ambitions, moving into banking and local politics. In 1979, he entered Parliament as the member for Huntingdon and proceeded under Thatcher to become parliamentary private secretary, whip, and then junior minister in the Department of Health and Social Security (DHSS). He moved on to become the chief secretary to the treasury in 1987 and the foreign office in 1989 and thereafter became chancellor of the exchequer. He was the epitome of a working-class Tory believing in increasing mobility between classes as a good thing and in meritocracy before the privilege of aristocracy.

Dean Acheson, the American secretary of state under President Harry S. Truman, once said that the "first requirement of a statesman is that he be dull. This is not always easy to achieve." In the case of John Major, however, many observers noted just how much he has achieved. Major has been termed "grey" and lackluster, a leader lacking real fire and personality; certainly in comparison to his predecessor these notes ring true.

These elements are more noticeable in terms of his working style than anything else. Major has a much more relaxed style than Thatcher, relying on career civil servants and inexperienced cabinets. His is a laid-back style of leadership, and the two quotes at the beginning of this section reflect the difference in perspective between two very different leaders. In that sense Major was seen as the ameliorator of Thatcherism, the best candidate to procure a "kinder, gentler" Britain in the years after Thatcher. Sixteen months after the Tory leadership battle, Major was reconfirmed in the middle of a recession with the largest popular vote ever recorded in Britain.

In that sense Major's term in office has been a partial success; he has rearranged the idea that Britain has a presidential-style leadership in the way that Thatcher presented herself to the public. Major is seen as an essentially decent person displaying good manners in politics, someone with a social conscience who dislikes snobbery, poverty, and racism. His primary mentor was not Thatcher but Iain Macleod, a reforming Tory chancellor who died in 1970 and believed in a classless society. His style in cabinet again is strikingly different from Thatcher's. When Thatcher was interviewed in the *London Observer* in February 1979, she emphatically stated her rejection of cabinet government: "As Prime Minister I could not waste time having any internal arguments." And certainly she did not in any sense of the word. Major, on the other hand, is a leader much more amenable to compromise and cooperation, managing cabinet meetings with more subtlety and finesse in comparison to Thatcher's strong-arm tactics. In fact it appears that he completely dislikes open disagreement, preferring a collegial atmosphere.

Despite his ability to compromise, Major's policies have in some ways been as radical as Thatcher's. He has continued with the privatization agenda in coal and the railways, from which even Thatcher steered clear, and in efforts to liberalize Sunday trading. Middle-class entitlements have been challenged, and changes in education and health are planned to shake up established views. In his policy on Europe he has departed from Thatcher, giving support to the treaty that she had strongly argued against. This issue again split the Conservative Party in two and threatened to bring the government down when Conservative rebels and opposition MPs dissented over the question of the EEC's Maastricht treaties. In July 1993, Major decided to entertain a vote of confidence in his government and his European policy, putting his career on the line and actually winning the vote. In an aside to the media in the wake of the victory, Major revealed his own sense of insecurity when he said, "What I don't understand is how a wimp like me goes on winning everything."

And it is the "wimpish" nature, the "nice Mr. Major" stereotype, which so clearly distinguishes him from Mrs. Thatcher. He has been seen as indecisive, as having short-term skills, a lack of vision, and lack of an overall philosophy to push through his ideas into a substantive Conservative agenda. He lacks a clear ideology in the sense of his predecessor, preferring much more the mode of pragmatism in politics. At the time of writing it was clear that Major was undergoing once more a crisis in the Conservative party, still deeply divided over Europe and having received on July 29, 1993, the biggest by-election defeat for a British government in the Conservative's fourteenth-safest seat, Christchurch. However, given his ability to bounce back, it remains to be seen how much this will affect his leadership. And with that in mind, with that level of continuity, it is interesting now to look at some of the discontinuities of British politics in more detail.

Political Culture and Change

Historically, British society has been noted for its fairly stable institutions and its apparently rigid social and economic class structure. There are other ways, however, of looking at society, and one of these is through the less tangible notion of **political culture**. Political culture is not an easy topic to define; it is a slippery concept which has been subject to various interpretations in the social sciences. It is indispensable, however, if we want to understand some of the forces and influences shaping the context of British politics. In this section we will be looking at British political culture and the changes it has undergone in the post-1945 period.

Defining Political Culture

The term "political culture" was devised mainly in the tradition of American political science in the 1950s and 1960s. Intrinsically, concepts from the field of social psychology have played an important role in defining the term. Gabriel Almond and G. Bingham Powell, for instance, provided a classic formulation which still carries a great deal of weight in contemporary social science:

> Political culture is the pattern of individual attitudes and orientation toward politics among the members of a political system. It is the subjective realm which underlies and gives meaning to political actions. Such individual orientations involve several components, including: (a) cognitive orientations, knowledge, accurate or otherwise, of political objects and beliefs; (b) affective orientations, feelings of attachment, involvement, rejection and the like, about political objects; and (c) evaluative orientations, judgments and opinions about political objects, which usually involve applying value standards to political objects and events.[8]

The crucial idea that politics involves a subjective realm, where citizens' attitudes, orientations, beliefs, and opinions play a part in the shaping of the political system, is central to the notion of political culture.

In more simplistic terms, political culture means the various patterns of beliefs, opinions, political attitudes, and practices that operate within the political life of a community. It covers a wide variety of societal norms and conventions; it signifies the way that people feel about politics, and it informs them in a behavioral sense. It provides the "rules of the game" within society and necessarily constitutes some of the most important political values to be found within the system.

British Political Culture in the Post-1945 Period

Given the previous definition it is important to assess the contemporary form and content of political culture in the United Kingdom. What role has it played? How has it changed in the period under consideration? And what does this change mean for British politics?

The United Kingdom has long been assessed as the epitome of stability and traditional values. The political system despite change has always focused on preserving the traditions, customs, and institutions that permeate the society. In the postwar period Britain experienced change that would delineate its form and experience throughout the period in question. Perhaps the most important signal of this was the accession of the Labour Party to government and its subsequent undertaking to nationalize many industries and create a welfare state in the United Kingdom.

The Politics of Deference

Because of the role of institutions and traditions within British society, the British public has been seen as a deferential people who passively acquiesce in the running of their political system. That is, when called upon to judge the elites who constitute the ruling classes, the average Briton sees them as more able and better suited to run the country than anyone else. Such **deference** to "superior" leadership and administrative capabilities reflects the old view that some people "are born to rule." It is a view rooted in the traditional class structure and the differences that existed and exist between the upper and lower classes within society. The ordinary people willingly accept the distribution of power in such a state, have no real desire to change the system, and thus reinforce the legitimacy of the system. Conventional wisdom has repeatedly stressed the view that the reason for Britain's unusual political stability has been the deferential attitudes the masses displayed toward their political elites. Walter Bagehot, who wrote a great deal about the British constitution, argued in 1867 that the masses were too stupid to understand the reality of government and were really duped by the "theatrical show" of the monarchy and other *dignified* elements of the constitution. The masses in Britain were patient and stoic in times of hardship and recession, preferring to pay obeisance to the system.

Almond and Verba, two American political scientists, confirmed some of these suspicions in the 1960s through the use of survey data.[9] Britain to them represented ideal conditions for a liberal democracy. The British displayed certain orientations that qualified them as fitting the category of "civic culture." A civic culture was described as one that allowed for a pluralistic vision of society in which dialogue, persuasion, and communication played a part; one that allowed "consensus and diversity, a culture that permitted change but moderated it."[10] Cooperation, compromise, and trust were important aspects of a system that had managed to survive and accommodate to change; the British citizenry were allegiant to their political system and not alienated from it, and clearly this had positive consequences. Their deference, however, was noted by Almond and Verba to be a little too perfect. If the British public had a fault, it was that they were slightly too ready to respect authority in general and their government in particular.

The Decline of the Civic Culture

If Almond and Verba painted an optimistic, rosy picture of British political culture in the late 1950s and early 1960s, by the mid 1970s social scientists were questioning and rapidly discarding much of this conventional wisdom. Surveys in this period indicated that the British were more prone to protest and other forms of political action than had previously been suspected.[11] Other writers argued that the notion of deference was too vague to be meaningful; one political scientist identified four different meanings of the term and at least five different ways in which it had been investigated.[12] Miners on strike, violent clashes on picket lines, violence in Northern Ireland, race riots, and mass demonstrations all served to undermine the traditional thesis of a deferential culture. The recent issue of the widely resented poll tax was a case in point, and it hastened the demise of Margaret Thatcher. No longer did it appear that the British were so prepared to respect authority at any level in the way that Almond and Verba had painted them. Samuel Beer in 1982 went further and used the term *collapse* rather than *decline* to describe the "civic culture." In such a situation British democracy was heading towards failure as its institutions were failing to meet increasing expectations among its citizenry.[13]

When Almond and Verba "revisited" British political culture in 1980 they found most of these elements confined to a small minority and deference by no means dead and buried. In fact it still existed as a persuasive element within society. However, there are serious problems with Almond and Verba's interpretation.

The evidence suggests that more than a substantial minority of the population in the United Kingdom are less enamored or beguiled by the constitution and the political elites than ever before. The miners' strike in 1974, which led to the fall of the Heath government, caused several writers to argue that democracy was in "crisis" and that Britain was in the process of becoming "ungovernable."[14] These fears of course proved to be groundless, but the late 1960s and 1970s did witness the emergence of unconventional participation in the form of strikes, demonstrations, and protest in all its varied forms on a large scale. Alan Marsh analyzed this decline of deference in his work *Protest and Political Consciousness,* published in 1978.[15] Providing survey evidence in support, he argued that many Britons engage in nondeferential forms of behavior; far from being allegiant and deferential, as Almond and Verba had argued, an attitude of protest is an integral and not a deviant part of the British political consciousness. And it is seen as a "legitimate pathway of political redress" by different sectors of the community.[16] In this view, then, Britain is not the deferential civic culture that Almond and Verba would posit, but rather a society that is on the road, and has been for some time, toward becoming a "noisy and disrespectful participatory democracy." Of course, just because people are taking part in protest activities does not mean the United Kingdom is drifting toward anarchy or that the social glue that held Britain together is now becoming unstuck. Rather it means that some substantial value change has been taking place in the United Kingdom in the last few decades and specifically after the postwar period.

Marsh argues along the lines of Ronald Inglehart[17] that **postmaterialism** has had a significant impact on the value structure of Britain. Briefly the Inglehart thesis is this: In First World countries the prewar and postwar generations differ in their structure of values. Older citizens were and are more concerned with maintaining a healthy economy—bread-and-butter issues—as well as domestic and international order, because they basically grew up in an atmosphere of insecurity, depression, and war. They display more sentiment towards material values. The younger generation, on the other hand, never experienced such hardships, and many of them took wealth or affluence for granted. Therefore they adopted a different set of postmaterial values, such as concern with freedom of speech, more political participation, and other matters of expression rather than economic problems. In other words, they were not concerned so much with distribution of well-being as with enlightenment and more individual expression. Well-being in the material sense was taken for granted.

Inglehart also found that on a cross-national basis, postmaterialists were more willing to take part in unconventional forms of political activity than citizens who expressed material values. In his analysis of protest, Marsh similarly found that young postmaterialists who were dissatisfied with British society are more likely to protest than other groups. In his sample of students, for instance, he finds that "an integrated syndrome of aggressive left-wing postmaterialistic ideological dissatisfaction is clearly responsible for the ultra-high levels of student protest."[18] The growth in various social movements in the United Kingdom supports such theoretical positions; the Campaign for Nuclear Disarmament (CND) and the Green party are two instances of groups that make radical demands on essentially noneconomic issues and at the same time draw a great deal of support disproportionately from the young. It also does not matter if the postmaterialist strand in society is a fairly small minority (perhaps 5 to 10 percent of the overall population); what is important is that they can have an impact on policy disproportionate to their size. In addition it is clear that these changes have been prompted by changes in the social and economic structure of the United Kingdom. There has been a significant decline in the number of people employed in manufacturing and a parallel growth in the service industries; moreover, despite the fact that environmental groups maintain a fairly small electorate, one can see that all the major parties have incorporated environmental issues within their political agendas. The traditional class-equals-party hypothesis that used to dominate British partisan politics has lost much of its influence in explaining voting behavior in recent years, and political scientists must proffer explanations for this decline in conjunction with the changing nature of the occupational structure and different value priorities that have emerged.

The Inglehart thesis that the younger generation is less concerned with material issues than the generation that had experienced hardship has some substance, of course. Younger people have been more willing to take part in demonstrations and protests over such nonmaterial issues as the environment, freedom of speech, and nuclear disarmament. However this is not the whole story; clearly other forms of protest have been directly concerned with material issues. Many strikes in the 1970s and 1980s still asserted basic economic class interests against political and economic hierarchies, the most protracted and violent of these being the miners' strike at the beginning of the eighties. Other issues were just as relevant, however, and signaled the decline of the "deferential" political culture as surely as did the rise of the "new politics" of postmaterial issues. The **poll tax**, for instance, which came to dominate the headlines at the end of the 1980s, is clearly an example of people asserting their political frustrations in the face of economic hardship.

Case Study: The Poll Tax Issue

Background

One of the most controversial political and economic issues that the Thatcher government faced was the poll tax. This was a long-standing problem in British politics that needed resolution;

the difficulty lay in how to achieve it. The issue was one of how to raise revenue to pay for local services; previously the method was based on **rates** (which stemmed from an ancient tax on property). Rates were problematic and unpopular for a number of reasons—for example, they are a very visible form of taxation, and young people between eighteen and thirty pay disproportionately less and poorer people pay more in proportion to their income than the wealthy. Rates did have some advantages—they were easy to collect and simple to administer—but overall, most people were in agreement that they were an outmoded and problematic method of raising revenue. Across the political spectrum people agreed that reforms were needed; again it came down to the problem of which reform and how to implement it.

Throughout the 1970s and 1980s, several alternative ideas were floated in an attempt to provide the solution. These included (among others) a local sales tax and a local income tax; finally, in a major effort in 1985–86, the government settled on the idea of the "community charge" to replace the rates. In many ways this was similar to the poll tax idea; the poll tax was to be based on the electoral register, the community charge on residence. The reform was included in the 1987 Conservative manifesto and was implemented after the party's general-election victory of the same year. Despite the original name, the charge soon became known as the poll tax, and the principle was clear: the idea was to charge an equal amount from each adult regardless of how much property he or she owned or how much income the person earned. It was an effort to control the spending of local governments and an effort to replace the device of rate capping (which at least had a progressive element) with a regressive tax. Many critics from the opposition and even many Conservatives argued that the poll tax was highly regressive. Individuals would be forced to pay the same rates despite major differences in income. More than that, it was a highly visible tax. Collecting such a tax would be highly problematic; it would be easy to evade, and the cost of administration would consume an enormous amount of resources, in effect far more than the old rating system.[19] The new system was seen as grossly unfair to women, who as wives and mothers did not necessarily work outside the home. The fact that the Conservatives wanted to implement it a year earlier in Scotland drew the wrath of the Scottish Nationalist contingent among other irate Scots who felt they were being discriminated against by Westminster. One report highlighted the dilemma of the McDiarmid family who lived on a housing estate in Edinburgh, Scotland:

Under the new system, the McDiarmids, who live in a $272 a-month three bedroom apartment in the Broomhouse project, pay the same per capita tax as the Government Minister for Scotland, Malcom Rifkind. Mr. McDiarmid says he earns about $8,500 a year and, under the old local taxation system paid $850 a year in real estate taxes and water charges, compared with the $1,332 he and his wife will owe this year [with the introduction of the poll tax].[20]

It was to some extent unpopular because it was based on erroneous assumptions on the part of the Conservatives:

Contrary to the theory behind the poll tax, the majority of the public did not blame their local councils and hold them to account since they took the view that it was an unfair tax that had been imposed onto local government by a central government that was seen as out of touch with the views of the ordinary man or woman in the streets.[21]

In short the tax was highly unpopular and politically controversial on all sides; the last time such a measure had been implemented was in the fourteenth century, and this ended in complete disaster with a peasants' revolt in 1381. In fact, the Conservative government in the 1980s had to call in many members who previously had seldom if ever attended to ensure that the measure made it through the House of Lords. With the stage set for a new and different revolt the new poll tax of the 1980s was a good guide to just how far deference had declined in the twentieth century.

Anti-poll tax groups spread far and wide throughout the UK quickly mounted opposition to the new tax; protests gained impetus as Scottish Labour Party councillors (who are directly involved with local authority finance) burned payment books outside government headquarters in Edinburgh.[22] Similarly large-scale demonstrations occurred throughout England in March 1990, culminating in violent demonstrations and public clashes with the police at the end of March.

The poll tax may not have been the direct cause of the downfall of Margaret Thatcher, but it is clear that indirectly it played a significant role in undermining her political position and credibility. In particular the leadership contest was heavily influenced by the divisive and controversial issue. Conservatives in marginal seats were to view the whole process as a disaster in electoral terms; in March 1990 the unpopularity of the poll tax was a major factor in the defeat of the Conservatives in a mid-Staffordshire by-election and in other local elections in May. Michael Heseltine (one of Thatcher's main rivals) sought to make political capital by making opposition to the tax a major plank of his challenge for leadership. After Thatcher's resignation from the fight, he was closely followed by Douglas Hurd and John Major. Ironically, when Major finally succeeded in securing the prime ministership, he gave Heseltine the job of secretary of state in the Department of the Environment with direct responsibility for reforming the poll tax.

Clearly the poll tax represented some elements of the protest culture that we have seen developing in U.K. politics over the last few decades. It was more than this, however; it was a revolt of the periphery against the center. Most Scots simply refused to pay the tax, for instance. It affected the have-nots more than the better off, it caused widespread antagonism against the central government, and it unleashed dormant feelings of nationalism and regionalism. In the end it had wider ramifications than its authors would have intended, but it serves as a good illustration of how far deference had declined by the 1980s as an adequate explanation for a consensual political culture in the United Kingdom.

Conclusion

It is clear from the preceding account that British political culture has undergone a number of changes since the end of the Second World War. Britain is not as homogeneous or consensual as some may wish it to be; the idea that its people have a strong sense of national identity is to some extent a convenient myth. It ignores the variations of race, nationality, and identity that constitute the contemporary social fabric of the United Kingdom. It overlooks the different forms of Scottish, Welsh, and Irish nationalisms that have diluted the sense of British identity. It leaves out the multiracial aspects of the United Kingdom and the different ethnic groups that play an important part. It assumes that British people share common values, common goals, and agreement on a political consensus. Certainly many people do hold such views and values, but they do not constitute such an overwhelming majority that we cannot say there are not alternative views and values that make British political culture a diverse and complex mixture.

There has been change in British political culture. As one can see, the high degree of political deference that characterized British political attitudes has all but disappeared. Political protest—whether concerned with nuclear disarmament, unemployment and social deprivation, or issues such as the publication of the *Satanic Verses* by Salman Rushdie—merely serves to highlight the changing nature of political participation. On the other hand, regime stability has not been threatened by new issues or postmaterial agendas; in general these do not engage large sections of the population willing to engage in direct action and unconventional forms of protest. In this sense political stability is preserved amidst political and social change, ensuring that political culture enjoys continuity in transformation.

Internal Wounds: Conflict in Northern Ireland

Origins

It would be impossible to understand the political conflict in Northern Ireland without reference to its long, tragic history of political violence and civil strife. History has shaped the conflict and provided the fuel by which the engine of political violence is still driven.

Britain has had an interest in Ireland from the Middle Ages until the partition of the island into two societies in 1921. Ireland, on the other hand, has never shared the same sense of interest in Britain; it was one of the earliest and most exploited British colonies, and the memories and scars of over four hundred years of British imperialism have left an indelible mark on the consciousness of the Irish people.

Despite the fact that the British have been interfering in Irish affairs since the twelfth century, the real origins of the Irish problem stem from the systematic **plantation** of English and Scottish settlers in the northern part of the island known as Ulster at the beginning of the seventeenth century. It was at this point that the distinction between natives (referring to Catholics) and settlers (referring to Protestants) became an important signifier in the conflict. The British came to dominate Ireland in their colonial struggle to the extent that it became an Anglo-Protestant state while the large majority of the population remained of Roman Catholic persuasion.

In the long run the Ulster plantation of 1609 produced a conflict of sentiments and identities between Catholic natives and Protestant settlers.[23] The new colonists were different not only in religious denomination but also in their social customs and agricultural methods. The Protestants had the mentality of frontiersmen carving out their own distinct identity, which in turn signified them as an alien community among the native population. Assimilation was out of the question. The Protestant community developed a siege mentality still widespread in Northern Ireland today.[24]

For their part the Catholics were suppressed to the lowest levels of Irish society and defeated in any attempts to regain their confiscated land. Massacres and forced subjugation became the lot of the Catholic populace. In 1641 Catholics owned 59 percent of Irish land; by the middle of the eighteenth century this share had been reduced to 7 percent.[25] Catholics were further marginalized by the enactment of the repressive **Penal Laws** which prevented them from sitting in Parliament, holding government office, or bearing arms of any sort. Catholic Mass, in turn, was forbidden, as was the establishment of Catholic schools. At the end of the seventeenth century the Protestant ascendancy had achieved almost total control over the Irish nation. In effect the seventeenth century was crucial in determining the relationship between Britain and Ireland. It was in this period that the majority group, the Roman Catholic natives, were colonized, subjugated, and made subordinate by a minority group of Protestant settlers who quickly assumed the political position of majority group in terms of the actual allocation of wealth, power, and status. In turn the Catholics were relegated to second-class citizenship within their own society.

The Protestant ascendancy also succeeded in differentiating these groups in terms of their loyalty to the regime. The Protestants were "loyal" to the British state and the crown and indeed owed their privileged position directly to Britain. The Catholics, on the other hand, were termed "disloyal" by definition because of their rebellion against British colonialism and its structure of governance in Ireland. This differentiation created the basis for a political identity that was to be reinforced by the various historical events in the next four hundred years.

In 1801 Ireland was formally incorporated into the British state under an Act of Union signaling the transition from informal to formal empire. Political policies were determined by the Parliament at Westminster, which endorsed a tight control over Irish affairs. By the beginning of the nineteenth century the record of Irish nationalism and the idea and reality of an Irish nation-state signaled defeat at all levels. Certainly the Irish had made some progress; in 1793 the repressive Penal Laws were abolished, but real power and control still lay in the hands of the vested Anglo-Saxon Protestant elites.

The **Political Union** of 1801 did not guarantee political rights to the Catholic majority; it simply reinforced their exclusion from political life, and it was the nineteenth century that saw the development of a modern Irish nationalism with organized groups attempting seriously to deal with the Irish question.

In the final decades of the nineteenth century, nationalism developed as a much more potent and significant force and was met simultaneously with stiff resistance from Irish Protestant and British Conservative groups who wished Ireland to remain part of Great Britain. Various bills were submitted demanding home rule for Ireland—in 1886, 1892, and 1912, for instance—and were all defeated in one way or another. In 1898 the Catholic **Sinn Fein** (Gaelic for "Ourselves Alone") was founded; it later became the political wing of the Provisional Irish Republican Army (IRA). They campaigned vigorously for home rule, but the idea was shelved until after the First World War, which abruptly took center stage in 1914.

The Great War of 1914–18 disrupted any hope for a peaceful settlement, and yet on the other hand its aftermath created the conditions for political violence and the establishment of the Irish state. When in 1916 the British executed the leaders of the Easter Rising (in which nationalists had attempted and failed in an armed insurrection), martyrs were created, spurring on violent campaigns for Irish independence. The IRA and the Sinn Fein were in the forefront of the guerrilla activity that sought to unseat the British hold on Ireland. Faced with the choice of outright independence or some form of partition of the country into two parts, the British government—under pressure on the one hand from southern nationalist forces and on the other from northern Protestant militants—chose the latter course of action. The negotiations began in earnest in 1920. By the end of 1921 a treaty between more moderate elements in the nationalist camp and the British government created the foundations of a divided island in which a twenty-six county Irish Free State was provided while the remaining six counties of the North were to be administered separately. Ultimately, Northern Ireland fell under British jurisdiction and control, but for the next fifty years it was to be in the hands of Protestants, who constituted a two-thirds majority of the population of the six remaining counties.

The Stormont Government 1921–72

After the partition of Ireland into two separate entities in 1920, an Unionist government comprised of Protestants continued the exclusion of the Catholic minority from the political life of the community. The track record of the Stormont government has been universally condemned for its treatment of its minority group. During this period, Britain devolved power to a Protestant Unionist administration designed to serve the interests of the Protestant population before anyone else. Catholics were excluded from the corridors of national power at Stormont and also at the local government level through the use of gerrymandering (distorting electoral boundaries) for political gain. They were discriminated against in housing, education, the economy, and in the composition of the forces of law and order.[26] All of this created a wide sense of resentment and feeling of injustice in Catholic attitudes towards the regime. It was a "government without consensus," meaning that it had not obtained legitimacy from a substantial minority of its population: the Catholics.

In the 1960s these attitudes were reflected in the growth of the Northern Irish civil rights movement (NICRA), composed of middle-class Catholics and professionals, who pressed for reform from the Stormont Parliament. Even mild reforms proved too much for some Protestant extremists like Ian Paisley, for instance, who condemned the NICRA and its goals and incited violence against the minority population engaged in peaceful demonstrations and marches.

Clashes between the groups involved created an escalation of violence within the province and in 1969 led to introduction of the British army—at the request of the Northern Irish Government—in an effort to keep the peace. Initially Catholics welcomed this move, regarding the soldiers as there to protect them from Protestant violence. But the army came to represent a problem as people were subjected to intimidation and harassment amidst a growing climate of fear. Increasingly, coercion and repression became the preferred instruments of the British state in dealing with the crisis. In August 1971 the policy of internment (imprisonment without trial) was introduced, leading, not surprisingly, to widespread resentment in the province. And in March 1972, **direct rule** was introduced; the Stormont Parliament was abolished and Britain began to rule Northern Ireland directly from the mainland. Thus it becomes ever more clear that the conflict is not a religious one between Catholics and Protestants; rather it is a political conflict in the sense that the two religious groups have conflicting loyalties to different political entities. The Catholics are perceived as being loyal to the Irish state, the Protestants to the British state.

The violence and civil strife that followed in the wake of the NICRA's attempts to secure social justice for Northern Irish Catholics did not mean that social protest was at an end in the province. Certainly as a tactic in securing political and social change it had been superseded by extremist groups on both sides. Some of them wanted revolutionary change based on nationalist and republican values. Others were equally as determined to prevent such change in the province and clearly sought to preserve the status quo (inasmuch as one existed after 1969).

Protest continued in various shapes and forms, with various goals and objectives, but without the organized coherence of a mass movement based on the ideals of attaining civil rights. The heirs to the NICRA's spirit and method therefore comprised disparate groups, some of whom had played a part in the original movement. Their leaders included John Hume, the founder of the Social and Democratic Labour party (SDLP), and others who came to campaign for peace and compromise in Northern Ireland in light of the political violence that engulfed the province following the resurgence of the Provisional IRA. Their Protestant counterparts and the British army had previously intervened in the conflict in 1969, positioning themselves between the extreme elements in the conflict. The escalation of violence in this period made any meaningful civil rights activity next to impossible: The "men of violence" had triumphed in reducing opportunities for negotiation and compromise and thus precluded any hope for a peaceful solution. A key element of the situation was the fundamental quantitative and qualitative difference between the NICRA and the "men of violence" in the development of **civil rights** in Northern Ireland. And this dichotomy is enhanced if one looks at the positions and practices of the Northern Ireland Social and Democratic Labour Party after the demise of the NICRA in the post-1970 period.

Northern Ireland and the "Troubles"

The period since the outbreak of the violence in the late 1960s to the present day has been known as the "Troubles." Over three thousand people have died during this period and countless others maimed and wounded on every side of the equation: northern Irish Protestant and Catholic civilians; the British army; members of terrorist organizations, and even people on the U.K. mainland and occasionally the European mainland who have been subjected to bombing blitzes and terror attacks by groups fighting for a cause that seems lost. Some Protestants have organized themselves into extremist paramilitary groups like the Ulster Volunteer Force (UVF) or the Ulster Defence Association (UDA). Some Catholics cling to the IRA as their means of salvation, or even to more-extreme groups like the Irish National Liberation Army (INLA). Still the killing goes on. In 1974 for instance a Prevention of Terrorism Act was pushed through Parliament after there were major bomb explosions in the English towns of Guildford and Birmingham. Police powers were extended, and the IRA was outlawed. Diplock courts introduced into Northern Ireland after this ended trial by jury and left decisions to single judges. The treatment of prisoners and the use of rubber bullets in Northern Ireland (killing several children) were condemned and attacked by the European Court of Human Rights.

At the beginning of the eighties, evidence was produced that the Royal Ulster Constabulary (RUC) had adopted a "shoot to kill" policy, and this occasioned the infamous Stalker affair. The British police officer put in charge of the investigation in 1982 was subjected to character assassination. He was suspended from work in May 1986, when he was about to conduct an interview with the chief of the RUC, John Hermon. The IRA brought its campaign to the mainland once again in a devastating bomb attack on the Conservative Party's annual conference in Brighton in 1984. After this the British Special Air Service (SAS) became involved, shooting eight IRA men and a civilian at Loughhall, County Tyrone, in 1987, and three alleged IRA bombers in Gibraltar in 1988 (the bomb was never found).

Political and Social Change 1970–1991

By the 1960s, a new, educated generation of Catholics had emerged in Northern Ireland. New demands, new aspirations, new political persuasions were formed to replace out-of-date beliefs and ideas, which nonetheless lingered in major sections of the community. In that sense the ideals of the NICRA and the new Catholic leaders were ahead of their time and therefore doomed to failure; their problem was one of unreceptive audiences. The myths and bigotry of four hundred years of history had precluded the prospects and hopes for success of such a farsighted organization.

After the demise of the progressive groups, the task of defusing the conflict and managing order was in the hands of the various Protestant and Catholic actors (many of whom craved disorder) and the British government, which introduced direct rule from the mainland in 1972, abolishing Stormont. The imposition of external control along with the introduction of British troops and the suspension of Stormont meant that any major solutions to the conflict would take place within the climate of political opportunities created by the British government.

Three major attempts to defuse the conflict and head in the direction of a solution were developed in this period. All proved unsuccessful. They included:

1. An attempt in 1973–74 to set up a Northern Irish Assembly and a Council of Ireland (with representatives from the North and South). The key to this solution was a process, labeled **power sharing** in which the assembly would vote for an Executive of six Unionists, four SDLP members, and one Alliance Party member ensuring a political and religious balance. After this process was enacted the extremist members of the Protestant Ulster Workers Council declared a general strike in May 1974, which brought Northern Ireland to a complete standstill for two weeks. Effectively the window of political

opportunity was closed, the political process of "power sharing" fell apart and Britain resumed direct rule amidst the continuing violence.

2. In 1985 an Anglo-Irish Agreement was enacted based on the premise that cooperation with the republic would procure legitimacy in the eyes of Catholics (North and South) and therefore support. It was also an attempt to avoid a repeat of the 1974 initiative which in the main was destroyed by Protestant loyalist groups. In 1985 the British government deliberately refused to consult or negotiate with the Unionist community. Instead it entered into a bilateral agreement which provided for regularly scheduled ministerial meetings between Dublin and London, giving the South some sort of role in influencing northern affairs. For this concession the British procured a degree of cross-border cooperation in dealing with terrorist groups and a vague recognition that the people of the North had the right to self-determination. This produced an extreme reaction on the part of some Protestants; they conducted mass demonstrations, marches, and strikes and resorted to violent intimidation of politicians involved. The bloc of Unionist MPs at Westminster even resigned enmasse. Neither these actions nor the actual agreement, however, had much impact in solving the constitutional and political impasse.

3. The third and most recent (at the time of writing) major initiative was developed after sixteen months of careful planning and negotiation by Peter Brooke, the Northern Ireland secretary. The idea was to bring all the political parties involved together for talks on Northern Ireland's future. The talks began on April 30, 1991, and were formally announced as over on the third of July by Brooke. They achieved little or nothing; everyone blamed everyone else for the abandonment of the discussions. One report noted that "nothing could conceal the crushing disappointment of his [Brooke's] announcement on July 3rd that the all-party talks on Northern Ireland's political future had formally been abandoned."[27]

Efforts at political solutions to the problem have not been matched by efforts to ameliorate or change the economic or social features of the sectarian divide. One of the themes running through the civil rights movement, for instance, was that Catholics were discriminated against under the Stormont government. Subsequent to the imposition of direct rule, the British government in 1973 set up a Standing Committee on Human Rights under the direction of the Van Straubenzee Working Party. This led in 1976 to the establishment of the Fair Employment Agency, which was empowered to investigate allegations of religious and political discrimination in employment and also given the ability to issue directives that were legally enforceable.

If the desired effect of this activity was to reduce differences in unemployment among Catholics and Protestants in the province, then the legislation must be regarded as a failure. More than twenty years after the outbreak of the "Troubles" it has been shown conclusively that Catholics in Northern Ireland are still two and a half times more likely to be unemployed than Protestants. The substantial problem that the communities are separate and unequal and that this is a salient perception in the eyes of the minority remains a continuing source of division and tension.

In December 1993, a new peace initiative emerged amidst a storm of controversy. Sir Patrick Mayhew, the Northern Irish secretary of state, revealed at the end of November 1993 that the British government had actually been engaged in prolonged and regular contact with the IRA. This was despite an official policy that there would be no negotiations or discussions unless the IRA ceased violence. In fact, John Major had stated that "talking to the IRA would turn my stomach. I will not do it."[28] Such secret talks and dialogue caused the Conservative government a fair amount of embarrassment. However, this was simply the prelude to a joint Anglo-Irish Declaration issued on December 15 by John Major and Albert Reynolds, the British and Irish prime ministers. The document, which appeared to contain something for everyone involved in Northern Irish politics, has drawn a fair amount of support from most parties concerned (except of course from the extremists on both sides of the divide). John Major, in appealing to the nationalist elements, declared that Britain had "no selfish strategic or economic interest in Northern Ireland." In an attempt to appease the Unionists, Reynolds assured them that a united Ireland would not be imposed without the "consent of a majority of the people of Northern Ireland."[29]

Peace negotiations in Northern Ireland tend to evoke cynicism and disbelief in even the most optimistic observers of the long-running conflict in the province. Despite the most recent Anglo-Irish peace initiative in December 1993, the Sinn Fein has opted for a noncommittal reaction. The men of violence easily manipulate such positions.

Clearly, the British would now like a solution to the problem. There is no real strategic or economic interest in a territory that costs them over £4 billion a year (for 1.5 million people, the most heavily subsidized population in the United Kingdom). The British remain there, however, because the majority still want them to be there and the majority of Protestants clearly want to remain part of the United Kingdom. As the Northern Ireland secretary, Sir Patrick Mayhew, said in April 1993 in an interview with the German paper *Die Zeit*, "as long as the majority wishes to remain we will pay the 4 billion pounds without complaining." The moderate majority of Unionists apparently would also like a solution despite the recalcitrant Ian Paisley. In October 1993, the Reverend Martin Smyth, the deputy leader of the Ulster Unionist Party, told the BBC that "we are not the negative people that everybody has sought to paint, we have a philosophy, we have a plan and we would like to see others using politics rather than force" in an attempt to provoke the IRA into a ceasefire. Some have likened the Ulster Protestants to the Serbians in recent months. Interestingly enough, the Ulster Unionists and the Social Democratic and Labour Party (SDLP), the two largest and most peaceful parties in Ulster, have made very encouraging responses to the peace proposals.

Changes in official Sinn Fein policy over the last few years also suggest a softening of previous hard-line strategies on several counts, including a legitimate role for the Irish government and an acknowledgment that the British are not really the imperialists they were once labelled. Clearly with a handout of £4 billion (or £3,832 per Ulsterman) they can hardly stick to their erstwhile Marxist dogma. And with the Israelis finally recognizing the PLO and F. W. de Klerk negotiating with Nelson Mandela in South Africa for peace, perhaps it is time for the IRA to recognize the validity of the Northern Irish majority's claims. Is it not a scathing indictment that while the Middle East sues for peace, part of the European Community continues to plant bombs?

Moving Toward a Solution?

In 1976, Richard Rose argued that there may be no solution to the problem in Northern Ireland. After more than twenty years of violent conflict, the idea that the problem is "intractable" still carries wide currency. Throughout this section I have tried to stress that political protest and change are multidimensional. In accordance with the view that we should not look simply to one source of protest or change, I would argue that any attempt to procure a solution to the Northern Irish tragedy must reflect its multidimensional character. When Richard Rose addressed the question in 1971, he concluded that Northern Ireland existed as a **government without consensus**; it was a regime that was neither fully legitimate nor totally questionable. Twenty years later the search for government with consensus and peace continues but has failed to adopt a multidimensional approach.

In other words all angles must be addressed: political, social, economic, and cultural among others. Any solution should aim at finding common nonsectarian grounds in dealing with the conflict. There is room for optimism because all we have had from most of the existing literature is highly pessimistic on the nature of the future in Northern Ireland. One area from which we could look for input is the "new Europe" emerging from the increasing integration of the European Community. One author has already pointed out that during the 1980s the European dimension became more influential, particularly with the development of a distinctive European political identity within the European Parliament. The result of this was that there was a "belief by many MEP's [members of the European Parliament] ... that the conflict in Northern Ireland constituted a blot on Western European civilization and detracted from the European Community's developing political image in the world."[30] The increasing power of Europe to influence member states may have some far-reaching and positive political implications for the future of Northern Ireland.

Part of the problem rests with the historical fusion of religious groups and political allegiances—Catholic with Nationalist and Protestant with Unionist. To some extent it is this overlap between identities that has provided the basis for political mobilization in the province. If these identities can be changed, transformed, or even abolished within the context of the new European scenario, then the future may turn out to be a brighter one for the unfortunate people of Northern Ireland. It should be reiterated that solutions do not rest exclusively within one domain; a multidimensional approach is important in offering the opportunity for the "intractability" of the Northern Irish problem to give way to peace and reconciliation.

Race, Ethnicity, and Immigration

In this section the emphasis will be on the problem of race and immigration in British politics. Questions of race and ethnicity are important because the traditional view of Britain as a culturally homogeneous nation is no longer valid. The U.K. is better characterized as a multiethnic, multiracial, and multireligious society comprised of distinct minority groups who fall into various categories. And the advent of this change in the composition of the population has a great deal to do with the end of empire, which is most significantly demarcated by the end of the Second World War.

Defining Race

Defining race has constituted a problem for social scientists, who often are confused over the boundaries delineated by race, religion, and ethnicity. Indeed there is a great deal of overlap between these categories. Here race is defined as a political or social construct rather than a natural one.[31] It is the state that defines race for its own political purposes. That is, by placing people within certain categories and definitions it makes them easier to control and manipulate. In other words race has very little meaning as a scientific concept outside of its political meaning; physically, humans are rarely black or white in color. The color of the human race ranges from delicate pink all the way to extremely dark. Functionally, race is a definition imposed upon groups or assigned by the immediate political authorities. Physical appearance in this case is not the determining characteristic in the definition of race; rather it is the political variable or formula utilized by the governing authorities that is important in deciphering the politics of race. In Britain one can quite clearly see this, since the term used to describe the minority immigrant population overall is "black." This is totally misleading and only serves to disguise and hide the differences among ethnic minority communities. The diversity is illustrated by the case of the city of Leicester, which has a large Asian community. One inhabitant in five of Leicester is Asian, and yet this ethnic minority comprises many different groups, religions, practices, and at least seven main languages. Race or ethnic minority, then, refers to groups that are generally located within a similar position in society by virtue of their immigrant ancestry.

What we should realize and decipher is the meaning of race for the state and the political authorities. We can see that there are quite clear-cut definitions that allow the state systematically to categorize the members of society. Throughout this section, then, the terms *colored* and *black* will refer basically to the immigrant populations as referred to in the literature. These terms are interchangeable in the sense that they denote a distinctly negative characteristic (at least negative within the context of racism in British society): belonging to a nonwhite minority within a white-majority state.

The Problem of Immigration in the U.K. in the Postwar Period

In 1950 in London I was at the beginning of that great movement of peoples that was to take place in the second half of the twentieth century, a moving and a cultural mixing greater than the peopling of the US which was essentially a movement of Europeans to the New World. This was a movement between all the continents. . . . Cities like London were to change. They were to cease being more or less national cities, they were to become cities of the world, modern day Romes establishing the pattern of what great cities should be in the eyes of islanders like myself. . . . They were to be cities visited for learning and elegant goods and manners and freedom by all barbarian

47

peoples of the globe, people of the forest and desert, Arabs, Africans, Malays.[32]

In his discussion of the condition of modern humanity in *The Enigma of Arrival* (1981), V. S. Naipaul poses the acute problem to be found in the delicate relationships of ethnicity, identity, and the nation-state. The modern state must deal with the consequences when cities become international, and fails because of the complexity of the problem and the lack of precedent to adhere to.

In the post-1945 period, Britain was faced with the prospect of large-scale influxes from its former colonies. Naipaul refers to his own experience in a postwar Earls Court boarding house in London. It was at "the beginning of a great movement of peoples after the war, a shaking up of the world, a great shaking up of old cultures and old ideas."[33] This great movement of peoples was of course to have major political and social ramifications for the context of British politics.

Racial and Ethnic Composition of British Politics

There has been substantial demographic change in the composition of British society, particularly in the post–Second World War period. Prior to 1945 the UK had experienced a long history of immigration, including Irish, Polish, Jewish, Chinese, and other settlers who sought a new life in Britain. It was after 1945, however, that the patterns of immigration changed the face of British society, making it essentially a multicultural, multiethnic, and multiracial society. In 1948, the British Nationality Act provided Commonwealth citizens with the chance to settle in Britain, and this had major consequences because it brought in many nonwhite immigrants. According to official estimates, by the beginning of the 1980s Commonwealth immigrants who had arrived since 1948, together with their dependents, numbered some 2.2 million, or 4 percent of the total British population. These new immigrants formed communities based on ethnicity, language, race, and religion.

The labor shortages in the postwar era brought workers from the Caribbean, Pakistan, and India, recruited by government bodies such as the National Health Service and the Transportation Services. It would be misleading to argue that many of these people were coming to a better life; in most cases they performed menial tasks that many in the native population were loathe to fill. They represented a new form of underclass—an immigrant urban proletariat.

In 1951, estimates of Commonwealth immigrants came to roughly 75,000 colored people and one-third million noncolored

Commonwealth citizens. In addition almost 500,000 Irish and one-third million aliens immigrated. After 1952, when West Indians lost much of their traditional migratory outlet in the United States, they turned to Britain; this immigration reached its peak in the mid 1950s. After this there was a major increase in immigration from India and Pakistan. In the case of the former, this was mainly a movement of Sikhs who returned to visit their families at intervals and brought the family over when stricter immigration controls appeared to be on the agenda.

By 1974 over 1 million new Commonwealth immigrants had come to British shores, 325,000 from the West Indies, 435,000 from India, and 150,000 from the African continent.[34] The change in racial composition was remarkable; before the Second World War the nonwhite population of the United Kingdom was a mere few thousand; by 1985 this number had grown to 2.4 million, or 4.4 percent of the population, a number comprising almost all the surviving post-1945 immigrants and their descendants.

Britain's Race Problem

Britain's race problem can to some extent be seen in the attempts of the political establishment, through the two major parties, to restrict immigration, leading to a form of institutionalized racism. In the late 1950s race riots in Notting Hill proved to be a watermark in race relations and set the pattern for subsequent controls. The direct result was that the Conservative government introduced the first postwar Immigration Act in 1962, restricting entry from the colored Commonwealth to those who were able to offer certain skills or even show that they had the ability to perform a specific occupation. In the Smethwick constituency election in 1964, the Conservative candidate, Peter Griffith, ran for office on the slogan, "If you want a nigger for a neighbour, vote Labour." The Conservatives won. In 1965 the Labour party (traditionally the party of minorities) also showed its racist colors amidst increasing racial tensions when it passed a law ordering the deportation (without a court hearing) of illegal immigrants of less than five years standing. Polls showed that the Labour party's reversal of position on immigration reflected the views of the public. After a 1965 White Paper was issued increasing immigration officers' discretionary powers, a survey showed that 87 percent were in favor of "a strict limitation on the number of immigrants allowed from the Commonwealth. . . ."[35] Thus right-wing views on the race issue were rapidly creeping into the mainstream of British politics.

The most notable and certainly the most media-grabbing point of the 1960s was the position of Enoch Powell on the issue. Powell, a member of the Conservatives, in a series of speeches laid down the grounds for public hysteria over race. Powell envisaged the submergence of English "civilization" under a tidal wave of alien peoples who appeared ready to wreak civil conflict upon the stable and "homogeneous" British society. In a public speech in Birmingham in 1968, he appeared to be filled with dread as he revealed that, "Like the Roman, I seem to see the River Tiber foaming with much blood"—an acute reference to how he believed British society would become a battleground between the different races should immigration continue unabated. He demanded that all immigration should be suspended, and even wives and dependents of immigrants already in the United Kingdom should be excluded. Instead, immigrants should be encouraged to rejoin their families in their native countries. Powell was subsequently dismissed from the Conservative Shadow Cabinet by Edward Heath, who at the same time endorsed policies that would limit immigration into the United Kingdom.

What is interesting about Powell was how widespread and popular his sentiments were at the time. Even in 1978, Mrs. Thatcher, who admired Powell, warned of the danger that Britain "might be swamped by people with a different culture."[36] She went on to say in the television interview, "You know, the British character has done so much for democracy, for law, and done so much throughout the world, that if there is any fear that it might be swamped, people are going to react and be rather hostile to those coming in." The Conservatives' ratings increased substantially after this, and they went on to win a major victory over the Labour party in the 1979 general election.

Public support in the 1960s for such sentiments revealed how intensely the issue was perceived. One poll revealed roughly three-quarters of the population in general sympathy with Powell's racist expressions at the time. In April 1968, one poll showed that almost 93 percent of the respondents favored a drastic reduction in immigration. The opposition was mainly concentrated in those groups who felt they had most to lose, such as unskilled manual workers, and also among the elderly.[37]

As a result of mounting race hysteria, a second Commonwealth Immigrants Act was rushed through Parliament in only two days in an effort to tighten the 1962 act, and in 1971 the Immigration Act tightened these rules even further, restricting entry to those with parents or grandparents born in the United Kingdom. Commonwealth citizens by this time, then, were granted only the same rights as all other foreigners applying to work in Britain.

Race and the Extreme Right in the United Kingdom

The equivalent to the French Front National (FN) is the National Front (NF) in Britain. And like the French party it makes an openly racist appeal, arguing in the same way that Enoch Powell did for the repatriation of colored immigrants. The immigrants are to blame for most of Britain's economic and social problems if the Front is to be believed; high unemployment, poor housing, drugs, and crime are all blamed upon minority groups. Like the French group, the NF is anti-Semitic, virulently anti-Communist, and anti–European Community. However, unlike the FN it has failed to attract much support and remains a fringe party by any standards. In 1979, it managed just 0.6 percent of the vote in the general election, although it has done better in local government elections in urban inner-city areas with substantial immigrant populations.

The tactics of the NF are typically protofascist and include demonstrations and marches by aggressive militant supporters. A large proportion of the demonstrators are "skinheads," youth who shave their heads and tend to be aggressive and violent in nature. In the 1983 election the NF lost even more votes.

By 1992 the tide of anti-immigrant sentiment in continental Europe had not really had much effect on the British mainland. As we have seen, there has been little support for explicitly racist parties. When Jean-Marie Le Pen, the French leader of the antiimmigrant party the Front National, visited the U.K. in December 1991, protests from the public and MPs were strongly evident. With tough measures against immigrants under the Thatcher governments and explicit details of racial discrimination available, Britain hasn't suffered the same backlash as in France and Germany. Many migrants to the United Kingdom in the postwar period have been treated as permanent settlers, not simply temporary migrant workers, and have been given the vote and social security benefits and allowed to hold political office. Parties like the NF (like all the other minority parties) are also discouraged by the electoral system of "first past the post," which prevents small parties from gaining seats and influence. Despite some increase in racial attacks in recent years and more activity by the neo-Nazi British National party, it appears unlikely that vicious racism will develop into a major problem in the near future. One former Conservative minister from the Thatcher period stated such a conviction when he dismissed the fascist parties as "simply too stupid, too coarse, [and] too absurd" to be a menace in Britain.[38]

Race and Race Relations

While racism has proved a problem for the British political system, it has encouraged the growth of a race-relations industry based on various organizations that work to improve the relationships between majority and minority communities within the United Kingdom. The Race Relations Acts in 1965, 1968, and 1976 made direct and indirect discrimination illegal in various areas of employment, housing, and education. The Race Relations Board was eventually replaced with the Commission for Racial Equality (CORE).[39]

Case Study: The Strange Affair of Salman Rushdie

From the beginning men used God to justify the unjustifiable.
—Salman Rushdie

Background

Before analyzing the Rushdie affair it is perhaps appropriate to give some details about the Muslim community in the U.K., around whom the controversy to some extent is centered. The number of Muslims in the U.K. has increased to over 1 million recently; two-thirds are from Asia, including 400,000 from Pakistan, 12,000 from Bangladesh, and nearly 100,000 from India. The remainder are from East Africa and the Middle East. Most of these Muslims have settled into large-sized communities in various urban areas such as Bradford and Birmingham.[40]

In addition, Muslims are the fastest-growing religious community in Britain; they tend to be younger than the rest of the population and to have larger families.

The controversy surrounding Salman Rushdie and his book *The Satanic Verses* has many facets and nuances which propel it into the center of political debate. When he wrote the novel it is unlikely that Rushdie could have foreseen the furor and animosity it would create among the Moslem community worldwide. He might have predicted the burning of the book by Muslim leaders, but certainly he would never have anticipated that a *fatwa* (death sentence) would be issued against him by the then spiritual leader of Iran, the Ayatollah Khomeni, on February 14, 1989. At the time of writing Rushdie remains under sentence, a victim of a dead man's decision. His plight is a cruel paradox within a British state apparently representative of liberal democracy and freedom of speech and yet adopting a position of appeasement in the face of the *fatwa*. Others have been attacked: the translator of the Italian version, Ettore Capriolo, was stabbed but survived at the beginning of July 1991, and the Japanese translator of the *Satanic Verses*, Hitoshi Igarashi, was stabbed to death almost two weeks later outside of Tokyo.

The two political acts—the burning of the book and the death sentence—pose an insoluble paradox for the British state. Just what is at stake? Freedom of speech, the protection of minority rights, the issue of a multicultural society, and religious tolerance (or intolerance as the case may be). The case of Rushdie offers a striking case from which to grapple with these issues.

There is no doubt that many Muslims regard the book as blasphemous, despite the fact that it is likely that most have never read it. But Muslims in the United Kingdom are not only demanding to have the book banned; they would like to have the British blasphemy law reformed so that it punished threats to their religion as well as to Christianity. The tension between the secular state and the Islamic perspective has increased over the years, and the Rushdie affair is only the tip of the iceberg. In fact, Muslims would also prefer to be subject to Islamic law in the U.K. rather than British law. They would like different social and educational arrangements, including single-sex schools for their children, special uniforms, and *halal* (religiously correct) meals. Muslim children should be allowed to forego art, music, and dance in the educational curriculum according to this view. Some fundamentalists even go so far as to demand their own parliament.

Some writers, therefore, have chosen to place the Rushdie affair within a wider political context rather than the immediate scenario. The burning of the book, as one author writes, was not a spur-of-the-moment event or the result of spontaneous anger. Rather it was a staged act to secure publicity; its goal was to rally Muslim opinion in the United Kingdom so as to defend Islamic traditions against Western values and secular traits. Similarly, the *fatwa*, this argument contends, was not based on the actual words in the book or the spurious charge of blasphemy but was called for in order to manipulate politics within Iran and secure political capital.[41] At the local level (within the U.K.), another writer stresses the importance of the different groups within the Islamic faith. The argument is clearly that the book burning had very little to do with fundamentalism, as is widely perceived, but expressed outrage among every section of the Muslim community. The majority of Muslims in the United Kingdom are Barelvis and Deobandis from Pakistan, for instance. These groups are concerned with preserving Islam as a social force and remaining independent from the state as much as possible. However, they do not represent the more extreme views of groups such as the Sunni fundamentalists, who follow the teachings of Jamaat-I-Islami. Differences among Muslims, although often obscured by groups out to secure political capital, of course suggest a more problematic interpretation of the events.[42]

Moreover the point is taken one step further by arguing that it was politically expedient for the British government to appease Islamic regimes by not taking stricter action on the matter. Defending Rushdie strongly and uncompromisingly was a difficult agenda for a government intent on maintaining trade and economic contracts with Iran and at the same time seeking not to alienate the minority Muslim vote in the United Kingdom.[43] In this author's view, the belief in freedom of speech and the preservation of this democratic right were sacrificed to the politics of expediency.

There appears to be no compromise on the part of Iran towards Salman Rushdie, even after five years of the imposition of the *fatwa*. And this is despite the fact that moderates within Iran have defeated the extremists in parliamentary elections. For his part, Rushdie embarked upon a series of publicity meetings with officials and leaders and made several appearances at universities around the world. On February 11, 1993, President Clinton's spokesman denounced the *fatwa* as a violation of international law. Germany, Canada, and the Nordic Council in Scandinavia have in various ways shown their displeasure and frustration over the situation.

The web of issues the affair has spawned encompass moral, legal, social, political, and economic angles; they in fact highlight the problems of democracy and a multiracial and multicultural state and in turn must be examined in that and the wider context.

Race in the United Kingdom: A Future of Harmony or Strife?

Race and the issues it raises will not disappear from the political agenda. Neither will they go away. The problems that exist within a multiracial state are problems that most governments would prefer to ignore because they are difficult, sensitive, and complex issues for which there is no quick fix and no easy solution.

At the beginning of September, 1993, a candidate for the extremist British National party was elected in the east London Millbank local council by-election. In turn this led to several violent clashes among members of groups such as the Anti-Nazi League and BNP supporters. In the last three years, at least four black youths have been murdered by white racists in the London borough of Greenwich.[44] Of course such groups can nowhere near garner the support that we see for fully fledged political parties like the French Front National. However, they do represent tensions in society and potential sources of conflict.

As with all questions of race, immigration, and ethnicity, the theme of identity is a recurring one. In this section, we have seen that various members of the political elite, from Enoch Powell in the 1960s to Margaret Thatcher in the 1980s, have been at pains to discuss and make efforts to preserve an explicitly British/English identity.

This is enormously problematic in a Britain that is multicultural and multiracial, and the problem is one that faces all societies in Western Europe. What constitutes a Briton, a Frenchman, a German, or an Italian obviously provokes widely differing responses and perceptions, but nevertheless appears on all of the political agendas of these societies. And it is interesting that the definitions of who is a citizen vary equally across these countries despite the movement toward European integration. This is a paradox that appears to have no resolution in the immediate future.

In the United Kingdom, the relationship between immigrants and the "host" society has progressed little beyond an accommodation of them—a condition of "social pluralism." In such a system people within "different minorities enjoy equality in respect of civil rights and obligations, but keep themselves separate in marriage and mutual hospitality, while rivalling one another in other contexts— such as in political organizations."[45] Similarly, Sheila Patterson sees such immigrant groups as adapting themselves to membership in the host society in certain areas, such as economic and civic life. And in turn the host society accepts them in certain ways but not in spheres that affect the "overall life of the society, such as religion, and cultural and family patterns."[46]

And clearly, under the operation of this **social pluralism,** the British sense of identity feels threatened by various other identities. In most recent times the global assertion of Islamic fundamentalism as a political and social force has started to have an impact in predominantly white Christian Britain. Demands for a Muslim parliament, the outcry over the *Satanic Verses*, and the changes in the laws regarding families reflect that social pluralism, as posited in the writings of Banton and Patterson, will remain the norm for many years to come. In other words it is unlikely that such groups will **assimilate** with the majority cultural ethos. In this scenario, social pluralism and the politics of accommodation will be the most important indicators of race relations in the United Kingdom. Until images of what it means to be British change, it appears unlikely that political responses and bureaucratic solutions will have much impact.

The British Malaise

In this section I will deal with what has come to be commonly described as a major societal problem in the U.K.: a general political, social, and economic malaise that is sometimes known as the British "disease." This disease is not characterized by any one symptom or cause but by a variety of problems that have developed over time.

The malaise has as its initial starting point the postwar era in which Britain lost industrial preeminence, was relegated to the status of a second- or perhaps third-rate power, and in general showed all the signs of relative economic decline. Of course this decline had been set in motion at the end of the nineteenth century with the arrival of the United States and Germany as prominent industrial powers, but it was not until the end of the Second World War that the problem began to become fully appreciated. Two world wars had left the U.K. in a state of economic exhaustion, stripped of its assets and export markets. Despite its symbolic prestige as one of the three victorious powers in 1945, its material, concrete benefits of victory were far from evident. The imperial possessions acquired over the previous two hundred years were given independence throughout the 1950s and 1960s, a process that was inevitable and limited Britain's world role. The transition to the status of a regional power was a difficult adjustment for Britain, and one that took on an increasingly somber reality. In 1962, Dean Acheson, the U.S. secretary of state, observed with painful accuracy that "Britain had lost an empire and not yet found a role." Even in Europe, Britain was having a difficult time. One sign of the decline was the decision to apply for membership in the European Community in 1961. Harold Macmillan was trying to reconcile the new Britain with a new future in an essentially regional institution. It was not until 1973, however, that the U.K. was finally allowed into the EC after several unsuccessful attempts. In the decline from world power to regional power, the British appeared weak and dispirited in comparison to the growth of advanced industrial, Continental countries.

At home and abroad the British economy was undynamic, and it appeared particularly weak in competition with the Germans or the Japanese. The picture then was one of relative decline in comparison to other industrialized states. Employment in manufacturing, for instance, declined by 13 percent between 1955 and 1973, whereas it increased by 155 percent in Japan. The continental Europeans simply produced more than the average Britons. By the end of the 1970s, the U.K. share in world trade was under 10 percent, gross national product was in rapid decline, and everyone was blaming everyone else. The British motorbike industry, for instance, which had dominated the world in the 1950s, had declined drastically at home and abroad by the late 1960s and simply could not match the design or performance of such Japanese models as Yamaha or Suzuki.

Britain managed the lowest growth rates of all the states in the Organization for Economic Cooperation and Development (OECD) in the 1960s and 1970s; between 1960 and 1975 it had fallen from seventh place in terms of GNP to the sixteenth position in the hierarchy. Moreover it had a reputation for being a strike-ridden society with poor economic management and poor-quality workmanship. Managers were blaming workers for sloppiness and inefficiency; workers were blaming management for poor practices and weak leadership. Limiting wage increases, developing relations with the EEC, and increasing economic growth have all proved in one form or another to be the spectacular failures of both parties in government. Trade union conflict and the battle over wages created a general crisis in the United Kingdom as the miners went on strike in early 1974, forcing the government into an emergency election. But the British disease was not related to one facet or area; it appeared throughout society to be "that sinking feeling."

By the beginning of the 1980s a great many books had already been written to explain and understand this problem, its symptoms, causes, and possible cures. In general they appeared doom laden and pessimistic, with titles like *Is Britain Dying?*, *The Death of British Democracy*, *The Break Up of Britain*, and *The Future That Doesn't Work*. They described in detail the symptoms of the disease: a sick economy, a welfare system bloated with bureaucracy, perpetual strikes by militant trade unions, and secessionist groups in Scotland, Wales, and Northern Ireland (in the last, terrorism was still having a major impact on the economy and society even though the United Kingdom was subsidizing it more heavily than any other region). The practice of **adversarial politics**, in which the reins of power swung back and forward between two ideologically opposed parties, was blamed for accentuating the disease. In fact William Gwyn divided the commentators on the British decline into two groups. One group he labeled the "Jeremiahs," who viewed these trends as part of a long-term general decline and had a generally pessimistic view of the future of the United Kingdom. On the other hand he identified a group he called the "Pragmatists," who argued that specific changes in personnel and policies and a revamping of institutions might bring about improvements and much-needed change. In essence this group was more optimistic about the future.[47]

There were, of course, many causes for British decline. Britain had to deal (or not deal) with at least two periods of decline. One was a period of relative decline, according to Paul Kennedy's theory that nations do not fall and rise absolutely but in comparison to one another. This period was from the late nineteenth century until the 1960s. The other period of decline was more absolute and stressed the total eclipse of the British economy by the Americans and the Japanese from the 1960s onwards. This latter time frame has clearly been a period of deindustrialization for the United Kingdom, which has had to cope with the abandonment of its shipping industries, the shutdown of large-scale manufacturing, and the obsolescence of much of its industrial plant. The country simply could not compete with the dynamism of the newly developing Asian economies.

However there is still a case to be made that this was also a period of relative decline; that Britain cannot be analyzed without taking into account the changes in the global political economy and without reference to other societies that were rising as fast as the United Kingdom was falling.

Britain in Political Decline

Britain's decline, however, wasn't simply an economic one, and some writers have made the connection that there is a clear connection between the state of the British economy and the perceived political crisis.[48] One argument is that the British economic decline has been caused by the failure of the British political system to develop a consensus on economic issues. In general, between 1950 and 1975 there was a broad political consensus on the management of the economy. It was a mixture of private and public in which the latter grew in scope and size under both Labour and Conservative parties and in which trade unions, industrialists, and governments collaborated. Under Labour governments, the social welfare programs increased as did nationalization of the private sector, with less resistance from the Conservatives than might have been expected.

By the mid 1970s this consensus had evaporated; both parties had mismanaged the economy. Compared to the booming Continental economies Britain appeared as the "sick man" of Europe. The left argued that the problems went deeper than superficial appearances might indicate; Britain's economic problems were part of a general crisis in capitalism that could only be dealt with through radical change.[49] On the other hand the right-wing side of the spectrum blamed the welfare syndrome of free handouts, which simply encouraged low productivity and laziness in the work force. Absenteeism and unemployment were only natural in a system that provided disincentives to work. For the right, there was too much state intervention; taxes went to pay for health and welfare services. Private funds that could have been used for investment were diverted into welfare. In addition trade unions, according to the right, exacerbated this problem with constant strikes and poor worker productivity; there were also poor relationships between management and workers due to an outdated and outmoded class system which permeated industrial relations.

Furthermore, the post-1970 period emphasized adversarial politics, with the two major parties (Labour and Conservative) simply attempting to reverse each other's policies at the first opportunity. In turn this resulted in inconsistency and prevented a political consensus on economic issues from emerging. Instead, the adversarial party system resulted in the manipulation of the economic system for political gain. The aim of political parties in such a system is not to improve the economy but to stay in power by winning elections.

Parties were pitted against one another. Labour advocated more not less nationalization of the private sector and increases in public spending and welfare programs. Margaret Thatcher and the Conservatives offered the reverse: sell public companies, reduce state intervention, and cut social welfare. Lower taxes to provide incentives for business and reprivatize industries that had been nationalized. Under such schemes, regulations and public investment funds were to be reduced and progressive income taxes slashed. Entrepreneurs were to be encouraged and public housing was to be sold. If anything Thatcher wanted to create a nation of home owners.

To some extent, Thatcher believed that what was needed was a shock to the system in order to provide a cure for the economic malaise that gripped the United Kingdom. Reversing national economic and political decline was the main priority. Thatcher specifically introduced a policy of monetarism in order to control inflation, and she wanted an enterprise economy, one in which the market and not the state was the predominant agent of economic recovery. It was a dramatic break with the past and the politics of consensus. In 1981 Thatcher had argued that consensus was simply a byword for the "process of abandoning all beliefs, principles, values and policies." The doctrine of Thatcherism had a major impact in breaking the postwar economic and political consensus, at least for the decade and more she remained in power.

Economically, the policy of privatization, with the sale of state-owned industries to investors and the work force (through shares), led to a major shift in resources. Among the large public-sector groups sold off were British Telecom, British Gas, British Airways, British Steel, and the water and electricity industries, and this has clearly led to a redrawing of the boundaries between the public and private sectors. Trade unions also fell under the legislative hammer of the Thatcher program. Secondary picketing and sympathy strikes were made illegal, while "closed shop" trade unions (unions in industries that made membership compulsory) were made increasingly difficult to operate. In short, industrial action was severely curtailed under Thatcherism.

Conclusion

Overall, has British national decline been reversed under Thatcher and the Conservative party in the 1980s and 1990s? Has there been the dramatic break with the past postulated upon the advent of radical policies?

The answer is yes, no, and maybe. In short there is no clear-cut way to assess the impact of Thatcher on the British economic and political malaise because all the evidence is not yet in; this will be a job for future historians. In saying this, however, I will offer some conclusions about the Thatcher era that have gained some consensus.

In essence the results that are in indicate that the Thatcher record is a mixed one with positive and negative aspects. Certainly in terms of the balance of payments, the indications are positive. The U.K. now has a surplus balance sheet in comparison to the negative position when the Tories first took office. On the other hand, inflation still remains a crucial problem, with very little change in the overall period. (Despite, for instance, being very low in 1987 at 3 percent, by 1990 it had increased again to nearly 11 percent.) This is a problem with no easy solution; it is difficult to tell the overall impact monetarism had on controlling inflation, particularly as nations operate in a global world economy and are subject to worldwide recession.

Manufacturing has fluctuated similarly. In the early 1980s nearly 20 percent of the manufacturing base became inoperative, and unemployment reached 3.5 million, a postwar record. Yet in the mid 1980s manufacturing picked up and output increased, even if only slightly. Then followed the downturn in the economy at the end of the 1980s. Certainly Thatcher tamed the destructive side of the trade unions and managed to privatize a great deal of the economy and transfer resources. In foreign affairs, with the victory in the Falklands, the special relationship with the United States, and her ability to project herself as a world leader, she restored some credibility to a nation which had seen its pride severely dented.

On the other hand, the economic record so far is debatable. The gap between the haves and the have-nots does not seem to have decreased significantly; the gap between the North and the South in the United Kingdom seems to have increased. Welfare institutions were attacked; the problems of poor people and the homeless received no significant attention. Record numbers of young people could be found sleeping on the streets of the major cities of Britain in the early 1990s. An apparently regressive tax (the poll tax) produced a popular revolt which in turn led (at least in part) to Thatcher's downfall. She left her mark on British politics without a doubt, but it remains a mixed picture, and her successor, John Major, will have to cope with it throughout the early and possibly the late 1990s. He does this, however, in the assurance that the Conservative party has maintained an unchallenged continuity in British politics since 1979, a record unparalleled in the postwar period.

Continuity and Change: A Conclusion

Many people throughout the centuries have admired the British way of life. From 1689, the constitutional settlement appeared to provide a balanced system. Government was secure and accountable to Parliament, and it ruled according to various laws and conventions. The French and British political systems could be contrasted from the 1830s onwards. France alternated between political extremes, while the British model was moderate and balanced; one was stable and the other unstable. Germany, Italy, and Spain all went through various periods of authoritarianism, and so it is not surprising that people looked to Britain as the epitome of liberal democracy. Certain features are important. There was a reconciliation or balancing of government authority and the limits to that authority. The "rules of the game" were firmly established: the rights of the opposition in Parliament were secure and the executive was accountable in Parliament. The legitimacy of Britain's political institutions remained solid despite a violent civil war in the seventeenth century, various peripheral rebellions in the eighteenth century, and continuing threats of violence in the nineteenth and twentieth centuries, particularly from Ireland. By and large, however, the United Kingdom has largely avoided the levels of political violence and instability that have plagued other European states.

While it would be true to say that Britain experienced a fairly peaceful evolution or transition to liberal democracy, clearly the issue of Northern Ireland remains a thorn in the side of the British state, a real element of discontinuity in its political development. The question of Northern Ireland is all the more interesting because it appears as a political anachronism in twentieth-century Europe. It may be seen as an ongoing politico-religious conflict in a continent that mainly resolved its religious turmoil several centuries ago. However, the fuel that fires such political violence might be attributed more to the sort of tribal tendencies that we have seen recently in Yugoslavia and for many years in Lebanon. The conflict has been "managed" to some extent through various measures, and while the picture is not entirely satisfactory, it does afford some positive outlook for the future.

Some discontinuities have also appeared at the level of British political culture. The decline of deference and the occurrence of more volatile expressions of political protest are important aspects of a new culture in the United Kingdom. Such important political trends have occurred in line with such societal trends as the decline in industrial and manufacturing bases in the economy and a subsequent increase in the service sector.

In addition we have seen other elements of change enter postwar British politics, including the arrival of a multiracial and ethnic society. In recent years the issue of Salman Rushdie and the *Satanic Verses*, as we have seen, has upset the religious sensibilities of Muslims in the United Kingdom. Some Muslims go so far as to demand their own parliament to cater to their own specific interests. And the question of the role of fundamentalist Islam in a liberal democracy is an important one for everyone who participates in the social fabric of the U.K.

The economic and social malaise known as the "British disease" has also had far-reaching effects in undermining the confidence of British citizens. The relative economic decline of the United Kingdom is obviously a long-term historical phenomenon, and it remains to be seen whether the Thatcher period will have any significant impact in terms of its reversal. On the whole, however, despite some of these discontinuities in British politics, there remains a society more influenced by long-standing traditions and political evolution than by short-term hiccups. Can we actually call the problem of Northern Ireland a discontinuity when it is a problem that has been around for at least four hundred years? After such a long political evolution, it appears unlikely that Britain will succumb to short-term pressures and will weather the tides of political and social change as it has done successfully over the years.

Key Terms and Concepts

Each term appears in the text in boldface type.

Adversarial politics
Assimilate
British disease
Charter 88
Civil rights
Common law
Constitutional monarchy
Convention
Deference
Devolution
Direct rule
Government without consensus
Penal laws
Peripheral nationalism

Plantation
Political culture
Political Union
Poll tax
Postmaterialism
Power sharing
Rates
Relative decline
Sinn Fein
Social pluralism
Sovereignty of Parliament
Statute law
Thatcherism

3
France

Historical Overview

There are certainly some major areas of contrast between the course of French political development and the evolutionary route that Britain pursued, and this has been particularly noticeable in the past two hundred years. Since the French Revolution of 1789 the nation-state has undergone major changes in its form and substance of government. France's three monarchies, five republics, and a puppet regime which exhibited fascist tendencies in the past two hundred years provide substantial evidence of a state racked by dislocation and discontinuity in its political process. Its most recent republic dates only from the 1950s and during the 1960s was subject to crises and discord even as it sought to provide the stability needed to maintain the French polity.

Why does France appear to have a tortured process of political development in comparison to the relative smoothness of the British version of events?

There are several factors that lie rooted in its historical consciousness. First, France in the Middle Ages did not have the same kind of centralization within the state that we find under the Norman system in Britain. The same forces pulling the nation to the center were not established in the French state, where the barons and aristocratic elements in society felt free to establish their own interests regardless of national perspectives. There was no national consciousness that could be compared to the version found in England.

The struggles among the various dukes over who was fittest

for the main role of kingship divided France into many rival factions and came to a climax in the Hundred Years War. This led to the establishment of a powerful monarchy that used the resources of the estates general (nobles, clergy, and townspeople) to finance the war. With the French victories in the long and bitter war against the English, the power of the monarchy reasserted itself, and the estates general lost any power or control that they exerted (and this had been brief to say the least). But after the French state had dealt with the expulsion of the English from its land, it soon became embroiled in its own Continental affairs with Spain and Italy on the one hand, and its own internal divisions between Protestant and Catholic groups on the other. Despite success in controlling these conflicts by the end of the sixteenth century, they reflect the fact that France was seriously internally divided and still largely fragmented in the process of nation building.

Absolutism and the French State

It was the French monarchy that constituted one of the major driving forces behind national integration and a national identity. But the monarchs' success in unifying the nation and creating an identity was also their own undoing.

If one state personifies the pursuit of **absolutism** in Europe in its history of political development, that state is France. Unification, centralization, and the extension of control were actively sought-after goals of the French aristocracy. By 1661, the notion of the absolutist state was well established under the feudal system that prevailed. Louis XIV's accession to the throne was the climax of this development to the point where he is reputed to have said *"L' etat, c'est moi"* ("the state is me"). Louis conducted the business of extensive centralization, relying exclusively on the kingship and conducting all the affairs of the French state from and within the bounds of his palace at Versailles. He completely ruined France by engaging in continual warfare, and he drove the state to the verge of bankruptcy by helping support the American colonists in their struggle against the British state. The overregulated economy, weighed down by restrictions, was hastily abandoned in favor of free trade and a market economy, but it was the last gasp of a dying *Ancien Regime*. In 1789 the French people provided the key to French politics by initiating a major and cataclysmic social revolution against the king.

The French Revolution provided us with an enduring set of words and ideas that are still highly relevant in our world today. The concepts of right and left, guerrillas, counterrevolution, and of course the revolutionary ideas of liberty, equality, and fraternity all stem from one of the most important episodes of political history just over 200 years ago. According to French commentator Alexis de Tocqueville, the revolution "roused passions such as the most violent revolutions had never before excited." The French Revolution was to constitute a major political discontinuity in French politics, but more importantly, it was to have major implications and consequences for future global political developments. When Chairman Mao Tsetung of China was asked what was the impact of the French Revolution, he replied, "It is too early to tell."[1]

What it is not too early to tell is the fact that France has exhibited a fair degree of continuity in terms of the legitimacy of the state in operation from this period onwards. There have been some major disruptions of course—restoration in 1814, revolution in 1848, a new republic in 1871—but none of these fundamentally undermined some of the basic tenets of the French Revolution and the effect this has had on French political life. David Bien and Raymond Grew point to this paradoxical context of legitimacy in French politics:

> Two characteristics of modern French politics follow. First, a significant segment of French public life has actively denied the legitimacy of each regime. So commonplace did such rejection become that it ceased in itself to be revolutionary. Thus familiarity has had an effect like tolerance, often allowing even fundamental opponents to maintain some peripheral contact with the political system. At the same time, issues of conflict that might be resolved or subject to compromise within the system are likely instead to be raised as a challenge to the regime itself. Second, each new regime, aware of its shaky legitimacy, stresses as much as it can its continuity with its predecessors in law, institutions, and even personnel. This has a paradoxical effect. It has reinforced the remarkable continuity across eight regimes in 160 years.[2]

In the political history of France, "discontinuity" appeared almost "continuous" in nature.

France since the French Revolution has produced five republics, some emphasizing the role of Parliament and some the role of an authoritative and powerful executive. For instance, Parliament was emphasized in the first republic during the period 1793–99. With the accession to power of Napoleon Bonaparte in 1799, the position of Parliament was weakened to a large extent through successive executive forms of government. These include the consultate (1799–1804), the First Empire (1804–14), the Bourbon Restoration (1814–30), and the Orleanist Monarchy (1830–48). During the Second Republic (1849–52) Parliament in France resumed its brief hiatus in the power

---

TABLE 3.1: Political Cycles and Regimes in France

Moderate Monarchy	*Liberalization*	*Conservative Reaction*
Constitutional Monarchy (1791)	Republic of 1792	Dictatorial government (1795)
Restoration (1815)	"July Monarchy" (1830)	Second Empire (1852)
Early Third Republic (1870–79)	Later Third Republic (1879–)	Vichy regime (1940–44)
		Fifth Republic (1958–)
	Fourth Republic (1946–58)	

Source: William Safran, "France," in *Comparative Politics*, edited by Jacobs, Conradt et al. (Chatham, N.J.: Chatham House, 1983), p.89.[3]

---

structure, but not for long. The Second Empire (1852–70) reimposed executive control at the expense of parliamentary politics. With the advent of the Third Republic in 1870, a long period of political continuity was assured, and the locus of political power reverted to the parliamentary structure at least up until 1958. The failures of the later Third and Fourth Republics to prevent France from sliding into chaos and near anarchy caused a reversion to strong executive leadership. The idea that the French political system has been subject to a series of cycles which involve continuity and discontinuity is nicely expressed in table 3.1.

The Fourth Republic (1946–58) was plagued by political instability. In its twelve years of operation it produced more than twenty cabinets; the system was unstructured and chaotic. There was a multiplicity of parties that lacked discipline, coherence, and the leadership qualities necessary to produce effective policies. Consequently, multiple parties existed within parliamentary coalitions, with politics taking place in an atmosphere of chaos. Issues were left unresolved, the political agenda was in dispute, and instability reigned under the system.

The appearance of the French Fifth Republic and a strong presidential system in 1958 was designed to counter the problems of parliamentary factionalism and the political instability that plagued the system. Michel Debre and Charles de Gaulle specifically wanted to create a system in which the French president was given an enormous amount of power. Such power would enable the executive to overcome any crises it might face, for crises had crippled the effective functioning of the Fourth Republic. The formulators of the constitution had at least two major prerequisites in mind when they made their decisions: (1) the authority of the state should be enshrined under the leadership of an extremely strong and powerful executive (i.e., the presidency); (2) the result should be the diminution of Parliament's power, and limitations and restrictions on its power to legislate.

The president of the Fifth Republic is elected by popular vote for seven-year terms and given enormous power, far more than his equivalents in any of the other European nations discussed. And these powers have been expanded upon to some extent by the various presidents in office since 1958. These are:

Charles de Gaulle (1958–69)
Georges Pompidou (1969–74)
Giscard d'Estaing (1974–81)
François Mitterand (1981–   )

Charles de Gaulle, one of France's wartime heroes, had been called back from retirement to help reconstruct France and provide it with a new regime. The Fifth Republic was molded in his image, that of a domineering autocrat, aloof from the daily dirt of politics. De Gaulle epitomized statesmanship and provided the French presidency with a very important role in framing the future of the country. In May 1968, part of the French population rebelled against this overbearing authority vested in de Gaulle when they took to the streets; the Fifth Republic, however, weathered the crisis and displayed a degree of continuity and stability in its democratic development.

It is often the case that crises at various levels serve to strengthen the system, not undermine it. In this sense the Fifth Republic was to prove the culmination of the successes and failures of previous systems; it combined republicanism with a strong presidential power base, a powerful executive with a parliamentary tradition. There is no doubt that executive power was given a predominant position, but this was regarded as important because previous legislatures that had dominated had failed to improve the political process in France. It is no mistake or error that there are more articles in the 1958 constitution describing presidential office than describing the role of the national assembly. Theoretically the French presidency is one of the most powerful executive offices in the world of politics. The French executive can designate the prime minister, dissolve the National Assembly, and invoke emergency powers when he feels the integrity of the republic is under threat (through Article Sixteen of the French Constitution). If used arbitrarily this power can allow the president to assume almost a dictatorial role. It is also within the power of the French president to bring certain issues to the people in the form of a referendum. As president, Gen. Charles de Gaulle was keen to set the mold and precedent which future presidents might follow.

Once in office de Gaulle moved swiftly to place his stamp on the new regime. One of his first acts was to announce that Algeria would be given independence; this move received massive support in two referendums from the French public. Despite resistance from extreme right-wing groups (including assassination attempts) and various uprisings in Algeria, the decision was carried through. In 1963, Algeria became an independent country. The Algerian crisis had been a test case for the strength of the Fifth Republic, one that it passed. At the time, many on the left and right felt that it would not outlive its creator, de Gaulle. They were proved wrong, however, as it has not only outlasted de Gaulle but weathered the storms and crises over the years and been accepted by the Socialists and the left who have maintained power since 1981.

The Fifth Republic

In 1958, the primary emphasis of the new French constitution was to restore a sense of law and order to the French political tradition. In this sense it was a conservative approach, with the accent on political stability rather than the political instability that had plagued France. But an increase in discipline at the elite level does not necessarily translate to the masses. The Fifth Republic did, in other words, provide essential stability and continuity to France, but difficulties and disruption remained an important part of French politics.

De Gaulle's electoral vehicle, the Union for the New Republic (the Gaullists), was a potent force in the aftermath of the French Fourth Republic. It successfully staved off challenges from both the left and extreme right and brought smaller parties of the right and center into its circle, managing to secure a majority of electoral support in the 1960s and early 1970s. State economic planning became a national agenda, as in most other European societies, in order to modernize the French economy, which had been severely damaged by the Second World War and the mismanagement of the Fourth Republic. The French economy was badly in need of modernization in the postwar period. France was largely an agricultural country until the end of the war, with almost one-third of its labor force in this sector; in 1954, for instance, 26.7 percent of its population were employed in agricultural occupations. By the middle of the 1970s this figure had been reduced to just over 9 percent. The move from rural areas into urban conglomerations in two decades by nearly 2 million people was a major factor in boosting French industrialization. Government ownership of key industries and a vast expansion of the public sector worked hand in hand with the private sector as energy, transport, and raw materials became more available and at a lower cost. Important areas of industry were given incentives to develop with subsidies and tax reductions; French manufacturers and distributors benefitted from planning and the knowledge of the market available under such a system. The mixed economy, of course, was not unique to France; it also found expression in other major European societies. In France, however, the governments of the Fifth Republic went some way to plan the economy in consultation with financial and business elites.

The French system of **indicative planning** was also fueled by large influxes of immigrant workers, as also occurred in the U.K. and West Germany after the 1950s. The fact is that it is doubtful whether France could have modernized so quickly or so effectively without this cheap source of labor. With an economic boom in the 1960s and 1970s, the French economy could not find enough French workers to fill jobs. With the influx of immigrants and their families from Italy, Algeria, and southern European states, foreign workers constituted over 4 million of the population by the late 1970s. And this immigration allowed France to complete its modernization programs. In the postwar era the performance of the French economy was a very respectable one, sharing the 1970s with the rest of the world, but weathering it.

Between 1945 and 1975 the planners and the bureaucracy were extremely successful in turning France into a modernized capitalist society; a highly urbanized labor force and rapid population growth led in turn to increased economic output and generated higher standards of living. The French economy was rapidly transformed from an agriculture- and manufacturing-based system into one primarily engaged in industry and services, with increasing emphasis on the latter. The average annual growth rate between 1958 and 1973 was 5.5 percent, a figure which exceeded that of any other European nation and was in fact second only to Japan's in the industrialized world.[4]

However the French economic "miracle" was a fragile one in some respects, based as it was on the authoritarian predispositions of Charles de Gaulle and a period of boom in the world capitalist system during the 1950s and 1960s. Social equity and the leveling of society did not appear to be the priority of the planners; instead, how to maximize economic output took precedence, and this approach began to meet with some opposition. Even today France has one of the highest levels of income inequality in the advanced industrial world and certainly one of the largest gaps between rich and poor, between the haves and the have nots.

The weakness of the postwar settlement appeared most dramatically in the form of an uprising in May, 1968, which had been preceded by several years of economic difficulties in the form of wage restraints, poor development of trade unions, and the lack of adequate provision of facilities for university students.

De Gaulle had dominated the French system for just over ten years, years that had seen major changes in terms of a new constitution and the way that France was governed. A former war hero, de Gaulle was a charismatic leader who, in drafting the constitution, provided the president with extremely strong power, enabling presidential control at the expense of parliamentary democracy. He once argued that the president "elected by the nation is the source and holder of the power of the state." In effect, de Gaulle became the source and the base of political power in France; by relegating the parties, prime minister, and Parliament to a secondary role, de Gaulle ensured a strong and continuous leadership, avoiding the pitfalls of multiple parties and coalition rule.

There were of course problems and limitations with this role, and in examining these we should look at the practical experience of the first Socialist government of the Fifth Republic, which was elected to power in 1981.

The Change to Socialism in 1981

On May 10, 1991, the French right announced the tenth anniversary of François Mitterand's rule by declaring *"Dix ans, ca suffit!"* ("ten years is enough!"). The Socialists responded with *"Dix ans qu'on seme"* ("For ten years we've sown"). Neither slogan at the time caught the mood of the general public.[5] When François Mitterand was elected to the French presidency for seven years in 1981 and when his Socialist party won nearly 38 percent of the vote in the June elections of the same year, a new shift away from the conservative leadership took place, and a discontinuity of political control was registered in the Fifth Republic. In institutional terms, things went on much as before despite previous criticisms of the constitution by

Mitterand and his party. Once ensconced in office, they ruled out any drastic institutional change. What was clearly different, however, was a marked ideological shift in terms of policy and orientation. By the end of the 1970s the right had lost its way, and the doors suddenly swung open to permit the entrance of the left.

Mitterand clearly had had a long and colorful political career. A resistance member in the Second World War, he opposed the Fifth Republic's constitution and even challenged de Gaulle in the mid 1960s for the leadership. When he took over the Socialist Party in 1972, he developed an electoral alliance of the left with the Communists but, significantly, he managed to reduce the latter to an insignificant role in the alliance. In 1981 for instance the Communists (PCF) managed only 16 percent of the vote and forty-four seats; in 1986 their share further declined to just under 10 percent of the vote and only thirty-five seats in the elections to the National Assembly.

After the Socialists had won a large majority of the seats and control of the presidency, they could turn to implementing their broad mandate and vision of a socialist France. This included nationalizing significant parts of the economy, introducing new types of relationships between management and workers, and decentralizing the highly centralized structure of the French state. In their first five years, the Socialists succeeded at least in carrying out the first part of their program. They nationalized six important industrial groups, two financial groups, and over thirty-six banks, and they complemented this by indirect ownership (similar to that of the British Labour government in the 1960s), buying the majority bloc of shares within various private industrial and finance companies. The welfare state was expanded to increase the minimum wage and provide pensions for the aged, health-care services, and family benefits, along with reductions in the retirement age (to sixty) and the average work week (to thirty-nine hours). Workers were encouraged to participate in the management of their jobs. The death sentence was abolished, among other reforms in the criminal justice system. In addition there was the policy of giving local authorities more power and say in the running of their affairs in order to decrease the power of the centralized state. After this intervention in the economy in 1981–83, the Socialists switched policies; they to some extent abandoned controls over prices and wages along with **Colbertism**, a tradition of state intervention (named for Jean-Baptiste Colbert [1619–83], Louis XIV's minister of finance). High inflation and large trade deficits forced Mitterand to adopt a policy of austerity, with real wages being reduced to provide incentives to industry and business. This advent of fiscal and monetary rigor, tax reductions, a little privatization, and a great deal of financial deregulation produced a mini economic revolution in France, enabling it to have a low inflation rate. Modernization was no longer driven by state-directed policies but by economic liberalism and greater individualism as entrepreneurship was encouraged. Low inflation, however, is not necessarily synonymous with low unemployment; ten years after Mitterand came to power the number of adults who were unemployed had risen by 1 million (to 2.6 million), or 9.3 percent of the labor force. The gap between rich and poor has in fact widened, and this problem has been exacerbated by the entry of illegal and legal immigrants (some figures put this influx at the rate of 100,000 per year).[6] Nationalization was partially reversed in 1986 when the victory of the UDF-RPR in the National Assembly resulted in the return of many industries to the private sector. (The Union pour la Democratie Français [UDF] is a federation of parties led by former president Valerie Giscard D'Estaing; the Rassemblement pour la Republique [RPR] is the Gaullist party led by Jacques Chirac.)

Despite the efforts of the Socialist government to stimulate the private sector and denationalize after 1983, France still has the most state-dominated economy among the G-7 industrialized countries (that is, the "Inner Seven" of the EEC). Recent figures show that out of every one hundred French workers, twenty-three are now on the payroll of the government (in comparison with eighteen in 1970) and approximately twelve more are still working for state-owned enterprises.[7]

When I discussed de Gaulle, I argued to some extent that he had established a strong presidency because of the chaos of the Fourth Republic, where unbridled and multiple political parties produced a fragmented and incoherent approach to politics. It was seen that the French president had an extremely strong leadership profile, one that could react to crises in a decisive if slightly authoritarian manner. There were, of course, some limitations on this power. If the president, for instance, does not have a majority in the National Assembly that supports his prime minister and cabinet, he will be forced to work with a prime minister and cabinet that may be opposed to his policies. As mentioned, this to some extent was the result in 1986 when the Socialist camp was defeated in the legislative elections, depriving President Mitterand of majority support. At this stage, political discontinuity entered the realm of presidential politics. Mitterand was forced to accept a center-right candidate, Jacques Chirac, as prime minister and a period of political **cohabitation** was entered upon, an uneasy sharing of power between reluctant political bed partners. In 1988, the president was again defeated in the legislative elections of June, thus ensuring that when he was reelected for a second term in May 1988, he fell just short of an outright majority of deputies. This development again illustrated that the French president was subject to certain constraints of party and parliamentary politics and that the constitution of the Fifth Republic was not as foolproof as de Gaulle had perhaps intended.

France in the 1990s: A Democratic Malaise

Recent signs from contemporary French politics point towards the symptoms of malaise throughout French democracy. The rise of Jean Marie Le Pen and his extremist Front National in domestic politics is symptomatic of this malaise. Peoples' interest in politics has declined significantly as the French have become disenchanted with the apparatus of the state and with the general practice of politics. Whereas Le Pen has no real difficulty turning out 30,000 supporters to a mass rally in Paris, the Socialists and mainstream right are having immense difficulties in persuading people to attend meetings and in stimulating active support. A survey taken in 1991 pointed out that 53 percent of the French believe that all politicians are corrupt.[8] Other French social commentators have argued that general feelings of disgust and contempt for democratic institutions lead to totalitarianism (something that would benefit Le Pen in the long run). Issues have become less important (apart from the race and immigration issue, which has become more important). In the 1990s, younger politicians have also signified their worries over such political apathy. For example, the mayor of Grenoble, Alain Carignon (a Gaullist), in an open letter to Mitterand published in the weekly *l'Evenement du jeudi*, argued that "the French have deserted their public life, and democracy is sinking. The only beneficiary is the extreme right."[9] Scandals and corruption have also crept into French public life. Not that they haven't always been there, but the mood of malaise further exacerbates them and brings them to the forefront of politics. Concern over insider trading, high-level corruption, mismanagement, and financial misdeeds employing party slush funds plague the Socialist government in the 1990s. To some extent one sees a return of the "diamonds syndrome" of French politics. The diamonds scandal emerged in October 1979, when then-President Valéry Giscard d'Estaing was found to have received gifts of diamonds from Jean Bedel Bokassa, the self-proclaimed emperor of a corrupt Central African Empire. This was reported in *Le Canard Enchaine*, the French satirical weekly at the time, and the scandal weighed heavily on D'Estaing all the way to the termination of his presidency. The current low public opinion of politicians, the resulting political apathy, and the malaise in French democracy seem to revisit the syndrome that pervaded France at the end of the 1970s.

A Crisis of Identity?

Although a particular sense of French identity had apparently emerged, it no longer seemed entirely secure at the end of the 1980s and the beginning of the 1990s. On the one hand there was a challenge from the new Europe and changes within the EC. If this had not threatened French identity, then perhaps it was in the process of subsuming it. Valéry Giscard D'Estaing, a former president of France and possible contender for the 1995 election stated categorically that "Europe does not cause us an identity crisis, but is an affirmation of our identity. . . . We know what we are, but the way in which we choose to express what we are has had to be redefined."[10] One question France appears unable to redefine, however, is exactly what does it mean to be French? Will France become a multicultural state in a multicultural Europe? Will Frenchness disappear in France?

Clearly the France of Marcel Proust, which was compared to an "immense human being" with a character, will, and particular pride, is fading away; a reformulation of identity, of citizenship, and nationality is perhaps one of the appropriate agendas for the French political system to focus on for the 1990s and beyond.

Political Culture and Change

> One moment, he is up in arms against authority and the next we find him serving the powers-that-be with a zeal such as the most servile races never display. So long as no one thinks of resisting, you can lead him on a thread, but once a revolutionary movement is afoot, nothing can restrain him from taking part in it.
>
> Alexis de Tocqueville[11]

The words of one of the foremost students of the French Revolution form a widely used description of the ambiguity of the French citizen in the arena of politics. It helps one to understand a system that has been punctuated by frequent bouts of political acquiescence followed by violent protests and revolutions. French political culture if nothing else is volatile.

The questions, then, that form the basis for this section are, To what extent does France have a volatile political culture? How do French citizens interact with their political system? What does it mean when they take to the streets and protest over issues they feel strongly about? Does France have a culture of protest?

To answer these problematic questions it is necessary to look at the relationship of the citizen to power, authority, and personal liberty in France because these have had a major influence on the way the average French person has perceived the system and its effect on political life in France.

A Civic Culture?

France was included in the landmark study conducted by Almond and Verba in the 1960s, but the data for political culture studies of France have not been as highly developed as for the U.K., Germany, or the United States. Survey data on political culture in France are scant, so that the social scientist is reduced to reliance on observations, newspapers, and other sources to gauge peoples' attitudes. In the late 1950s and 1960s the French experienced rapid modernization within their economy, and evaluations of the Fifth Republic as a regime rose accordingly. It is a subtle irony that modernization went so well as a direct result of the mass of immigrant labor, which nowadays is made the scapegoat of many of France's economic ills.

The predominant view in political science is that on both micro and macro levels the French public displays an ambivalent attitude towards various forms of political authority and elites. A **dualism** exists in the sense that "close up" authority, which manifests itself before their eyes, is regarded as anathema. On the other hand there is respect for distant personages who wield power over their lives. The French prefer their leaders to remain aloof because it suits their fundamental position on individual liberty.

Two basic tenets of this culture distinguish it from its British equivalent on these issues. On the one hand a strong tendency towards individualism, displayed in a general distrust in the state and the agencies of the state, permeates French political culture. It is believed that individual concerns and goals clash with the collectivist goals of state action, and so public and private should be kept separate. However, the French do emphasize other associations and institutions as a form of defense and protection against the state. They seek refuge in their families, trade unions, the village setting, and their region as a balance against what they regard as the negative, all-encompassing actions of the larger state. Such mechanisms of defense and response are the product of a highly individualistic society.

On the other hand, there is a prevalent culture of **statism**, historically a product of the French Revolution in general and the Bonapartist organization of the state in particular. In this cultural view it is the state that is responsible for solutions to the problems of society. You may note that this position appears to contradict the idea of individualism previously described. However, again this is a reflection of the dualism within the political culture. The French, as an "administered" people, remain the subjects of the very institution they distrust. One only has to look at the role of the French civil service and its huge administrative capacity to understand the importance of the bureaucratic norm that pervades French society. One political scientist, Henry Ehrmann, concisely describes this ambivalence: "The French citizen's fear and distrust of authority and his simultaneous need for strong authority feed on both his individualism and his passion for equality."[12]

This view is reinforced by an examination of French political history. One of the patterns that emerges is that, after each revolt or rebellion against the political establishment, there is a retraction; at least in part, there is a restoring of that which had been overthrown. It should be noted quite emphatically that there is never a full restoraton of the prior status quo, but the pattern does indicate that, despite individual expressions of rebellion, the average French person is still interested in maintaining a relatively conservative political system. After degeneration into near anarchy during the Fourth Republic, the imposition of discipline in the Fifth Republic was a much-appreciated restoration of political order through strong authority.

In the contemporary period of French history both these concepts, individualism and statism, appear to be undergoing revision. As we noted, political culture is rarely a static phenomenon; France is currently engaged in both the decentralization of the state to invigorate autonomous forces and by efforts to foster more associational initiatives to achieve collective goals.

The key to understanding the political culture is to understand the complexity of the abstract notions that constitute it. Often ideas that seem contradictory and "difficult" play a role in explaining how and why the political culture has developed. What we find in the end is that it is a product of its historical background. Shaped by revolution, ideology, instability, and a great deal of social violence, France, not surprisingly, is a good example of discontinuity. Its political shape is very different from that of the British system.

A Culture of Protest

Protest and political action are not new in French politics. They are not a recent trend, but rather, an almost established norm of the

French political system. The events of May 1968 when barricades were erected in Paris and police clashed violently with students and youth were not exceptional in French society. They merely served to prove how much of a protest culture had permeated the system throughout the years.[13]

In general, violent and not-so-violent forms of collective action have maintained a conspicuous presence within the gamut of French political history. The French in general are much more prone to take part in demonstrations than any other European people.

The 1960s, for instance, were a time of tremendous social and political upheaval in Western Europe in specific and the world in general. This upheaval was made manifest by "unconventional" behavior and expressions of protest against various political systems. In the United States new tensions were created by such traumatic incidents as the assassinations of major political and social leaders, including John F. Kennedy and Martin Luther King, Jr. In Italy, Spain, West Germany, Mexico, and the United States, student rioting took place on an unprecedented scale. Nowhere was this more apparent than in the events of May 1968 in Paris. The "events of May" 1968 constituted a month-long battle of student collective action and workers' strikes against the forces of law and order. They provide some of the most recent evidence of the ambivalent nature of French political culture.

May 1968

The problems that erupted in May 1968 may seem to have originated in rather petty circumstances, but they constituted a serious crisis at the time for the French political system. The dispute began at the University of Nanterre, located in a Parisian suburb; parties to the dispute were the university administration and the students who went on strike. The latter were upset at a lack of facilities, overcrowding, a rigid curriculum, and the absence of student participation in the affairs of the university, among other complaints.[14] These specific issues at Nanterre were soon seized upon by a vocal left-wing minority who managed to spread the discontent across French campuses into a general attack against the inadequacies of the national educational system. Anarchism and rebellion against the authorities spread to incorporate workers who realized the benefits of jumping on the "revolutionary" bandwagon after the students appeared to win major concessions from the government. Spontaneous strikes saw between 6 and 7 million participate in demonstrations and France practically brought to a standstill. Even the trade unions and representatives of the workers were caught by surprise and actually did little to encourage or organize the strike into a more effective instrument of collective action.

The authorities' reaction was to immediately repress these disruptions with special riot police, tear gas, and excessive crowd-control measures. Charles de Gaulle, the French president, appeared on the verge of using the army to put down the rebellious groups involved. De Gaulle, however, sought an alternative solution to the violent crisis by attempting to use his preferred instrument, the referendum. In the case of a negative response to his proposal in the vote he agreed to resign. The appeal, however, failed to gain consensus; few people appeared interested in the referendum proposition. Instead he quickly utilized Article Twelve of the constitution, calling for fresh elections and dissolving the National Assembly. This proved to be a masterstroke; in promising law and order and by providing the scare of a totalitarian and Communist threat to the Fifth Republic, de Gaulle and his party won an electoral landslide and further increased their own legitimacy and the Fifth Republic's at the same time. Once again the legitimacy of the post-1958 settlement had been put to the test and survived the crises.

The events illustrated that consensus in this period had prevailed over conflict; the varied mixture of anarchy and existential philosophy of the students had failed to take root among the general population. While the May events were a violent confrontation, they were not experienced in terms of radical revolution. While protest and the capacity to protest are clearly important elements in French political culture, a pervasive obedience to authority is also an important reality. When de Gaulle switched the focus from street politics to electoral politics, the protests and strikes were subdued. And in turn order was restored, with the beneficial result for the restorers of order that they won their most decisive victory over the left. Once again there was apparent the paradox in the elements of a citizenry who believe in the freedom to resist but also the obedience that restores order. Tolerating authoritarian values and the right to revolt in the same breath represents an enduring continuity in French politics.

Contemporary Political Culture

A new French political culture appears to be in the process of emerging in light of recent events and circumstances. The political currency of the 1980s—**cohabitation, consensus, *ouverture*** (openness to dialogue)—appears in the 1990s to be giving way to political conflict, and this conflict centers around the questions of race and immigration and the general democratic malaise that has reinforced such problems. Several trends testify to the overall decline in consensus: the dramatic decline of the power base of the Communists with the collapse of the Soviet Union and Eastern Europe and subsequently the complete decline of Eurocommunism as a credible electoral choice; the dramatic shift to the right in French politics at all levels, and the fact that the issue of race has come to occupy such a large part of the political agenda.[15]

The Le Pen phenomenon and the rise of race and immigration will be placed in greater context in the section on race, immigration, and ethnicity, but it is important to realize that these questions have now become firmly ensconced in the milieu of French political culture in the 1990s. A right-wing party with a specifically anti-immigrant set of policies poses a new challenge to the French republic and its status as a liberal democracy. It signals the rise of political disaffection within the French community and is clearly related to an economic and political sense of malaise. It appeals to general discontentment, and what is interesting is the movement of the mainstream right, not to the center, but increasingly further to the right. This development eschews the politics of consensus and cooperation, instead embracing the politics of extremism, of alienation and decline. Several commentators have noted that race appears to be the only issue on the agenda.[16] It is a politics that demands scapegoats and finds them readily presented. It is a politics that eschews consensus in appealing to a form of *insecurite*, broadly meaning the "fear and uncertainty prompted by economic recession and social change."

One possible qualifying explanation is that this development is in itself part of the evolution of the political culture of the Fifth French Republic. It may be that the questioning of the consensus that constitutes the general political culture is a healthy and democratic political process in itself, which strengthens rather than weakens the orientations around which that culture is based. In this sense it remains to be seen whether the issues of race, immigration, and a reinvigorated far right will produce a crisis, and whether that will have a profound or superficial impact.

Internal Wounds: Anti-Semitism Past and Present

Racism created myths which it subsequently attempted to bring into existence. Myth as reality is best explained by an extreme example. The Nazis created a department in their interior ministry concerned with unravelling the supposed Jewish world conspiracy. The bureaucracy acted as if such a conspiracy really existed, and so made it come true as a foundation of national policy. The myth had been turned into reality.[17]

Overview

The quote above summarizes much of the author's view on racism: that it operates through the use of the myth. These myths are turned into reality for explicit political purposes, and this is manifestly the case when we come to examine the politics of anti-Semitism, an open wound on the landscape of French society and politics. These negative feelings towards Jews gained popularity and respect in parts of Europe during times of economic and political crisis, particularly towards the end of the nineteenth century. People found an outlet for their frustrations by scapegoating this particular ethnic group. These ideas are gaining credibility in certain quarters even today as France faces economic and social malaise.

Anti-Semitism in France has had a fairly long history and has proved to be a phenomenon with a degree of political continuity. Perhaps one of the most notable starting points would have to be the famous **Dreyfus affair** in the late nineteenth century. The scandalous 1898 mistrial of a famous French army captain, Dreyfus, with its specific anti-Semitic motivations, had wider implications in that it became the backdrop to a violent conflict over values among the French political elites.

In 1894, a Jewish officer attached to the French general staff, Capt. Alfred Dreyfus, was accused of providing the Germans with state secrets. In a military trial rigged with false evidence, Dreyfus was sentenced to life imprisonment on Devil's Island, one of the worst French penal colonies. The country was divided over the issue; the left in general tended to side with Dreyfus and defended traditional republican virtues of equality. These *Dreyfusards* included the writer Emile Zola, who wrote a famous letter entitled "J'accuse!" ("I accuse!"), a scathing indictment of government and military collaboration in the Dreyfus affair. On the right, there were the *Antidreyfusards*, who represented the aristocracy, right-wing Catholics, army elites and anti-Semites, who generally favored values that belonged to the Ancien Regime prior to the Revolution. Finally, in 1906, Dreyfus was freed, but the scars of anti-Semitism and the political divisions these engendered remained.

L'Affaire, as it became known, turned into a "violent conflict over values among the country's elites. Both sides went to fanatical extremes; guilt or innocence of Dreyfus was not a question of evidence but of unshakeable dogma."[18] On the one side was an anti-Semitic group who believed in general what Maurice Barre had said when he argued after 1898 that there was no need to show that Dreyfus had betrayed France because "that he is capable of treason I believe by knowing his race."[19]

In France the most important right-wing movement of this period was the militant Roman Catholic, anti-Semitic group Action Francaise, born during the Dreyfus Affair; this group desired a return to the Ancien Regime. This development had important implications; for one it illustrated that the mainstream of French anti-Semitism attempted to link nationalism with social and political reform. Above all, anti-Semites were interested in national unity (and it is interesting to note that in the case of Le Pen and the FN, not much has changed in this regard).

Anti-Semitism and the Far Right

Since the postwar exodus from North Africa, French Jews number roughly 650,000; they form the largest Jewish community in Europe outside the former Soviet Union.

At the elite level the attitude may have changed; under de Gaulle, for instance, the French government was openly critical of Israel. This attitude, in turn, created a "Jewish vote" potentially hostile to the French Fifth Republic. This situation subsided with the advent of subsequent administrations.

On the other hand, the intolerance of the extreme right towards the Jewish community may actually have increased. Anti-Semitism has always been a theme and a preoccupation of the intolerant right, and it has found its way into the Front National's agenda in a fairly explosive manner recently. No longer a peripheral issue, it has become a much more central aspect of French racism. This has occurred in several ways.

In a behavioral sense, at least 20 percent of all racist attacks in the past few years have been directed at the Jewish community. In opinion polls, one in five French people believe it is impossible for a Jew to be a loyal citizen. The number of Jewish graves that have been desecrated in France has increased dramatically in recent years. For instance, between August 1980 and April 1986, an average of 56 graves a year were desecrated (a total of approximately 337 in this period). Between April 1988 and May 1990, however, this figure increased to an average of 156 graves a year (312 in total).

Revising History

In addition, in terms of the media and rhetoric of the Front National and in terms of French academic life, the issue of French Jews has become more significant. And once more, recent fascist propaganda materials in France simply represent a long tradition. In the late 1980's Henri Roques completed a Ph.D. dissertation at the University of Nantes in which he defended those who had denied that Jews were massacred in Nazi camps in the Second World War. In several universities the issue of anti-Semitism has spilled over into the academic community and indeed been promoted by academics. In January 1990, an article published by Bernard Notin, a lecturer at Lyons 3 University (and a member of the FN's scientific council) cast doubt on the existence of the gas chambers and the Holocaust. This article was published in a prestigious magazine subsidized by the National Scientific Research Council. In Aix-en-Provence, a university town that voted heavily for the Front, several neo-Nazi groups formed in the local military training school and among the law faculty. In 1986, for instance, two lecturers at the military school who protested over the teaching of Nazi military songs were dismissed after other teachers complained that the two were interfering with the curriculum. At Paris 2 University in 1989, the Groupe Union Defense (GUD), which is connected to the law faculty, publicly advertised a "striped pajama party with Zyklon B cocktails." These are only a few illustrations of events at the university level, but they serve to illustrate that revisionism and the denial of the gas chambers are becoming important in the themes of the far right.

Jean Marie Le Pen, the leader of the Front National, has for instance stated in public that the Nazi gas chambers were a "minor" detail of history or an "incident"—in effect dismissing the significance of the Holocaust. In fact there is a burgeoning literature on the subject; several of the Front National propaganda papers such as the *National Hebdo*, the *Present*, and the *Identite*, have pushed anti-Semitic themes in their publications. In October 1989, Roland Gauchier, the editor of the *Hebdo* which sold 100,000 copies, referred to the power struggle between Jews and Catholics, which he argued posed a "fantastic planetary-scale struggle between Catholic Christianity and international Jewry."[20] In its January 1983 issue, the *Present* argued that Paris had become the "capital of the Jewish world" and continued to denounce alleged conspiracies organized by B'nai Brith, the Jewish community's Masonic movement. Even outside of the official extreme right Front National propaganda a

84

large propaganda literature on anti-Semitism is available. Once again much of this represents a continuity in French political life. As one author puts it,

> In February 1984 the pro–le Pen newspaper *Present* published an article by Romain Marie (now a Euro-MP) criticising the "tendency for Jews to monopolise all the highest positions in the Western nations." Such slogans confirm that in looking at racism and fascism in Western Europe today we are not looking at something new, we are looking at an extremely well established tradition which is now reasserting itself.[21]

This reassertion of tradition is also echoed in other areas. Revisionism on the subject of the Jewish community has appeared in the form of reanalysis of the Vichy Regime, the Nazi puppet government of France during the Second World War. During this period at least ten thousand Jewish people were deported from free zones (where the Nazis had no control) to concentration camps under the rule of Marshal Petain, a notorious anti-Semite (and leader of Vichy France) and Darquier Pellepoix, commissioner for Jewish affairs at the time. There was no law at the time that Jews had to be delivered to the gas chambers, and yet Vichy officials extended this "convenience" to the Gestapo. At Le Pen rallies today, Marshal Petain and his anti-Semitic nationalist program are consistently commended, and on national television Le Pen argued that Petain had been unfairly condemned. Some authors, in fact, attribute the resurgence of present anti-Jewish feeling to a failure to condemn the wartime persecution of the Jews under the Vichy regime. Until 1983, for instance, Vichy's complicity in the Holocaust was never mentioned, and no one involved had been brought to trial for war crimes. A film uncovered in France in 1954 showing French police helping the Nazis was removed from public access. Even as late as the 1970s, Prime Minister Giscard D'Estaing appointed Maurice Papon to head a ministry; during the war Papon had repeatedly signed orders for Jewish children to be taken from safe foster homes in Bordeaux and sent to the death camps. Time and time again the French right wing failed to condemn these practices, and many in effect supported anti-Jewish measures well into the war. One author, Bernard Henri-Levi, goes so far as to argue that the Vichy regime was not necessarily an aberration in French politics; in his view France adopted fascism with such great ease that no adjustment at all seemed necessary.[22] While Henri-Levi overstates the case, there are obvious parallels between the rhetoric and propaganda of the 1930s and early 1940s and the current speeches and writings of Le Pen and his followers. In both cases the appeal to anti-Semitism is clearly evident.

Conclusion

Anti-Semitism has left a scar on the French body politic that refuses to disappear and in fact opens up periodically. Shortly after the desecration of an ancient Jewish cemetery and impalement of a disinterred corpse on a parasol (known as the Carpentras atrocity), French television screened Alan Renais's famous documentary on the concentration camps of the Second World War, *Night and Fog*. This illustrated how sensitive the French psyche was to the reopening of old wounds.

Anti-Semitic behavior has increased throughout the 1980s as seen by the number of attacks on Jews and the rehabilitation of such anti-Semites as Petain. Anti-Semitism has become a growth industry and one of the main preoccupations of the reinvigorated far right. In the program of the Front National, the ideas of anti-Semitism, continued from the Vichy regime, are no longer simply an implicit component but an explicit and integral part of the doctrine. Anti-Semitism has moved from the periphery of the agenda closer to the center. In this case then it would be fair to argue that the more things change, the more they remain the same.

Race: Ethnicity, and Immigration

France has been taking in immigrants since at least the 1880s, but the most salient period for our purposes is the large-scale immigration since 1945. France brought in workers from two sources during this period: from colonies and excolonies and from southern Europe (Portugal, Spain, Italy, and other Mediterranean countries). What was different in the postwar period was the predominantly North African immigration into France. This had a crucial effect on French views of racism and national identity because it evoked images of the Arab world and in particular the Islamic world (which for many French appear inseparable). By 1970 this immigration amounted to 3 million foreign workers (one-third of whom were non-European). Migrant labor was developed under guest worker schemes in both Germany and France, in France under the auspices of the Office National d'Immigration (ONI). There are now roughly 3.6 million of these immigrants within French society according to INED (the National Institute of Demographic Studies); according to the interior ministry, the foreign population is closer to 4.5 million.

Policy Response

France began tightening controls on the entry of immigrants from Africa in 1970 and 1972 and again in 1974; since 1974 France's borders have been officially closed. A voluntary repatriation scheme was initiated in 1977, and in 1980, the law was changed to allow French-born North Africans to be deported. The Bonnet law of 1980 forced approximately four thousand migrants a year to leave; many of them had lived and worked in France for years and had children with French citizenship. In 1986, the right-wing minister Charles Pasqua approved a measure to remove the basic rights of due process to immigrants facing deportation. One year later, seventeen thousand of these deportations took place.

Race and religion, it seems, have become the new, perhaps the only pressing issues in French politics. In June 1989, Francis Leotard (president of the Republican party) argued that [race] "has become the only domestic issue."[23] There is no doubt that racism and the far right have had a political impact on French politics in a historical sense, but only in the recent past has this been translated into mass support for a full-fledged political party, the Front National led by Jean Marie Le Pen. And no more dramatic or explicit indication of this can found than in the rise of the FN and the substantial increase in its share of votes from the French electorate.

The fact that Le Pen has risen as a popular political star has taken everyone by surprise, not least the mainstream French politicians. From 1945 to the 1970s the extreme right's share of the vote has in fact been fairly minute. Even in 1974, when Le Pen ran for president, he received only 0.74 percent of the poll; he won only 4.38 percent of the vote when he ran for the National Assembly in the same year. Fourteen years later, in 1988, he gained 14.39 percent of the vote in the first round of the presidential election—only 5.5 percent behind the outgoing prime minister, Jacques Chirac. The support of 4.5 million voters for a party with an explicitly racist component represents a substantial proportion of an electorate of 38 million people.[24]

Immigration, Race, and Islam

The question of immigration and the role of Islam is at the heart of the race, religion, and immigration question in France. It is not a new question, but it has only recently been exploited. There have been large numbers of non-Europeans in French cities for a long time. By 1931, the influx of foreigners into France during the 1920s had increased the population by 3 million, which in percentage terms is roughly equivalent to the percentage of foreigners in the total population today (i.e., 6.8 percent in 1982 and 6.6 percent in 1931).[25] But in the late 1950s and 1960s, with growing decolonization, the modernization of the French economy, and the concomitant increase in competition, there was a very large-scale immigration of labor from Muslim societies to Western Europe. The period between 1962 and 1968 for instance, saw a steady influx of more than 100,000 workers a year. And in general these workers were used as cheap sources of labor. In fact it has been argued that without this work force, France would not have been able to press ahead with its modernization programs.

These minorities are here to stay, and several questions are raised by the interested parties in French society. First, will they be assimilated into the majority society and lose their distinctive views? Second, what will happen to these societies if Muslims are integrated and assimilated?

There is no doubt that the authorities, the political parties, and the general public see a real problem in the immigration question and its relationship to French identity and values. By the early 1980s, the Muslim North Africans seemed largely unassimilable. Certainly, a minority of intellectuals was agreeing with Louis Pauvnell, the right-wing editor of *Le Figaro*, who during May 1985 argued that pluralist education was failing to assimilate Muslims to French values. In October 1985 Le Pen's attitudes towards foreigners won a 31 percent approval rating in the polls, and as many as 28 percent approved of his defense of traditional values. It seems that many people who even detest Le Pen and what he stands for worry about the problem of assimilating the younger generation of **Mahgrebin** (people from the Mahgreb, the mainly Islamic countries of North Africa). As Robert Pandraud (the former minister for public safety) in Jacques Chirac's government argued, "When you go for a walk in Nice or Marseilles, you realize that the emergence of Islam on the far shores of the Mediterranean is sending shivers up people's spines."[26]

Charles Pasqua, a right-wing populist influential in the Gaullist party, argued this:

> Immigration is a more serious problem than we imagine. The Mahgreb is going to wake up and the countries of Eastern Europe will also have their immigrants. If we don't come up with answers for these deep fears Le Pen is going to ride high on them.[27]

Case Study: Jean-Marie Le Pen and the Front National

> Experience shows that the framing of a future, in some indeterminate time, may, when it is done in a certain way, be very effective, and have very few inconveniences: this happens when the anticipations

of the future take the form of those myths, which enclose with them all the strongest inclinations of a people or a party or a class, inclinations which recur to the mind with the insistence of instincts in all the circumstances of life; and which give an aspect of complete reality to the hopes of immediate action by which, more easily than by any other method, men can reform their desires, passions, and mental activity.[28]

The real problem is that there are people who think like Le Pen.[29]

The aim of this case study is to take a specifically political view of the rise of Jean-Marie Le Pen and the Front National. The intent is to place him and his movement within a context of political science and history that allows us to develop frameworks of explanation. Three questions are salient to the case. First, what is the breadth and scope of Le Pen's and the Front's political support? Second, where can we locate Le Pen and his historical roots? And third, why has his strategy been successful in the attraction of electoral support?

Support for Le Pen

One of the most interesting aspects of Le Pen's appeal in contemporary French politics is that the increase in the vote for the Front National has not been limited to one particular level. It has increased at the local, regional, national, and supranational (meaning European) levels. It has increased across the board and the French political landscape. In June 1984, for instance, the FN received 11 percent of the vote in the European elections. Again in the 1988 elections, in seventy-six out of ninety-six departments, Le Pen polled upwards of 10 percent; in eight of these he received between 20 percent and 30 percent. In Bouches-De-Rhone, a traditional stronghold of the Socialists, he received 26.39 percent, in comparison to Mitterand's 26.96 percent (or just a few percentage points short). In by-elections, Le Pen has scored a series of electoral triumphs. For example, in one of the Marseilles seats the FN received over 47 percent of the vote in the second ballot, and in Dreux their first ballot percentage increased from 16 percent in 1988 to 42 percent in 1989.[30] They even won a canton election in Salon-De-Provence, which the Socialists had held for over fifty years. In 1986, when Mitterand introduced proportional representation, thirty-five FN deputies gained access to the National Assembly. That number was reduced to one with the reintroduction of the first-past-the-post system in 1988.

The Scope of Le Pen's Appeal

As mentioned previously, the support for Le Pen and the FN is national, not parochial. The majority of it is still strongest in the built-up industrialized regions of the North, the Parisian heartland, and the Mediterranean regions, especially in urbanized areas where unemployment, housing, crime, and drug problems are acute (which areas also have high immigrant populations). However, the FN is also becoming increasingly popular in areas where immigration does not appear to exist as a problem. Second, there is a simultaneous appeal to disgruntled youths, workers, and part of the middle class. The number of workers and middle-level employees backing Le Pen rose from 37 percent in 1984 to almost half his support by 1986. At the same time the FN electorate became younger and more middle class. In 1988, for instance, the greatest support for Le Pen came from small shopkeepers, artisans, shop assistants, and professionals. As one journalist who spent several months in the Front pointed out:

> The Front is a hodge-podge: one enters it with his own rebellion, resentment, rage at living in bad housing, having too little money, and so many other reasons for repressed aggression. Everyone brings in his own hatreds, and then, picking from the other's plate, acquires other ones, egged on by the experienced militants.[31]

Le Pen has come to epitomize the opportunistic politician, one who appeals not only to the right wing but also to out-of-work Communists and to the chic bourgeois who claim to be fed up but are unable to explain why. And part of the explanation is linked to the way in which Le Pen has managed to exploit and control the question of immigration.

Variants and Roots of the Front

Some versions of the extreme right differed from Le Pen. For example, Charles Maurras, leader of the Action Francaise, was an explicit opponent of the Republic in expounding his view of "integral nationalism" and the primacy of the state. One view of the difference between the French mainstream and far right is that, whereas conservatives strive to maintain the status quo, the extreme right would like to restore the status quo ante. Although this maxim may be useful in describing the Royalists and views prevalent in the Action Francaise, which had some predominance in France during the 1930s, it is not so helpful in terms of analyzing Le Pen and his particular political strategy.

A more useful way of locating Le Pen from the point of view

of practical politics would seem to lie in the more recent past, in particular the 1950s and the rise of Poujadism. In 1954 Pierre Poujade led a protest movement of "little people" in which he gained the support of small shopkeepers, artisans, and small farmers by rallying them around the threat of downward mobility.[32] The right-wing government of the time had passed a bill with provisions for more careful income tax scrutiny, and this threat to the lower middle classes of downward mobility was a fertile ground for right-wing extremism. Poujadism as a movement is similar to the FN today in that both can best be defined in terms of what they are against rather than what they are for. Poujadism was against taxes, big business, politicians, civil servants, technocrats, the rich, the state, the Jews, financiers, intellectuals, and cosmopolitans. Many of the negative positions that characterize the Front National are similar, and it is a salient fact that the same so-called little people, the lower middle classes and artisans, are among the most ardent and loyal followers of Le Pen (31 percent in the 1988 elections). In fact the Poujadiste movement won 2.5 million votes in the 1956 election in a time when the Fourth Republic was in crisis. The Fifth Republic does not appear to be in any immediate crisis, and Le Pen achieved 4.4 million votes in the last presidential election, or just over 15 percent of the vote. The fact that the Poujadiste movement in the early 1960s was absorbed by both Gaullism and the reactionary Algerie Francaise Group (Keep Algeria French) is paralleled in a theme of Le Pen's movement in that there is a nostalgia for French Algeria. Once again it is a case of tradition lingering over into the 1980s and 1990s. Even in the late 1980s and early 1990s some of these scars and wounds apparently have not yet healed in French society.

A Sorelian Framework and Le Pen

One framework or view that could be used to discuss Le Pen and the issue of racism in France, or why Le Pen has gained support, is Georges Sorel's idea of a myth. For Sorel, a French philosopher, a myth was not a primitive legend about gods or supernatural heroes; neither was it a fully elaborated ideological system or blueprint for utopia. Rather the myth was a vague but effective symbolization of the hopes, aspirations and dreams of a group of people. Sorel saw ideologies and utopian views as rational constructs; the myth, on the other hand, relies on irrationalism. Sorel believed the ability of reason to explain the world is limited. On the other hand, he doubted that anyone could make use of reason in any case. The **political myth** relies on passion, not reason. Sorel believed democratic values and institutions to be a charade, and he treated such with condescension and contempt. Democracy, in Sorel's view, simply allows politicians and intellectuals to confuse, to fool the masses and cheat their way to power. And again for Sorel, it is only intuition and instinct and not reliance on the scientific method that can help us to understand politics. All great social movements are "pulled" by the power of a myth that is essentially closed to analysis.

In many ways, particularly in substance, fascism was less an ideology and more a myth in the Sorelian usage of the term. It can be seen as a system of images defying logical definition or rational analysis, filled with contradictions if submitted to either. This view is relevant in several senses to the context of political life in France in the 1930s and early 1940s, when fascist right-wing views exerted a tremendous influence in politics vis-à-vis the Action Francaise in ways comparable in some respects to the Front National.

Yves Simon, a French historian writing in 1941, referred to the Depression of the 1930s and the French movement towards nazification as the "twilight of the myths." There were numerous leaders and parties but no available ideology, only a certain amount of image based around opposition to communism, atheism, freemasonry, and the Jews. The prejudice and bigotry that existed in France among the far right were not related to any one particular cause but to these vague elements. Fascism in essence had to be anti-something; its appeal lay in a general resentment. Simon believed that France had destroyed itself from within by this period; it was a time of destructive passions and ideologies lacking "the protection of an unquestioned system of beliefs, visions, and aspirations."[33] The French right found a hero in Hitler. One should note that anti-Semitism was not a major theme or essential aspect of fascist doctrine; this was Hitler's own myth. It was not shared by Mussolini or other fascist leaders, but the organized violence, the destructive tendencies offered by fascism did require an object, a scapegoat. Fascism had to be directional in some sense, and it was directed against the Jews in France as in Germany. Substantial sections of the population in France, particularly the middle classes, believed that France was better off in the hands of Hitler than in the hands of the Jews. To some extent these myths have been exploited by Le Pen.

The Role of Myths

The Myth of Identity. For Le Pen the myth of French identity and the idea that this identity is under attack are primary issues. He is convinced that sacred French values and ideas are being undermined.

92

And for Le Pen it is convenient to discuss this threat specifically in terms of the immigrant population.

And it is acutely a French identity, a French civilization and value system, that is seen as under attack from foreign influences. Le Pen is not really interested in assimilation; for Le Pen the real problem lies in the danger that the foreigners may actually be assimilated. It is far easier to deal with the enemy without than the enemy within, he believes. Once they are assimilated, once rich and powerful, when they try to behave and look like us, when the "them" and "us" distinction disappears and becomes the "we"—this is where the real problem lies for Le Pen.[34] This is when rootless cosmopolitanism undermines the French nation and its spiritual values. History lecturers like Christiane Pigace at the University of Aix-en-Provence are attracted to the far right and its view of French identity. She joined because she wanted to promote something she calls "the rebirth of our identities" through the establishment of a party educational wing.

And the "rebirth of identity" has been couched in fairly radical terms, at least from the formation of the Front National in 1972. Its theme then was to save France from the barbarian hordes and from everything else. The Ordre Nouveau's young revolutionary nationalists summed up this messianic vocation in the following way:

> The revolution's aim is to pull the old regime down completely and build the New Order from the ground up. We're real revolutionaries for we're determined to go to the very limits of this necessity at any cost. Toppling a decadent regime and its henchmen, totally transforming a society which has collapsed under the weight of its shortcomings and vices, we'll build a new world, rid of worker exploitation, a world of beauty, courage and justice.[35]

The Myth of the New Man. Fascism to some extent combined the "cult" of the hero with a mass movement. It was dedicated to the protection of traditional values. The idea of discipline was combined with the prospect of the "new man," one of the elite of heroic supermen earlier described in Nietschzean philosophy. This myth of a "new man" was connected with a desire for renewal, for revival, for reinvigoration. It was designed to save a society in crisis. In the series of dinner debates he conducted during the 1988 presidential campaign, for instance, Le Pen characterized himself as the "outsider" running against a group of useless cronies. He in effect represented a "new man," a leader of the people in the face of a stagnant political elite.

93

Le Pen thrives on media coverage and publicity, actively embracing it. As Shields notes:

> In the first stage of his campaign in summer 1987, he conducted a *tournee des plages* reminiscent of the "caravan" which he himself had orchestrated for Tixier-Vignancour in the 1965 presidential campaign. Speaking without notes from the podium in a giant marquee, and surrounded by the tricolour symbols and insignia of his movement, Le Pen displayed his considerable skills as an orator in a bid to keep the minds of the holidaying French fixed on the forthcoming election. Though the *tournee* met with mixed success, it allowed Le Pen to steal something of a march on his rivals and to maintain a constant public profile throughout the summer recess.[36]

It is this love of the grand gesture and the symbolic act that fuels the "myth" and pervades Le Pen's strategy.

At the 1990 Front National congress in Nice, for instance, after being elected for another term as leader, Le Pen declared, in suitably embattled martyr terms, "Follow me if I move forward. Prod me on if I falter. Kill me if I turn back."[37]

Le Pen: From Fringe to Mainstream

However, given that there are aspects of Le Pen's appeal that seem to fit within the framework of the political myth, this is only part of the story. The other major part of Le Pen's appeal lies in the fact that he has left the fringe right and moved much closer to the traditional right in a very short period of time.

A second political framework useful in locating the Front National is the idea of the **catch-all party** propounded by Otto Kircheimer in the early 1960s to describe the Christian Democratic parties in Western Europe. For Kircheimer, "national societal goals which transcended group interests offered the best sales prospects for a party that was aiming at establishing, or enlarging an appeal previously limited to specific sections of the population."[38] In order to show how this thesis relates to the Le Pen phenomenon, I will briefly describe it and then illustrate to what extent it fits Le Pen and the Front National. Over twenty-five years ago, Kircheimer posited that a major transformation of Western European party systems was taking place. Political trends indicated that previous parties of mass integration were changing into parties that had no fixed ideological resume. This tied in with the prevalent literature which declared that ideology per se was coming to an end. Parties were realizing that the route to power lay in successful marketing strategies oriented to winning elections rather than ideological pronouncements.[39] Mass integration parties aimed at capturing hearts and minds selectively, whereas catch-all organizations concentrated on a wide electoral appeal. Kircheimer constantly used market analogies to substantiate his views—the idea being that parties differed from one another only in order to make themselves recognizable.

Thus, Le Pen is interested in giving his party a wider electoral appeal than simply an anti-immigrant position. In other words, he wants to go beyond the boundaries of the political myth.

And this might be seen to follow from Gaullist attempts to achieve the same thing. For the Rassemblement pour la Republique (RPR), the philosophy based on de Gaulle was simple: There exists no absolute truth in either strategy or politics. There are only circumstances. And it is to these circumstances that the Front National, with its ambiguity and lack of ideology, has been able to adapt itself. Even if Le Pen uses the issues of race and religion as his main planks, he is not confined to these. Le Pen's party is no longer based on single issues but on multiple issues. It is true that it wants a radical revision of the nationality code, a version of the right of immigrants to automatic French citizenship and selective repatriation. Le Pen, however, has many positions on other topics. In regard to crime and law and order, for instance, he has a traditional conservative stance and advocates the return of the death penalty. He favors the promotion of the family and family values and an end to state-reimbursed abortion. He seeks the abolition of income taxes along with the implementation of an unfettered popular capitalism. He is for conservatism in religion and the defense of traditional education. He is concerned with the question of French identity and the role of France in the world (particularly with the advent of the single European market in 1992). At the FN's conference in April 1990, one of the major topics was pollution. Thus, Le Pen's votes appear to have roots encompassing everything from the fear of AIDS and drug abuse to unemployment and recession. And one of the interesting things about this is the way in which the party has managed to connect these issues (most of which relate spuriously to one another) and convey them in terms of some sort of political program. Race and crime, race and unemployment, unemployment and drugs. The exaggeration of such tenuous links has in fact been the political forte of the Front National. As one journalist put it:

> Amid much vague rhetoric, the Front's single unmistakable thesis is that immigrants, essentially Arabs and Africans, are equivalent to crime and disruption, and should be sent home. The rest of the party line appears to depend on the audience; it can include anti-Semitic innuendo, the Vichy regime's gospel of family, work and nationhood or talk of denationalizing French industry.[40]

Second, because the vote of the far right has increased at all levels on a national scale, Le Pen has definitely increased the appeal of the Front beyond the boundaries of its natural constituency. Le Pen himself has interestingly disavowed many of the reactionary and extreme ideas that came for instance from the work of Charles Maurras, and Le Pen is seeking to work within the parliamentary framework even if he is antiparliamentarian, seeking not to destroy the republic but merely to improve it. It is this pragmatic departure from previous far-right-wing tendencies, which wanted to get rid of the republic and many of the things it stood for, that is gaining electoral appeal. So Le Pen is concerned with traditional values and French identity but not with the idea of restoring the pre-1789 value system and certainly not with revolution.

By 1986, the sociological profile of the Front National was no longer that of the typical right-wing French party (not to mention the extreme right). And in part this has to do with the failure of the right and the left to present their case and certainly to take clearly articulated positions on the issue of race. The Communist party, for instance, has been in decline for a long time, and recently this decline has gone hand in hand with the rise of the front.

The left is faced with an enormous dilemma over the position of Islam; they have in essence failed to deal with the problem of immigrant communities. Yet traditionally it has been seen as the friend of minority groups and has typically supported their rights. In 1990 there occurred a widely reported incident regarding whether two Muslim schoolgirls in Creil should be allowed to wear their traditional headscarves in class. The left was split into at least two groups. One pointed to the long French tradition of secular state education and anticlericalism; which had helped to define French socialism in the first place. The other argued that religious cultures should be respected. A third, feminist, viewpoint, which also finds sympathy in the left of course, is that the headscarf issue concerns the oppression of Muslim women. Since the left is divided, Le Pen and the media have been free to exaggerate and exploit the headscarf issue out of all proportion and catapult it into the wider debate on immigration. Naturally Le Pen suggested repatriation, which would not only solve the problem of education but also, he claims, issues of mosque building, drugs, AIDS, law and order, and traffic congestion in Paris. Le Pen is at his opportunistic best in exploiting such tensions. The left simply has failed to deal with the more complex issues of race, personal freedom, women's rights and national identity. It has failed to define these in terms of an agenda. And the voting percentages show that Le Pen is making large inroads in the Communist vote, particularly in the South. In 1988 some 16 percent of the Front National vote came from workers. In the June 1984 European elections, the Front had received just 0.7 percent of the vote—less than the PCF. The Communists over the past fifteen years have in effect seen their vote drop from 25 percent to just over 10 percent, and it is unlikely to recover after the events of the past few years in Eastern Europe and the collapse of communism.

Furthermore, although Le Pen has been taking votes from the left, he has also been taking more votes from the so-called respectable right, the Gaullists and the Union for French Democracy (UDF). Clearly the conventional right is as unstable as the Communists and even more divided, since it is made up of several groups—the Gaullists (RPR), the UDF, and the Republican Party, all of which are divided by programs and leadership ambitions. In the first round of the presidential elections in 1988, for instance, the Le Pen vote was an average of 27 percent of the total right in six regions and an average of 38 percent in another eight (out of a total of twenty-two). In fact Le Pen had an average vote of 17.5 percent in the ten largest French cities. Again, because the traditional right is essentially divided over the Le Pen phenomenon, it has been divided at the polls. This division has led to some electoral alliances with the UDF and the RPR in municipal by-elections. In addition, however, it has also led to the inability of the established right to significantly increase its electoral support. Unstable voters in the end seem to shift their support away from the establishment towards Le Pen.

The other interesting question facing the traditional right is how much in common do they have with the Front. Charles Pasqua, a neo-Gaullist who was Chirac's campaign manager and interior minister, argues that there is no essential difference in values between the RPR and the Front. In 1981, Chirac's campaign for the presidency echoed many of the themes espoused by the Poujadists and similar movements of the 1950s and 1960s: opposition to big government, budget deficits, and bureaucracy. In 1988 Chirac received a pitiful 19.9 percent in the first round of the presidential election, only 5.5 percent more than Le Pen. The fact that Le Pen doesn't exactly fit into the extreme right-wing mold has in fact brought him closer to the mainstream right in terms of policy and agenda. There are common themes running throughout the UDF, the RPR, and the Front, such as economic liberalism, moral regeneration, law and order, and the defense of national and cultural identity. Again the argument is one of degree and involves the media.

If Le Pen has captured the headlines on these kinds of issues it is because to a large extent he has presented positions which outright the right and not because he has had that much different to say. Because immigration in the 1980s had become part of the mainstream political debate, it was convenient for Le Pen to secure the monopoly on that debate by exploiting it to the maximum. We have seen that there is a fair degree of intermarriage between the extreme right and the mainstream. And even if Chirac says that he feels as close to Le Pen as he feels to a martian and doesn't want anything to do with him, the fact is that Chirac was still talking about race and the "problem" of immigration.

Lastly, within the idea of the catch-all party is the point that the media and consumerism have played a large part in the rise of Le Pen, and this is generally related to his packaging as a product. For instance Le Pen has always been eager to shake off his erstwhile role of street politician and bully boy; he has been somewhat successful in presenting his case in an effort to gain more legitimacy. To some extent Le Pen and his party have Thatcherized themselves over the past ten years, to the extent of changing their wardrobes (gone is the khaki garb, replaced by well-pressed blazers and suits). Le Pen has even changed his diet and hairstyle. He is a master of the television medium as a rhetorician, aided by the malleability of far-rights views. He understands how to tap dissatisfaction and discontent, and therein lies his opportunism. The lessons in politics for both Le Pen and the failing conventional right involve consumer-oriented political marketing: appealing across the boundaries of class, ideology, and narrow vested interests to many different groups.

Again the media's best uses of propaganda in this sense lie in the area of passion, not necessarily rationality. And certainly the repackaging of Le Pen and the Front, and the desire to succeed within the established political context (within the framework of the republic) is part of the overall presentation. In fact Le Pen has gone full steam into the parliamentary process, successfully engaging contests at all levels of election: local, regional, national, and European. It is Le Pen and his party that have managed to disengage themselves from the conventional, stereotypical image of the extreme right. Gone are the neofascism, monarchism, ultra-Catholicism, socioeconomic populism, all of which have been starved of a forum under the Fifth Republic. Le Pen has essentially sought to campaign within the prevailing political context.

The media are of course related to propaganda and mobilization. They are particularly well linked to the construction of the political myth because this is the most elusive structural aspect of ideology. Jacques Ellul points out that modern propaganda is not necessarily about changing ideas but about provoking action; its purpose is not to change adherence to doctrine but to promote irrational persistence in a process of action. Its goal is no longer to lead to a choice but to loosen the reflexes; no longer to change an opinion but to arouse an active, myth-directed belief.[41] Le Pen and his party have become a consumer package in their use of media techniques and marketing strategy. This in itself brings them closer to the mainstream of modern politics.

Le Pen and the Front National's Program

What exactly do the Front National and Le Pen have in mind when they discuss solutions to the immigration "problem"? According to a fifty-point plan drawn up by Bruno Megret, the party's theoretician, and released in late 1991, the solution is to "protect the French." This would include preventing all immigration of non-Europeans and also making life as difficult as possible for immigrants now residing in France. With these proposals the right of relatives to join their families in France would be completely abolished. Foreigners visiting France would be subjected to paying a large deposit (an amount of FFr 100,000, or $18,000, has been suggested) to be recouped on departure, so as to prevent "false tourists." In addition Le Pen has suggested a complete ban on tourist visas for Africans and Arabs from North Africa. Foreigners entering the country without a certificate proving them free of AIDS would be subject to an obligatory AIDS test. In addition foreigners living in France would fail to qualify for family benefits, and their children would be subject to maximum quotas in schools. Priority in jobs and subsidized housing would be for French nationals, a tax would be imposed on employers hiring foreign workers, and goods produced in France would be labeled "produced in France with French labor." Illegal immigrants would be expelled; unemployed immigrants who exhaust their unemployment benefits would also be expelled, as would foreigners convicted of a crime. The present nationality law, which provides the right to citizenship for persons born in France or married to a French citizen, would be abolished. The laws on naturalization would be tightened, and in effect all naturalizations since 1974 would be reexamined. All of these rules, of course, would not apply to citizens of the EC countries.

Conclusion

Despite the fact that Le Pen is a product of the modern French context, he does have a series of historical precedents to draw upon.

He seems to have rejected some of the more romantic notions of the far right in favor of the practical ones, but he still relies on an ambiguous ideology and political myths to fall back on. The Front National is clearly less of an ideological crusade than a movement of opportunism and a channel for discontent. Le Pen relies not only on the ambiguity of ideology and the political myth but also on practical and effective media campaigns; together, they form a blatant reliance upon consumerism to get the message across.

The appeal of the Front National to some extent addresses the paradox of an apparently unassimilable Muslim minority. Specifically, Le Pen opposes the so-called Western vice of "ruthless cosmopolitanism," while simultaneously advocating liberal free-market economics to cure France's ills. After the election in 1988, a young female supporter of Le Pen declared on television that the "future belongs to us." With the concoction of ambiguous myth and pragmatic politics that Le Pen has conjured up, he will certainly influence the future political agenda if nothing else.

Problems in Empire

France has always regarded itself as being of some considerable importance to the rest of the world, whether in its role of empire or its self-styled championship of Third World causes. This sense of importance can be traced back to the period of the French Revolution. Revolutionary thinkers thought that the ideas and practices of the Revolution should be exported to provide liberty and freedom to other peoples in Europe at the time. Armies were mobilized on this basis, and French nationalists exhorted these armies to perform the mission of spreading French culture and civilization to the rest of the continent. However, French efforts to expand went far beyond the boundaries of Europe, and more often than not the French failed to bring civilization to their destinations. The French Empire was second only to the British version and still retains more influence in its pre-1945 colonial possessions than the British can manage. One writer regards this empire as "subtly structured":

> [one which is as] rewarding as any in history, [and] maintains France as a world power, perhaps the only cultural superpower, one that is based firmly and squarely on illusions. Freed of its colonies, it is master. Having killed hundreds of thousands in colonial wars, France is a Third World symbol of liberty, equality and brotherhood.[42]

The duality of the French role in empire is aptly expressed by such statements. On the one hand, France and the Revolution repre-

100

sented hope and freedom for oppressed peoples and societies. Yet on the other hand the very nature of empire and imperialism represents racism, exploitation, and degradation for the majority of peoples in the Third World. This uncomfortable contradiction has proved a difficult and agonizing dilemma for the French to resolve. In part it is the dilemma of a country that has real cultural ties providing a continuation of closeness between France and its ex-colonies (in particular in Africa). After the process of decolonization France again saw itself as the standard bearer for enlightenment in the Third World, the nation that had provided the Declaration of the Rights of Man; but again the gulf between rhetoric and reality, between ideals and substantive achievements, is perhaps more prominent than the place in which they meet. And this is not only seen in African nations but also in many of France's overseas departments in the postwar period.

Contemporary Colonies

Despite the fact that much of this empire has been scaled back or lost in various Third World wars of national liberation (Algeria and Vietnam for instance), France still retains considerable influence and power in many regions of the Third World. In fact France is the only European society to maintain a military presence in many of its colonial outposts in French Equatorial and French West Africa. For instance the French state still exercises jurisdiction over five overseas departments (which had the status of colonies until 1946), including Reunion in the Indian Ocean, Guadeloupe and Martinique in the West Indies, French Guiana in Latin America, and the two islands of St. Pierre and Miquelon off the coast of Newfoundland, Canada. In addition to this there are New Caledonia, Futuna and Wallis and French Polynesia in the South Pacific, and the island of Mayotte off the coast of Africa.[43] Overseas departments and territories maintain representation in the French parliament as well as having locally elected assemblies. However, recent reports suggest that there are major problems in these areas of the French Empire, perhaps the most important being that there are major discrepancies between the standard of living in France itself and in its overseas empire. After the Socialists came to power in 1981, the plan and the rhetoric was to reverse such differentials and bring France's overseas operations into line with the twentieth century, even offering them the right to self-determination. This was a failed realization, however; self-determination was shelved, and resentment started to grow against the colonial overseer. Riots and disturbances in Reunion in February and March 1991, in which at least ten people died, have aggravated the difficulties involved in attempting to maintain an essentially outdated and archaic system of administration in the former colonies. Increasingly it is difficult to reconcile the position of these societies to the world that emerged after 1945 and the massive process of decolonization that emerged in the Third World, particularly with the realization that the idea of colonialism was no longer morally acceptable in the modern world. Legislation to try and ensure that national French practices met with local conditions has had a mixed record in the history of the departments. The last decentralization law, that of 1982–84, for instance, intended to give local populations a certain degree of administrative autonomy, but it has clearly run into problems with its ambiguous institutional structures. The problem is, of course, the attempt to provide administration suitable for a developed society but not necessarily for one that still maintains many colonial economic practices. In other words it appears "out of sync" with the contemporary realities of societies that are essentially underdeveloped. One author, in fact, describes the small Pacific colonies as the *confettis de l'empire* still retaining their links to the *metropole*. He argues that

> The history of the French Pacific, like that of all the regions colonised by exterior powers, is a blend of domestic developments in those territories (in both indigenous and settler communities) and the policies and actions of the "mother country." The impossibility of separating one from the other—either in history or in historiography—provides a continued justification of "imperial history."[44]

Sweeping changes have occurred, of course, in the last half century; nearly everyone has health and education facilities, and electricity is generally supplied. The number of children in secondary education increased markedly in many overseas departments. There are, however, many local problems that are not receiving adequate attention, and this has led to expressions of frustration and violence.

Moreover, immigrants from the French West Indies and Reunion often find that they suffer from an identity crisis in mainland France, where they are the victims of racism and unemployment. In effect the children of the immigrants who arrived during periods of economic boom are caught in a time warp of identity and lost expectations. As one writer put it, "Just as French citizens of North African origin are not tempted to go and live in Algeria, French-born young people whose parents came from the West Indies or Reunion are not generally attracted to the idea of returning to settle in the lands of the ancestors."[45]

The idea of the state as the emancipator and bringer of liberty to backward regimes went hand in hand with the idea that France had a unique "civilizing" mission to fulfil. France was seen as a model for the rest of the world, and the superiority of the French state provided a peculiar attitude of self-righteousness in the process of colonialism. It also provided a sense of justification to the dictators France supported throughout the Third World. When the Communist world began to collapse in late 1989, the idea of individual freedom spread throughout the Third World and began to undermine the statist approach.

Relationship to the Third World

French policy towards the Third World stems from France's previous policies toward its colonial empire and the fact that in the post-1945 period of Cold War it attempted to pursue a foreign policy independent of both the Western allies and the Communist bloc. Its overseas colonies were mainly established during the period of the Third Republic (1875–1946) and the period of new colonialism that the European powers embarked upon in the late nineteenth century. This effort went hand in hand with the notion that eventually colonial peoples would be assimilated into the French nation—an objective rendered moot by the growth of nationalistic sentiments within these states.

However, France continued to believe that it fulfilled a peculiarly special role within the Third World: although it was a member of the Western alliance, it did not fit into the bloc led by the U.S. military, and so it could always retain a certain degree of independence. France was not nearly so obsessed as the United States with the "Communist menace." The French (at least rhetorically) were concerned with offering a more progressive message of national liberation, human rights, and economic development; France's message had a universal quality to it. In most cases France was more interested in providing a model and an option for the path of development rather than reducing embroiling Third World nations in a "one or the other" ideological confrontation as symbolized by the Cold War. France has developed a fairly liberal policy towards its Third World charges; over the years it has initiated bilateral treaties on developmental aid, security, and developing business links. Economic and military assistance has been forthcoming, although in some cases this has simply helped to maintain authoritarian regimes who have actively suppressed their populations (Chad, for instance).

De Gaulle, even in providing independence for France's colonies in the early 1960s, sought to preserve close ties at every level with the new states. He provided economic and technical assistance and even maintained troops to protect some of them (such as Chad) from invasion. Such policies, in the main, were accepted in France.

Aid and investment in the Third World were enhanced under the leadership of François Mitterand, who tried to double the percentage of gross national product spent for this purpose by the end of his first term in 1988. According to one account, Mitterand's three goals for the Third World were (1) to help the developing countries achieve self-sufficiency in food production and energy; (2) to encourage a level of industrial development that met each country's ability to absorb new technology; and (3) to encourage more cooperation among the advanced capitalist societies to lessen the gap between North and South, rich and poor—particularly by tackling the controversial problem of Third World debt.[46] Regional solutions to regional problems were to be encouraged (in contrast to policies of his predecessor); human rights were to be increasingly emphasized despite the fact that France continued to be a major arms supplier to the Third World.

Some success in foreign policy has been offset by such spectacular failures as the unilateral withdrawal of forces from Chad while Libya remained ensconced and the major incident of the destruction in a New Zealand port of a Greenpeace ship due to enter the region of French Polynesia to check on nuclear testing.

Mitterand's administration since the early 1980s has been actively concerned with raising the Third World's level of priority in French politics. The Socialist party has always labeled this an important agenda item, and the French president's experience as minister for overseas territories in the early 1950s reinforced this priority. In appointing Claude Cheysson as minister for foreign affairs and Regis Debray as his personal advisor on Third World problems, Mitterand was clearly drawing on very sympathetic elements for the conduct of policy towards the Third World. It has been a tradition in France to donate large amounts of aid to the underdeveloped countries, and in the Fifth Republic there has been the view that France should not only move towards donating 0.7 percent of its GNP in aid but also recognize the Third World's view of a "new international economic order."

Claude Cheysson, for instance, has launched a concerted campaign within the European Community to coordinate and harmonize aid and investment programs in the Third World, particularly with regard to former colonies in the ACP (African, Caribbean, Pacific) regions. Similar attempts have been made to utilize the agencies of the United Nations.

While such activities have generated a great deal of talk and high expectations, it is clear that the Mitterand government (although apparently committed) has run into obstacles, bureaucratic and political. Efforts to establish an independent aid agency were blocked by bureaucrats in the different ministries concerned with aid programs. Going beyond the boundaries of France's accepted colonial obligations proved fairly futile and could not be sustained. Finally, aid and trade seemed to go hand in hand with preferential agreements that affected France's image. Aid disappeared and turned up in the hands of Christian Nucci, the minister-delegate of cooperation and development, and this scandal reinforced a negative image of foreign aid.

Despite these events, France is still perceived in a fairly favorable light by many Third World nations. It has been willing to intervene in various trouble spots such as Chad, Zaire, and Lebanon, even sending the second-largest European contingent (after the United Kingdom) to fight in the gulf war of 1991 (France's largest fighting force abroad since the war in Algeria). This more positive side of active foreign policy is of course balanced by unsavory connections with some fairly authoritarian regimes.

France is also interested in promoting democracy in many of its former colonies, particularly in Africa, and this may raise as many problems as it will solve. Presidents Mathieu Kerekou of Benin and Moussa Traore of Mali have already stepped down, the former as a result of losing an election in March 1991 and the latter forced out by a general strike. An active change in position by François Mitterand provided an early warning notice for Francophone Africa's dictators at a summit meeting in 1990. Previously France had shored up African dictators and strongmen, providing them with military assistance and stabilizing their currencies. Now, Mitterand argued that there would be "no development without democracy and no democracy without development" and appeared determined to initiate a general trend in the West to provide aid to countries that made progress in these directions.[47] Cynics might argue that what were once assets for the French are now liabilities, but with the general winds of change blowing in favor of democracy around the world (e.g., Eastern Europe in 1989), it is not difficult to see why France found it politically expedient to climb onto the bandwagon of democracy.

It is not only politically expedient but also beneficial for France to push these former colonies towards multiparty democracy. And the reasons are obvious: the eccentric policies of colonial France failed to work. They failed to produce sustained development and rather produced inefficient, corrupt regimes. In turn, France may no longer be able to prevent younger generations of Africans from asserting demands for democracy. Examples are numerous. Felix

Houphouet-Boigny, in charge of the Ivory Coast and Africa's longest-running dictator for over thirty years, was siphoning off French foreign aid to provide himself with a massive fortune estimated at around $12 billion. In fact his country's debt was roughly equivalent to the president's personal wealth. In Gabon, President Omar Bongo continued in power despite a dreadful human rights record. Mitterand's paternalistic attitude towards erstwhile dictators in Africa has in fact been compared to Giscard d'Estaing's backing for Bokassa in Central Africa in the 1970s—a scandal that erupted over diamonds that d'Estaing accepted in return for political favors. So a French policy that was out of tune, paternalistic, and inefficient is in the process of being replaced with a more modern attempt to deal constructively with the problems of development in Africa.[48]

Some see Mitterand as obsessed with human rights (*les droits de l'homme*), themes that have a long history from the time of the French Revolution, and as president he has continually sought to identify French interests with those of such higher aims. However it appears that Mitterand is interested not only in the concept of human rights but also in action by the French state and himself to try to procure political change. A "new French diplomatic concept, called *le droit a l'ingerence,* the right to interfere, . . . Mitterand is pushing hard as a new world order doctrine he can leave as his legacy."[49] The idea of course is that giving aid and help is not enough; undemocratic states should be uprooted and human rights upheld by intervention and force if necessary. After Mitterand's intervention in the gulf war and diplomatic missions to Yugoslavia, it seems that this credo make take hold in French foreign policy and determine a new stance towards France's empire in the future.

Conclusion

France is an example of political discontinuity. It has distinguished itself in this way for at least the past 200 years, as a society prone to revolutionary convulsions in which citizens feel torn between adherence to authority and the need to rebel. For most of its political history, it has been an uneasy paradox to live with. The political success of the Fifth Republic is in some ways undermined by the nature of this ambivalence, and this in itself proves that legitimacy is by no means consensual. It seems unlikely, however, that the French in the future will revolt in the absence of a need to do so, or merely for the sake of rebellion. Political change will take place if there are substantial reasons for that change to occur. If the government appears too aloof from the masses, alienation may set in and lead to revolt in the final analysis.

In some ways France is a polarized country with large discrepancies between the haves and the have-nots at both economic and political levels. Apart from the sense that pervades the political culture that the elites are simultaneously to be obeyed and held in distrust, there is a developing feeling of alienation amongst the French citizenry. And we have seen this expressed in terms of support for Le Pen and the Front National. In part this support has the character of a protest vote, but it is deeper and more widespread, a form of democratic malaise. A regime that is distant from its people, who feel alienated, frustrated, and excluded from politics, represents a problematic challenge to France in the 1990s.

In an interview in 1989, President François Mitterand seemed to reflect the acute mixture of optimism and pessimism in France when he stated, "I believe in the future of the human race. . . . Man is indeed capable of overcoming any difficulties. We are still in fact in the era of prehistory. My optimism is made up of a myriad of pessimisms."[50] And it is in this challenging sense that France will move forward, a nation of ambivalent discontinuities, into the twenty-first century.

Key Terms and Concepts

Each term appears in the text in boldface type.

Absolutism
Ancien Regime
Catch-all party
Cohabitation
Colbertism
Consensus
Dreyfus affair
Le droit a l'ingerence

Les droits de l'homme
Dualism
L'etat, c'est moi
Indicative planning
Mahgrebin
Ouverture
Political myth
Statism

4
Germany

Historical Overview

Germany like France has had a long and difficult history of political development; indeed its historical development has provoked sharp debate among historians. The last hundred years have proven to be a tumultuous period in terms of the legitimacy and continuance of the state in Germany. The guilt and embarrassment of the stains of Nazism still cause the German people angst and emotional trauma. They do not have the long history of continuous political development that the British can celebrate and enjoy. Rather, history is problematic for Germans, who agonize over past mistakes and present tensions.

In part, this problem is related to the fact that geographically the country lies in the heart or center of Europe and has natural boundaries on only half its borders: the North Sea and the Baltic Sea to the north and the Alps to the south and southwest. The position of Germany's flat northern plain has ensured that throughout much of European history the area has been a major battleground and the scene of continual invasions. And until the end of the nineteenth century, therefore, the nation state remained politically divided and militarily weak.

The First Reich

Whereas in England the question of who should rule was resolved in the seventeenth century with the ascendancy of parliamentary government and a centralized unitary state, and in France, the formation of a centralized bureaucratic state was well under way by the eighteenth century, the situation was very different for the German nation. In fact Germany was fragmented into many different principalities and cities from the medieval period of the thirteenth century onwards. This fragmentation increased with the Protestant Reformation led by Martin Luther; northern Germany rebelled against the centralized authority of the Roman Church and its system of heavy taxation, embracing mainly the Lutheran credo with some pockets of Calvinism. The south, on the other hand, remained mainly Catholic. This confessional split along geographical faultlines even today characterizes the divide between north and south. The religious question produced two wars and reasserted the role of the princes in politics as key players in the German state.

The divisions in Germany during the period following the Protestant Reformation is in direct contrast to the route the English Reformation pursued and the impact it experienced. Luther argued for the authoritative rule (**Obrigkeit**) of princely power against any rebellion that might have been attempted by the peasants and lower classes. In turn, this produced a fragmented populace who offered loyalty to the demands of the prince and remained obedient to authority; the feudal characteristics of a decentralized state permeated the German nation well into the nineteenth century. The Thirty Years War (1618–48) was catastrophic for any hope of German unity. It ended in the **Treaty of Westphalia** (1648) which divided Germany into 360 separate political units. The split between Catholic and Protestant represented a major dislocation and discontinuity in German political life that even remains important in a contemporary sense because of the subsequent voting patterns of the different factions.

The Second Reich, 1870–1918

A Germany of many different states represented less of a threat to other European countries than a united Germany, but it was only a matter of time before the larger of these territorial states would begin to absorb the smaller entities. Prussia in the north became the main instigator. Rich in resources and a major military power on the European continent, it grew more and more powerful under Chancellor Otto von **Bismarck**, who oversaw the defeat of Austria-Hungary and France through wars in 1864, 1866 and 1870–71 and, by absorbing other German principalities, established a German empire in Europe. Thus Germany became the last of our four cases to achieve unity. The aristocratic princely rulers transferred power to an imperial emperor, and the states were subordinated to an imperial government run by a chancellor and a collection of aristocrats (the **Junker classes**). The fact that power was retained in the hands of a few elites meant that, whereas Germany had embarked upon a rapid transition to modernity in terms of its economy and industrial capabilities, there was no concomitant experience in the social and political spheres. Political and social power remained firmly in the hands of the Prussian aristocrats; the impetus for change in these spheres could not come from the middle classes in a similar manner to the experience of Britain and France. Political authority within the German state was still entrenched among the same bureaucratic and military elites that had persistently controlled German affairs from the eighteenth century onwards. Germany retained an autocratic regime where democracy was preached but never practiced. It had an elected parliament with severely limited powers, and this meant that the imperial urges of the kaiser, unchecked by the democratic impulses of the modern state, were to cost Germany dearly. In direct comparison to Britain, which had in the main solved major questions of identity and legitimacy, and France, which had at least embarked on the process after 1789, Germany by the end of the nineteenth century was still missing crucial attributes of nation formation. Its experiences in this area left the state unprepared to enter the modern age.

Bismarck, the man who had achieved German unity in 1870, was sacked in 1890 by the new German kaiser, Wilhelm the Second, a romantic nationalist who was to lead Germany into a catastrophic world war in 1914. In the interim, the kaiser installed more generals at top levels of the administration, initiated a major program of naval armament, and harbored dreams of Germany as a major imperial power. In turn Germany became involved in all sorts of disputes, from South Africa (where it supported the Boers against the British) to the Balkans (where it supported the Austrians against Russian claims). In short, by the beginning of 1914 it had succeeded in achieving exactly what Bismarck had set out to avoid: the Second Reich was surrounded by enemies and the political system had spun out of control. The assassination of the Archduke of Herzegovina in Sarajevo was the spark that ignited the First World War in 1914, but German military and aristocratic dreams of expansion had been driving that way for at least the preceding twenty years.

Germany and Two World Wars

The First World War (1914–18) was to cost the new German state and indeed all of Europe a heavy price in physical and social destruction. By 1917 Germany was mainly a military dictatorship and had lost much of the legitimacy it had gained since 1870. Between 1916 and 1917, 700,000 Germans died from starvation after a severe winter and food shortages under the devastating effects of the Allied blockade. In the end, Erich Ludendorff, one of the main German chiefs, was forced to ask the kaiser to abdicate and allow the remaining civilian leaders to form a republic and enter negotiations for peace with the Western Allies.

The German Second Reich was in ruins in 1918, its leadership and people demoralized by defeat after a war they could not understand how or why they had lost. Disaster seemed to follow disaster. In 1919, a new regime was formed from the ashes, the **Weimar Republic** (1919–1933); it was geared for the advent of democracy under popular elections with the introduction of a constitutional assembly.

The Weimar Republic, however, was too weak to repair the damage of defeat and instability that plagued the German system. Germany was forced to pay massive reparations to the Allies by the provisions of the peace treaty of Versailles; it lost all of its colonies and was deprived of large amounts of territory. Alsace-Lorraine in the West was transferred to France, which also occupied the industrial heartland of the Ruhr, and a substantial section of Prussia in the east was transformed into a "Polish Corridor" to the Baltic. Germany was demilitarized and labeled with the responsibility of causing the war by the victors, the Western Allies. The Versailles treaty, which blamed Germany for the mass destruction in this period (the notorious "**war guilt**" clause) was severely resented by all Germans and to a large extent created the grounds upon which it would embark upon the second major disaster for Europe and itself twenty years later—the Second World War. Under these conditions it should come as no surprise that the Weimar Republic lacked popular support and overall legitimacy among the German people.[1]

The Weimar Republic had even more problems to deal with than the Versailles treaty, despite the fact that many of its difficulties were a direct consequence of the postwar settlement. Weimar was characterized by permanent economic and political instability. It was consumed with repaying the sums the kaiser had borrowed to finance the war; its economic instability was exacerbated by reparation payments and French control of the industrial Ruhr area. In 1923, inflation spiraled to the fantastic figure of 26 billion percent as the currency became worthless. For example, a kilo of potatoes that cost

20 marks in Berlin in January 1923 cost 90 billion marks only nine months later in October.[2]

Democracy is unlikely to flourish in any country under such economic circumstances. There were several factors involved in the collapse of the democratic republic. For instance the idea that a regime must be legitimate and acceptable not only to its elites but also to its populace is a crucial theme in political development and continuity. The Weimar Republic was a discontinuous element in German history, and because of its weaknesses it failed to produce a system capable of enjoying and maintaining popular and elite support. In this sense it represented a unique element that was not related to previous German political development. Without a long history of democracy, its institutional structures and administrative elites were still primarily rooted in an authoritarian value system; it was a poor fit. With unification achieved only in 1870, Germany had still not resolved the crucial problems of a common political identity and a democratic political culture that were so important to the development of European liberal democracies. Crises plagued the system at every level: a crisis of economics, a crisis of politics, and a crisis of confidence in the ability of democracy to solve Germany's problems. In the end the institutions of the Weimar Republic were not strong enough to overcome these problems and prevent authoritarian extremes from entering and dominating the German political system.[3]

The straw that broke the back of Weimar was the Great Depression of 1929. Between 1929 and 1933 the economy was devastated by worldwide economic recession, and economic crisis pushed the political crisis to the forefront. As the economy deteriorated a series of presidential decrees designed to reform the economy, initiated in 1930 by Chancellor Heinrich Bruning, spelled the beginning of the end for democracy in Germany. By 1932 the government had moved this development one stage further, introducing rule by emergency powers granted under Article 48 of the Weimar constitution. By this time, however, the conservative leaders of industry and military had moved to support the return to authoritarianism. With the country almost on the verge of civil war and political violence the norm rather than the exception, the president, Paul von Hindenberg (a former First World War general) appointed an extreme right-wing candidate to the position of chancellor in January 1933. With the accession to power of the leader of the **National Socialist party (Nazis)**, Adolf Hitler, the nails in the coffin of the Weimar democracy became permanent fixtures. Within the next two years Hitler had taken almost total control of society and politics.

Hitler and the Third Reich

The failure of the Weimar Republic to overcome its problems represented the failure of the democratic experiment in this period of German history. If Weimar was democracy, then democracy didn't work for Germany according to the people in charge of its future in 1933. Hitler moved quickly to consolidate his grip on politics, revising the constitution in March 1933 by forcing through parliament an enabling act that granted him dictatorial powers. The Weimar Republic gave way to Hitler's **Third Reich** and the symbol of the new Nazi Germany, the swastika. From this point Hitler moved swiftly to create a new National Socialist order. His Thousand-Year Reich, however, lasted only twelve years and collapsed with the defeat of Germany in the Second World War.

Hitler and the Nazi party enjoyed considerable mass support in Germany and achieved at least a superficial kind of prosperity in their years in power. Unemployment was very low, inflation was curbed, and massive public works and rearmament programs provided the economy with a veritable boom. At the same time that Germans came to enjoy the "success" of the Nazis, especially in comparison to the "failure" of Weimar, Hitler had different plans for the rest of the population, particularly the minorities. The Nazis administered systematic imprisonment, torture and eventual elimination of millions of Jews, Gypsies, handicapped people, homosexuals, and political dissidents throughout their period of rule, including the Second World War. In all 6 million Jews along with millions of others died in the **Holocaust**. Civil liberties were suppressed, political opposition banned, and censorship imposed as the Nazis tightened their grip on German society.

The end goal of the Nazis, or at least of Hitler, in the 1930s was to prepare Germany for a war. The German state was to expand, and expand it did, marching into the Rhineland in 1936, annexing Austria in 1938 and Czechoslovakia in 1939, and dividing up Poland (or at least part of it) that same year. The British policy of appeasement lay in ruins as Hitler knew no boundaries (his ultimate goal was to take over the Soviet Union and transform the Russians into a race of slaves who would serve the Third Reich). In September 1939, after Germany invaded Poland, the British government finally gave up its policy of appeasement and declared itself at war with Germany.

Change in the Post–1945 Period

With the victory of the Allied forces and the defeat of Germany in 1945, the German nation was at its lowest point in its overall political development. The defeat it suffered was far greater in scale than even its position in 1918. Germany was economically, socially, and politically destroyed; the political and moral fabric of its nationhood had been reduced to ashes, and from such a position it could only improve.

And it did improve in a remarkable way—so much so that on its fortieth birthday in 1989, it was the political and economic success story of Europe, an affluent participatory democracy, an economic superpower. The transition is all the more remarkable given the state of Germany after the war and considering its long history of discontinuous politics. In large part the reconstruction of Germany was undertaken by the Allied powers and in particular by the United States. Germany was divided into several zones of occupation under the control of the different Allies in this period, and they pursued policies of demilitarization and denazification in a general sense. (At the Yalta conference, shortly before the war's end in 1945, such an idea had been proposed by the United States, Britain, and the Soviet Union.) This wartime alliance, however, was certain to break down given the East-West divide and the deep divisions between ideological camps. The Soviets, for instance, started transferring power to the German Communists in their zone of occupation; the Western Allies began to support the creation of Western-style political parties in their particular areas.

In March 1947, the seeds of a divided Germany were sown with the failure of the allies to overcome their ideological differences in the administration of Germany. The world thus moved closer to the Cold War between East and West that was to characterize international relations over the next forty years. In the summer of the same year the **Marshall Plan** for the reconstruction of Europe set out by the Americans was rejected by the Soviets and their satellites in Eastern Europe. After this the Western Allies began to make preparations for a separate German state in their zones of occupation, and in 1948 they called for the establishment of an independent West German state in the three Western occupation zones. In June, the Western powers introduced a currency reform, which in turn provoked a Soviet blockade of the Western sectors of Berlin; an airlift of supplies by the West to West Berlin increased tensions between East and West, but it had the desired effect of removing the Soviet blockade in 1949. In May 1949, following the removal of the blockade, the occupying Western powers allowed the Germans to introduce a **German Federal Republic (F.R.G.)** and a democratic constitution, the **Basic Law**. Shortly afterwards, in October 1949, a second German state was announced in the Soviet zone. This was the **German Demo-**

cratic Republic (G.D.R.), otherwise known as East Germany. The Allies and West Germany declared the "illegality" of the new state, and West Germany from this period on claimed the right to speak for all Germany, both East and West. Similarly the Soviets in this period viewed the Federal Republic as simply "part of Germany." Germany was divided once more, and this time the division was to prove substantial, ideologically and economically. The Western part stood firmly in the capitalist, Western sphere and became enormously successful. The Eastern half remained firmly within the Communist, Eastern sphere and as we have seen since 1990, became demonstrably unsuccessful. In part the existence of the democratic Federal Republic encouraged several waves of refugees; between 1949 and 1961 over 2.6 million refugees left the GDR, a number that appeared to threaten the economic and political stability of the state. East Germany and the Soviet Union felt they had to take action on this matter, and on August 13, 1961, the East–West border was closed. Five days later they began to erect a wall (eventually extending 103 miles) designed to keep East Germans from escaping to the West. And this was the situation between 1961 and 1990; for nearly thirty years the ideological divisions were symbolized in concrete in the shape of the **Berlin Wall**.

> The Wall was ugly and obscene, though no uglier than other walls in Belfast and Cyprus and Beirut; no uglier, for that matter, than the miles of metal fencing along the southern border of the United States with Mexico, and certainly more flexible than the border kept tightly shut on both sides between the two Koreas. But the Berlin Wall stood in the spotlight, in center stage, central Europe, at the one spot where the forces of NATO and the Warsaw Pact directly faced each other.[4]

Germany and the Federal Republic

West Germany was concerned from the outset with establishing a democratic system of government, one that would not be susceptible to the failures and weaknesses of the Weimar Republic or to the vagaries of fascist politics. To this end, the Basic Law banned extremist political parties and weakened the role of the president in an effort to prevent a repeat of Hitler's rise to power; emergency powers for instance were no longer under the president's control. Similarly the strengthening of the position of chancellor increased the chances that such a figure would not be prone to intrigue or factionalism within the various parties. The new constitution also allowed for a "constructive vote of no-confidence" to develop stability in government. Such a motion allowed parliament to remove the chancellor but only if it was able to agree on a successor. In the new federal system the role of the ten states (**Länder**) was to play an important part. A constitutional court allowed for the process of judicial review to take shape. At a later stage in the Federal Republic's history, a 5 percent threshold law introduced the requirement that political parties needed to receive more than that percentage of the popular vote in order to gain seats in the Bundestag. The new German parliament consisted of the Bundestag (the lower house) and the Bundesrat (an upper house). Having established a constitution and reconstituted their society with a political framework, the Germans (now armed with Wastern aid) could reconstruct their economy and society and provide the state with a degree of continuity that its predecessors never witnessed.

Economy and Society

With the basic building blocks of society in place, West Germany began to rebuild its economy. It achieved this under the direction of a series of strong executives and governments from 1949 onwards. The first chancellor of the new republic, Konrad Adenauer, leader of the Christian Democratic Union, set the pace between 1949 and 1963, working closely with the economics minister, Ludwig Erhard (who was to become the next chancellor). Both men succeeded in creating a new Germany in the 1950s and 1960s; through what is now known as the "economic miracle" (**Wirtschaftswunder**), it became rich and successful. How did the West German state recover so quickly from the ravages of war? The key in the Federal Republic after 1949 was that it placed its faith wholeheartedly in the free market, with the state playing a supportive role. The state for instance would intervene only to stabilize the deutsche mark or maintain a steady money supply. Erhard devised the idea of the social market system as a response to West Germany's difficulties. This social market blueprint, as suggested by its name, had two major components. The social part was based on a doctrine that became familiar in Western Europe after the war: the welfare state in which welfare provisions were retained at the level of central government. Increased spending on welfare functions actually increased economic demand while at the same time providing basic social services; the idea was to stimulate collective consumption more than individual consumption. The increased role of the Land governments also meant a transfer of some central-government functions to the states. The role of the public sector in creating large-scale welfare measures also provided a stable environment in which business could operate.

Second, the idea and reality of the market came to fruition under Erhard's sponsorship. Industries did not undergo nationalization as in the United Kingdom and France, and West Germany did not follow the views of the socialist party (the SPD) or the trade unions and their ideas for reconstruction. Rather the large firms that had been tightly controlled by the Nazi government were broken up. The emergence of small, competitive firms engendered an entrepreneurial spirit that created more capital in the early years of the republic; by the late 1950s, however, the industries reverted back to a more concentrated form. Chemical, steel, and electronics industries, for instance, came under the control of a few large companies. Along with the support of the public sector, banks and industry groups played a role in coordinating such industries. In 1948 a major currency reform also pointed the way forward to a new dynamic capitalism; the reforms were designed to benefit large property holders, and those with little savings were to be discouraged. The aim was to allow investment patterns of growth to take root in the republic rather than consumption-based growth; exports rather than imports along with the development of heavy industry were encouraged under this system. The net result was a period of unprecedented growth for the economy. During the 1950s the economy averaged almost 8 percent growth a year, regressing to around 5 percent in the 1960s. Within eleven years of its establishment, the Federal Republic in 1961 had surpassed any previous value of industrial production by more than 150 percent and by the 1980s this same production had outstripped any of its nearest neighbors in Europe.[5] Inflation was kept below 2 percent in this first ten-year period, and despite fairly high unemployment the reconstruction of the economy had begun to take shape.

The takeoff in the West German economy improved the standards of living and earnings of individual Germans in a major way; wages continued to grow dramatically, educational facilities were expanded, and the growth of the mass media combined with other expansion create a genuinely affluent postindustrial society in a relatively short period of time. Changes in the occupational structure were similar to those taking place in France during the same period. The role of agriculture was dramatically transformed; official statistics show that whereas in 1950, just over 20 percent of the population was employed in the agricultural sector, by the end of the 1970s this number had decreased to roughly 5 percent of the population. At the same time, the number of persons working in the service sector had increased to almost half the population (the defining watermark of postindustrialism).[6] By the 1960s the West German economy was so strong and the achievement of full employment had been so rapid that the country was forced to fill vacant jobs with foreign workers (*Gastarbeiter* or "guest workers") from the less-developed countries of southern Europe and Turkey.

The boom period of the German economy lasted substantially through the 1960s and early 1970s, but like all European economies, it was affected by the oil shocks of 1973 and the subsequent worldwide recession. Economic growth was reduced to just over 3 percent, while inflation reached an all-time high in the postwar period at just under 5 percent. Similarly, unemployment began to increase steadily as the recession took hold and Germany lost out in industrial competition to Japanese industry, where wages were much lower and shipping and consumer electronics more competitive. In this respect the German society started to echo the problems of the other major European nations—the United Kingdom, France, and Italy—all of whom were similarly affected by the twin evils of high inflation and high unemployment (or "stagflation").

Despite these problems, there is no doubt that the West German economy evolved to become one of the most dynamic success stories of postwar Europe, certainly more successful than it had been during the dominance of Prussia, the Weimar Republic, or the Nazi control over German society. As a capitalist society and a liberal democracy, West Germany proved to be a model of stability and growth in the post-1949 period.

West German Politics after 1949

The success of the West German economy in the postwar period went hand in hand with the establishment of a working, multiparty democracy. Various measures (as previously mentioned) were taken to ensure the stability of such a system after a long period of discontinuity in German politics. And what emerged was a creditable and democratic form of parliamentary government generally based on coalitions between the political parties.

The most important figure is of course the Chancellor; chancellors since 1949 are listed in table 4.1.

The first chancellor, Konrad Adenauer, proved to be a hard act to follow. His nickname, *Der Alte* or the "old one," referred to the fact that he gained the chancellorship when he was seventy-three and served for fourteen years until he was eighty-seven. Adenauer was a charismatic politician who exercised decisive leadership and was sometimes capable of authoritarian views similar to those of France's Charles de Gaulle. None of the chancellors who followed

TABLE 4.1: Chancellors of the Postwar Federal Republic

Chancellor	Years	Parties
Konrad Adenauer	1949–63	CDU/CSU
Ludwig Erhard	1963–66	CDU/CSU
Kurt-Georg Kiesinger	1966–69	CDU/CSU/SPD
Willy Brandt	1969–74	SPD
Helmut Schmidt	1974–82	SPD
Helmut Kohl	1982–	CDU/CSU

possessed the same qualities. Erhardt and Kiesinger suffered in failing to maintain the strong image that Adenauer had established. Willy Brandt and Helmut Schmidt succeeded in establishing solid international credentials for West Germany as statesmen. Brandt was responsible for **Ostpolitik** (Eastern Policy), in which he forged detente and understanding with Eastern Germany and the Soviet Union to provide a relaxation in Cold War tensions. Both Brandt and Schmidt were popular even though the economy was hardly a success in these periods. The present chancellor, Helmut Kohl, came to power in 1982 after a constructive vote of no-confidence in the SPD government. Kohl oversaw the successful return of the conservative Christian Democrats (CDU/CSU) to political leadership. The fact that there are three main political parties operating at a national level allows changes within the coalitional structure of politics and provides for a fluid political system.

When Chancellor Kohl took over from Helmut Schmidt in 1982, he was faced with several important tasks—tasks that had apparently overwhelmed the SPD/FDP coalition government and led to its downfall when the FDP switched loyalties to the CDU/CSU. The first goal of the new CDU/CSU-FDP coalition was to try to revive an ailing economy plagued by the twin problems of inflation and unemployment (common to all the countries compared here). Moreover there was the problem of finding a solution to the difficulties raised by the stationing of new American missiles on German soil, a highly controversial topic throughout the eighties, particularly in light of the development of Green politics. The increasing difficulties posed by the large numbers of foreign workers in Germany and various outbursts by terrorists and neo-Nazi movements simply served to exacerbate the problems in West German society throughout the eighties.

In all of these cases the Kohl government enjoyed only limited success. The economy in German society is of course of prime importance, especially because of the fact that when Germany has had severe economic problems in the past, extremism has come to the surface and with horrendous consequences. The disastrous Weimar Republic and its economic record was not something German leaders wanted to repeat.[7] Overall the German record on keeping inflation in check has been fairly good in comparison to that of its European neighbors. At the beginning of the 1980s inflation peaked at around 5 to 6 percent; by 1986 the economy was experiencing − 0.2 percent deflation, but the figure has since crept up to around 2.5 to 3 percent. West German workers on the whole faced far better conditions than their counterparts in other developed industrial nations. Unemployment grew throughout the 1980s (as it did in all of the societies in Europe under discussion).[8] At the beginning of the 1980s, just under 800,000 people were unemployed; ten years later the figure had risen to over 2 million (between 8 and 10 percent of the work force). Structural problems in the economy had begun to take their toll. Industries such as mining, shipbuilding, steel, and textiles all suffered in a similar way to British industries faced with increased competition and lower costs from the newly developing economies of the Asia-Pacific region, such as Japan, South Korea, and Taiwan.

Despite these problems some growth was achieved, but German success has been limited. It would have been surprising in fact if the F.R.G. had not been subject to the slowdown and other vicissitudes in the world economy and their debilitating effects. The Kohl coalition succeeded in pushing growth from a meagre 1.4 percent in 1983 to around 3.5 percent by the end of the eighties. In 1990, the West German economy grew by 4.5 percent. With the reunification of Germany, of course, it remains to be seen whether this economic recovery will continue and develop. In 1991 the rate of German growth was expected to decrease to 2.75 percent and even further, to 2.25 percent, in 1992.

Domestic issues such as the assimilation of different groups and foreign workers (*Gastarbeiter*) into German society has also proved to be controversial and difficult. And clearly this problem will not go away in the immediate future. Suffice to say at this point that the influx of settlers from East Germany and Eastern Europe, which reached a fairly massive scale in the 1980s in comparison with average postwar figures, coupled with the numbers of *Gastarbeiter* from countries like Turkey and with other refugees (of either the "political" or the "economic" kind) have led to a major social dilemma in German society.

Conclusion

Throughout the postwar period the history of West Germany, in terms of both economics and the development of a valid political democracy, has been one of success. With the reunification of Germany at the end of the 1980s, that success story appeared on the surface to be threatened by various circumstances, not least the disastrous state of the East German economy, the revival of right-wing xenophobia, and the threat and reality of large-scale strikes (which rocked Germany in April 1992).

Unification has proved to be immeasurably more difficult, complicated, and expensive than most politicians and analysts were willing to predict or even realized in the early days when heady optimism about this historical process was the vogue. The dynamic political change that occurred has, as one source has argued, all the qualities of a fairy tale, taking on good, bad, and ugly proportions.[9]

There is little doubt that German reunification has exacted a heavy price for the Federal Republic, but equal hardship is borne by the East German state as it tries to cope with the social, political, economic, and psychological drama that has presented itself. It would be naive to think that the entire process could have proceeded without some real dislocation and traumatic effects, given the entirely different nature of each society. But given that we see dislocation, the pessimistic response may be the more inappropriate one. We have seen that when Germany has been in economic and political difficulty throughout its history, it has resorted to dictatorship and war. But historical circumstances have changed. Germany is no longer the victim of excessive war charges. It now lives in an age when colonialism is no longer morally acceptable and therefore does not feel the need to conquer new territories. Moreover, Germany is now democratic and has been since 1949; it is unlikely that any dictator like Hitler could make a reappearance in a society that has proved to be a stable and enduring democracy for the past forty-five years. In short, Germany may be better equipped than any other Western European country to endure and weather political problems and economic difficulties—even given its difficult and turbulent political past. In this sense German political continuity is ensured.

Political Culture: Change and Discontinuity

Since German history has been essentially fragmented and divided, it is hardly surprising that German political culture has undergone a great deal of change. The major changes, however, have been most notable in the post-1945 period. This era formed the climax of an eventful and discontinuous series of events in German history. The collapse of the monarchy, the collapse of the Weimar Republic, and finally the collapse of the Third Reich with the end of the war brought about a need for stability and peace in German history. Ironically, this was achieved with the partition of Germany into two separate societies, East and West.

The trauma of division and the often violent history of the German people serve as a guide to their political culture, which was the legacy of authoritarianism. One has to bear in mind that Germany in comparison to, say, France or the United Kingdom has a relatively short period of liberal democracy to fall back on. And even at that, its longest period of democracy was when it was divided, the western half divided up among the Allies, and the eastern a satellite of the Soviet Union. So to some extent when we discuss Germany in this context there will unavoidably be references to West Germany, as this is the society on which we have more information and the one that belonged to the Western camp throughout the period. At the end of this section there will be a brief discussion of the problems of forming a new Germany that integrates the East Germans, who after all have experienced a different political culture during the past forty-five years.

A Democratic Political Culture?

In 1949, democracy was a relatively unknown virtue in German politics. In the space of just over thirty years, the Germans had experienced three regimes, all of which had failed. The brief hiatus of democracy under Weimar (1919–33) had been insufficient to instill democratic values into the populace. In fact the weakness of the Weimar Republic provided further cause to eschew democracy as a good form of governance. Germans were much more attuned to authoritarianism and dictatorship; democracy was an almost unknown quantity and quality in German political life.

It is all the more interesting then that forty years after this fairly pessimistic scenario, the West German state was one of the leading examples of an advanced, industrial liberal democracy in Western Europe, having finally solved in large part its crisis of legitimacy and forged a respectable democratic identity and image in the eyes of most Western nations.

In 1949, German political culture, attitudes, and beliefs reflected the prior legacy of the Third Reich, a culture shaped by the nazification of Germany between 1933 and 1945. After 1945 the task of German and Allied elites was to develop a new form of political culture for Germany. In this they faced an uphill task. Not only had Germany been defeated in the Second World War, but its political institutions were external impositions of the Allied powers. Could Germans render allegiance and loyalty to a new set of federal institutions based on democratic politics? Or would the same old problems simply resurface to engulf German society? It was in this setting that a key aim or goal of the German elites was to develop a working commitment to democracy and the Federal Republic that was instituted in 1949 under the new West German Constitution, the Basic Law.

Prior to the advent of the boom in comparative politics in the late 1950s and 1960s, much of the research that was conducted on German political culture tended to focus on why Germany had experienced authoritarianism in such an extreme manner. Why did Germans become Nazis? What was it about the German personality type that made it susceptible to authoritarianism? For example, this type of research produced works such as *The Authoritarian Personality* by T.W. Adorno and associates (New York: Harper and Row, 1950). As Eva Kolinsky has noted, such studies focused on:

> socialization processes in the family and on decision making in the public and private spheres and argued that the political institutions and attitudes that originated in Imperial Germany produced a personality type with an authoritarian or fascist potential. Democratic or liberal values could not emerge in an environment built on obedience, fear, repression, and on the desire of the apparently powerless individual to himself exercise unlimited power if the opportunity presented itself.[10]

In the 1950s this research focus began to change as democratic institutions became operative and the engine of the German economy gained momentum. In this new atmosphere, aided by the advent of opinion polls and new research techniques, political scientists began to focus, not on why people were authoritarian, but on why they would support democratic institutions. What were the factors that encouraged and enhanced political stability in the political system? In the following section I will assess the results of this change in focus.

Balancing Consensus and Conflict

If anything the postwar success story of German (at least specifically West German) political culture has been the balancing act sustained between conflict and consensus. West Germany is the political, economic, and social model of success in Western Europe after 1945. It has coped most successfully with the changing social and economic environment, the generational differences between prewar and postwar cohorts, and the development of issue politics (for instance, struggles around environmental and nuclear issues in post-1945 German politics). Germany as a result has quite clearly developed into a full-fledged participatory democracy where mass participation is valued for society as a whole and not simply at the elite level.

I will deal with these aspects separately so as to arrive at a general conclusion on German political culture and how it may develop in the future. The fact that most of these aspects are interrelated should serve as a key to understanding the analysis.

Changing Social and Economic Environment. It would be difficult to assess the contemporary political culture in Germany without reference to the economic and social context. When West Germans, for instance, were asked in the late 1950s about their political institutions, they did not appear particularly fond of them; they were not "proud" of them, as Almond and Verba put it. The same could not be said about the economic system and the general German national character; Germans quite clearly expressed more faith in the performance of the economy than in the performance of democratic institutions.[11] In the mid 1960s this view was supported in a study that claimed that West Germans adhered to the rules of democracy; the implication was that the Germans were not necessarily attracted to democracy because it was an intrinsic good but simply because it performed well.[12] Thus in the early stages of West German democracy, its political support appeared to be conditional—conditional on whether the economy was functioning successfully. This prerequisite provided the basis for the new German political culture. Thus economic downturns or crises within the economy represented a threat to the stability of this newfound "democratic" culture. Since the failure of the Weimar Republic and the poor management of the economy in the 1920s had given rise to extremist parties, many feared the repetition of such circumstances. This fear in effect prompted the new constitution makers in West Germany to design some safeguards against the dangers of extremism (whether of the left or of the right). The 5 percent threshold clause, for example, means that small parties or groups have difficulty gaining access to the Bundestag: they need to achieve over 5 percent of the popular vote before they can gain representation within the German parliament. In effect the clause provided an institutional backup to the efforts to produce a democratic political culture. It is clear, then, that in the beginning the German political system and its various governments relied less upon

diffuse support for the entire political system, regardless of performance, and more on **specific support** for a particular government, contingent upon its performance in the economic arena. In the mid-1960s, for instance, support for the National Democratic Party (NDP), which espoused neo-Nazi ideals, increased at a time of rising unemployment, economic stagnation, and weak performance. This support weakened when economic performance picked up and increased again in times of economic downturn, such as in the recession following reunification. The idea that democracy is adhered to in Germany because of its efficient performance is sometimes referred to as *Schonwetterdemokratie* or "fair weather democracy."

Over the years, the correlation between economic performance and political support and attitudes has decreased as German citizens advanced other forms of increasingly democratic activity. The most obvious example lies in the extraparliamentary activity of the Greens and similar groups. Particularly in the 1980s, the correlation between performance and political support appears to have significantly weakened as German citizens overall came to exhibit much more diffuse system support. Conradt made this point when discussing replicas of the Almond and Verba study, which showed that Germans had more wholeheartedly accepted democratic institutions.[13] The public had in effect developed into a sophisticated citizenry capable of rejecting or accepting policies and programs without necessarily rejecting such national institutions as parliament or the party system. And in part this might be attributed to the overall economic security of the system. The fact that West Germany has weathered (and indeed not really been susceptible to) the major economic crises of the postwar period has given the public a fairly long time in which to get used to the idea and the institutions of democracy and to accept them as part of their political system. Therefore it is important to look at the basically secure economic and social environment in which the German political system has emerged, ensuring a firm basis for the continuation of the democratic process in the German state.

Other developments in West German politics which in part stem from this socioeconomic dimension have also played a role, however. Notably, I am referring to the role of generational change and its political significance.

Changing Attitudes: Generation to Generation. A large part of the study of political culture is devoted to how and why attitudes change. People are shaped by their political, social, and economic environment but in turn also play a role in shaping it. The crucial element in German attitudinal change clearly lies in the difference between the prewar and postwar generations. Most of the prewar generation acquired their political socialization mainly under the influence of either the Weimar Republic or the Third Reich of Adolf Hitler—which may or may not have left profound effects on their thinking. The younger generation, especially since the mid-1960s, grew up in times of unprecedented prosperity and economic security, not to mention political continuity. It did not endure the hardships of war or deprivation that marked the older generation.

There is little doubt that the political culture experienced under the totalitarianism of Hitler had severe and negative consequences for the German nation. The Third Reich exercised almost absolute control over the development of the individual. Its authority was not to be questioned, and the individual was to be subjugated to the will of the state. Orders were to be obeyed, not questioned. In such a system the average citizen represented nothing, while the nation-state constituted the life force. This was a political culture of intolerance and authoritarianism which debased and dehumanized its subjects in every sense of the word. To proceed from such a culture to a democratic one, overnight or within a few decades, appeared an uphill task if not impossible in 1949. And this is why the remaking of German political culture in subsequent years appears all the more remarkable.

In the section on British political culture in chapter 2, I discussed the applicability of Ronald Inglehart's theory of value change to postmaterial attitudes of the postwar generations. In Germany in the postwar period, this theory is even more applicable because a new German social movement and political party, **Die Grünen**, or the Greens, came to epitomize the ethos of postmaterialism in Western Europe.

The Greens

Inasmuch as the Greens were a product of their political, social, and economic environment, in turn they helped to shape and form that environment. Previously we noted that there were many economic and social changes in postwar Germany, and these changes provided an environment conducive to the emergence of a new postmaterial agenda. Traditional religious ties and values were decreasing; economic affluence and a leisure-oriented life-style, together with greater education and expanded mass media, increased the average citizen's awareness of politics.[14] The traditional class and occupational structure continued to change as the agricultural sector suffered at the expense of a vastly increased service sector. The "economic miracle" was in turn accompanied over time by increasing support for the institutions and values of West German democratic institutions. And it is in fact the spread of this democratic value system that has encouraged and facilitated the growth of the Greens.

Not only did successful social and economic change help to produce an environment in which the Greens could flourish; it also provided an arena in which a more sophisticated and politicized citizenry could in fact turn to alternatives to express dissatisfaction with the political regime in question. In the late 1970s the major parties' share of the votes began to decline as political and financial scandals at the elite level surfaced and pressure groups and citizen initiatives began to play an active role in West German politics.[15] The Greens emerged in this atmosphere of citizen initiative politics, being launched as an official political party in 1980. In 1983 they managed 5.6 percent of the vote and twenty-seven seats in the Bundestag; by 1987 they accounted for 8.3 percent of the popular vote and forty-four seats. The Greens advocated a political program, agenda, and political style totally different from those of the established parties. Their rise reflected the new postmaterialism that had taken root among certain sectors of the public. The pillars of their program are ecology, social responsibility, grass-roots democracy, and nonviolence—a heavily postmaterial agenda. The movement's support among the new German middle class and students reflects a style that challenges the elites and the value system of the material culture, in which economic priorities are still entrenched. In the new politics in Germany, freedom of speech and political participation are valued as intrinsic elements as opposed to the old class-ridden, material agendas. This development is in line with the creation of a democratic political culture that has been actively learned in the past forty years.

The Greens clearly reflected an active postmaterial stance towards politics compared to the major parties. They have consciously made an impact out of proportion to their size and strength. For instance, between 1983 and 1987, Green deputies introduced fifty-eight bills (pieces of legislation) while SPD deputies introduced eighty-five, the CDU/CSU, fifty-eight and the FDP, fifty-seven. Furthermore, Green members of Parliament introduced as many motions to amend bills or to pass resolutions as the SPD did.[16]

In the first all-German elections, in 1990, the Greens' share of the vote, and thus their share of the seats, fell from 8.3 percent in 1987 to only 4.1 percent, a loss of more than half. And even this total combined the seats of the West German Greens and the East German Greens/Bundnis '90. In some ways this decline reflected the divisions within the party over reunification and the ability of SPD leaders to hijack potential Green votes by appealing to new-left and environmental issues. However, despite some marginalization of the Greens after the 1990 election, they still maintain a place in German politics, and if the politics of postmaterialism continues to have an impact out of proportion to its strength, the Greens will continue to have influence in the "new" Germany.

Conclusion: A Political Culture in Flux

Despite the progress since 1989 toward reunification of Germany and the difficulties associated with that, perhaps one of the most difficult tasks for those involved is the psychological, cultural, and social reconciliation of the former two states. One has to understand that these were two completely different states, with different ideologies, different political, social, and economic systems, and vastly different life-styles. Especially for the people of the East (who were in fact being co-opted by the West) reunification proved in many ways to be a traumatic, unsettling event which caused a great deal of insecurity and hardship. The G.D.R. was an authoritarian regime where people were simply the passive subjects of the state and the government met dissent with an iron fist. Individuality was frowned upon; strict family discipline was encouraged; order and obedience were the rules of the day, causing people to suppress their emotions and beliefs. As a result, people grew up in a stunted way, suffering from depression, deprivation, and submissive character traits. Insecurity, feelings of inferiority, and a sense of helplessness were common traits of the East German character. It should therefore come as little surprise that such dependent subjects would have great difficulty adjusting to the suddenly newfound freedoms of the West, of democracy and independence. If the "revolution" in East Germany was fueled by material deprivations and the need for consumer goods, then reunification must have proved disappointing to many hopefuls. Only a few years after the wall was removed, disillusionment and disappointment had become prevailing emotions in the East. The stark reality of the market economy in which people have to compete and perform, and the massive increase in unemployment (something previously unheard of in East Germany) caused widespread resentment and bitterness among "*Ossis*" (easterners). What really happened in the "new" Germany was not a coalescence or compromise of value systems but simply the wholesale transferral of West Germany's political, social, and economic system to the East—an event inevitably bound to cause severe societal dislocations.

Previously in this section it was noted that West Germany had been fairly successful in adopting the elements of a participatory political culture. The Greens, for instance, had established themselves as a healthy counterpoint to the established party system. Pressure groups and citizen initiative groups had contributed to a participatory democracy in which citizens did not just vote (as part of their civic duty) but played an active role in trying to influence the political process. This was a positive development, as one Social Democrat leader noted: "The alternative Green movement is a sign of creativity in the Federal Republic which is not present to the same extent in France or the United Kingdom. German politicians should welcome the challenge they present."[17] The Greens and the politics of postmaterialism had in fact confirmed just how well democratic attitudes had taken root in the West German nation. These developments were clearly out of step with the culture of East Germany, as became apparent when unification came home. The rise of extremism and authoritarian attitudes are a worrisome possibility in the near future.

The German political culture thus appears in a state of flux as the result of the unification of two states that have experienced two vastly different types of political culture and learning experiences in the post-1945 period. Only time will tell whether democratic attitudes will be learned and loved in the East and the wholesale adoption of these values will take place, or whether the dark sides of German nationalism and extremism will rise once more to reassert themselves in times of crisis.

Internal Wounds: The Problem of Reunification

[German novelist Gunter Grass] reminded everyone at an early stage that the last period of German unity (the seventy-five years from 1871 to 1945) was the most spectacularly dreadful in all German history.[18]

The Wall Comes Tumbling Down

It is an historical fact that a united Germany is an unusual entity in European history. Between 1870 and 1945, Germany was united, and from 1990 to the present day it has been reunited, but the rest of the time it has been divided, as seen in the historical overview. The foremost advocate of German unification in the twentieth century was—unfortunately for Germany and for Europe—Adolf Hitler. It was he that dreamed of a thousand-year Reich (which really lasted only from 1933 to 1945). Hitler's idea of unification, to bring all Germans under one rule, was ultimately responsible for the destruction of other European states and peoples. The German state under Hitler proved, of course, to be a disaster for other nations, and some had grave doubts whether reunification was a good idea for Germany or for Europe. In this section I will not deal with the history of German unification because it has already been covered in section 1 of this chapter. Rather I will deal with the more recent past and the problems that reunification poses not only for Germany but also for the rest of Europe.

For Unification

The majority of the public and of politicians, academics, and current-affairs specialists clearly favored reunification as events unfolded in late 1989. In fact it was difficult to find someone who would criticize these events. The chancellor, Helmut Kohl, had spelled out a ten-point plan for German unity, and it appeared to be only a matter of time before the process would be fulfilled. The argument was a strong and potent one: The world had come to accept that national self-determination was an intrinsic right of all peoples. To deny such a right to Germany would be tantamount to hypocrisy on the part of the West, which had developed this notion as a fundamental part of its political creed; a divided Germany in this sense was seen as an unnatural artifice. It was also pointed out that Germany had paid for its sins and that these should be laid to rest, given the fact that the majority of its population had been born since 1945 and were therefore not responsible for the past events.

What is more, the proponents of unification argued that by the late 1980s historical circumstances for the first time favored reunification. The fact was that in 1945 the new postwar European order was constructed specifically in and around the role of Germany. It sought to achieve two major purposes. On the one hand was an external containment function; containing the power of the Soviet Union and any expansionist tendencies it might have was first and foremost on the minds of the Western Allies. The second purpose was to control Germany. Europeans did not want another war, and German power was better divided than united. Stability was much sought after in the post-1945 period; indeed it was a prerequisite for the reconstruction of Germany and Europe, and the Federal Republic of Germany was the fundamental cornerstone and front-line state of the Western alliance.

However, the enormous changes in the late 1980s, which were to shatter the post-1945 European order, destroyed most of the premises and assumptions on which division was maintained. One man initiated a series of major reforms and political initiatives within the

Soviet Union which was directly instrumental in changing the entire shape of Europe in this period. Mikhail Gorbachev, the then–Soviet leader, in 1985 initiated programs of *glasnost* (openness) and *perestroika* (reorganization). Their consequences had a major impact on events leading to German reunification four years later. In fact the consensus at the time was that German unification would not have been possible without Gorbachev and the changes he introduced into the Soviet system.

The revolution that Gorbachev sought to effect within the Soviet Union had at least three major implications for West Germany on the eve of its reunification and its fortieth birthday in 1989. First, it reduced the West's perceived threat from the Soviet Union. As a result, West Germans were less keen to bear a share of responsibilities for the North Atlantic Treaty Organization (NATO). The second result was an enormous movement of hundreds of thousands of ethnic Germans across borders from the Soviet Union and Eastern Europe back to their "homeland." This event increased sentimental feeling and energy to work in favor of a united Germany. And finally, the boundaries created and perpetuated by the Cold War in the post-1945 period began to dissipate.

Against Reunification

During the euphoria at the beginning of reunification, it would have been difficult to find a group of people to openly criticize the notion, the sentiment, or the reality of the movement. Overall German reunification was regarded as a good thing, a process that would end years of artificial division created by the ideological conflicts of the Cold War. However, there were some skeptics as indicated by the statement by Gunter Grass at the beginning of this section. Grass even wrote a book to express his anti-unification position—*Two States—One Nation? The Case against German Reunification.*[19] He wrote that Germany would eventually be feared and isolated in Europe once more; the echoes of its tragic past would stifle the initial jubilation of unification. This problem was compounded for Grass by the belief that the West German state was (had been) also part of the problem. Neither East nor West could fulfill all the aspirations of the German citizenry. For Grass the preferred solution would have been a confederation with eastern and western parts of Germany linked together but separate, not united. The delusion of the Federal Republic—that it could absorb the easterners and provide them a good life—was a lie that would have to be maintained by a smooth and invisible repression. A similar argument was offered by Hans

Magnus Enzensberger in his book *Political Crumbs*.[20] Enzensberger extended the argument to take in the European Community: repression will occur in a supranational scenario as technocrats at every level come to wield power. The EC would be the ultimate administrative state—the Federal Republic of Germany writ large. Control and repression would not flow from the barrel of a gun but much more insidiously, from the software of the computer. Enzensberger's analysis could, of course, also be applied to the rest of Western Europe; administrative organs have been strengthened, undermining the democratic elected authorities and therefore political accountability throughout the 1970s and 1980s. The tendency of the modern state is to grow administratively. This central fact will not fail to have political and social implications for the societies of Western Europe in general and Germany in particular.

Warnings, fears, and cynicism about Germans and the German character were not limited to certain of the German intelligentsia but also voiced by governmental parties, such as the British cabinet and the French government.[21] A great deal of this uncertainty and cynicism was rooted in an awareness of Germany's problematic past. Reference was continually made to the Nazi period and fears that Germany might once again dominate the Continent. Gunter Grass specifically associated German unity with Auschwitz, one of the worst Nazi concentration camps during the Second World War.

Character Assassination?

Part of the debate on reunification was also concerned with the fears at the elite level among British and French policy makers. Both of these societies has been on the receiving end of the First and Second World Wars, so to some extent this was not an unnatural development. Nor was it necessarily new; a former French statesman once said, "I love Germany so much that I rejoice there are two of them." However, fears of a reunited Germany were sharply criticized in European circles, particularly when a memorandum of a meeting among Margaret Thatcher, various British and American academics, and cabinet officials in the United Kingdom on March 24, 1990 was leaked to the press. The meeting was concerned with the German national character in particular and reflected the concerns of British elites over German unification. The Powell Memorandum, named after Charles Powell, Thatcher's private secretary, attributed various very negative characteristics to the German character. These included: the Germans' insensitivity to others; their obsession with themselves; a strong inclination to self-pity, and a longing to be liked.

More permanent attributes were angst, aggressiveness, bullying, egotism, an inferiority complex, and sentimentality. Fears about the future of Germany in Europe were raised at the meeting: Would Germany re-emerge as a destructive power? What exactly would its role be? And the political hopes reiterated were that Germany would essentially be constrained within the context of the new Europe; for Thatcher, that meant a European Germany and specifically not a German Europe.[22]

A second controversial discussion resulted in the sacking of Nicholas Ridley, Thatcher's trade and industry secretary, in July 1990. Ridley had just given an interview to the *Spectator* magazine in the United Kingdom and had made some very controversial remarks about Germany and its role in the new Europe. On European Monetary Union, for instance, Ridley argued that "This is all a German racket designed to take over the whole of Europe. It has to be thwarted." On giving up British sovereignty in Europe he was even more adamant: "I'm not against giving up sovereignty in principle, but not to this lot. You might just as well give it to Adolf Hitler frankly."[23] These and several other comments in a similar vein caused a great deal of outrage—not only in Britain, where Thatcher was forced to replace Ridley despite objections that he was merely voicing her private concerns—but also in the major European capitals. Concern over the dangerous reawakening of Germany as a European superpower was not limited to key policymakers in the U.K. The issue of whether German nationalism would be revived was also of concern to France and to Germany's long-suffering neighbor, Poland. France felt slightly left out in the ensuing German rush to unification; its role in the process was unclear and there was some worry among the elite (including Mitterand) concerning failure in the early stages to secure guaranteed borders from the German side. Poland also was concerned, having been the previous victim of German economic expansion; there was criticism of German chancellor Helmut Kohl, who up until March 1990 had refused to give clear guarantees on the permanence of the German borders with Poland that had been established after the war. Newspaper headlines betrayed some of the concerns: "French Concern at German Changes," "Dangerous Reawakening of Old Fears," "Angst on Reunification Reflects Economic Reality," "Misgivings on Germany"—both in the United Kingdom and in the United States.

In the early stages of reunification the French government and business elites were also wary of the new Germany. They feared that

France would lose its position on center stage in Europe, they feared that Germany would overshadow France on the economic level, and they feared German ambitions. These fears subsided, however, as France realized that Germany would have to take on a bigger role in Europe as a whole and that France would be at the core of a developing European Community in a French-German axis.[24]

Other Problems of Unification

There are, of course, other and perhaps more important problems associated with unification. The economic problems were of major concern after the initial euphoria. East Germany was a second-rate industrial state; its economy was not even close to the strength or vitality of its Western partner. Decades of dependence on the Soviet Union, centralized economic planning, and bureaucratic red tape under a Communist regime had left it massively underdeveloped; the revolution in East Germany at the end of the 1980s was probably born more out of the need and desire of the people for consumer items than from any real desire to procure democracy.

The challenge of reunification was squarely put on West Germany; it was East Germany that would be incorporated into the Federal Republic, not the other way around.

There was and is an enormous problem with refugees in the early stages of the reunification, and this has essentially continued to the present time. When Gorbachev began to lose control of the political reforms in the Soviet Union, the GDR also slipped away from the grasp of the Soviet Union. Accordingly East Europeans became free to do it their way (what is now known as the **Sinatra Doctrine**).[25] As a result, floods of East Germans decided to leave immediately. In May 1989, for instance, Hungary opened its border with Austria; three months later, tides of East German refugees were heading east. In the G.D.R. the demonstrations simply grew larger and larger, with demands becoming more and more vociferous. When the Berlin wall was opened on the ninth of November in an effort to quell the problem, the demonstrators demanded more than freedom—they demanded democracy. Finally on the third of December 1989, they achieved their desire; the loss of the G.D.R. was perhaps the death blow to the Soviet empire and certainly one of the most significant events in the end of the Cold War.

In elections subsequently held in the G.D.R., a center-right coalition of parties that closely resembled their counterparts in West Germany won in a landslide. The chancellor, Helmut Kohl, managed to gain approval for a currency union beginning the first of July 1990 after winning in another landslide in the Western half, and reunification proceeded at a hectic pace.

Economic Difficulties. In the early stages of economic union, most East Germans expected or anticipated that, after decades of economic hardship and deprivation, their lives would be transformed almost overnight. Seventeen million East Germans may have perceived that bringing them up to the highest economic standards in the EC would not be much of a problem for the richest state in the European continent. This was not the case. In fact many experts were predicting that economic hardship would be the predominant fact of life for at least the first ten years of the program of reunification. East Germany had, after all, experienced a centrally planned economy in the postwar period. Forty years of this had produced underdevelopment; any move from a command economy to a social market economy was bound to be fraught with major difficulties and economic hardships. For example, inflation is likely to rise in Germany (and therefore in the rest of Europe).

No one anticipated the scale of the economic underdevelopment of the G.D.R. economy in comparison to its western counterpart on the eve of reunification. Organization for Economic Cooperation and Development (OECD) figures had given the impression that Eastern Germany had a fairly strong and prosperous economy, not too far removed from that of the West. But it was an economy of stagnation, not dynamism, and the amount of effort and finance needed to bring that economy into line with West Germany's was and is enormous.

The negative consequences were drastic. The East German economic system fell into a state of near-total collapse, with business closures, redundancies, and unemployment. By July 1990, eastern industrial output had decreased by 40 percent; over the next ten months it fell an additional 40 percent. One year after unification, unemployment (which had officially been unknown in the G.D.R.) had increased dramatically. By the end of August, 1991, 1 million were unemployed, nearly 1.5 million were partly unemployed, 360,000 workers were given early retirement, 78,000 people were in job training, and 261,000 were in temporary work—out of a population of 16 million East Germans. As the *Economist* put it:

> It is not surprising that Germans were delirious in the days before and after unification, and eager to be misled by government promises of a smooth transition. A couple of months later, their euphoria had turned to gloom. The collapse in the East astonished even the pessi-

mists. Obviously, the German economic miracle was over; the only question was how to cope with the riots and recriminations to come.[26]

The riots never came, but the gloom failed to disappear. Comparisons inevitably were drawn between Eastern Germany and Italy's *mezzogiorno* (or southern region). The fear was that the East would remain heavily and perhaps permanently dependent on the West in the same way that the mezzogiorno depends on the northern part of Italy for economic assistance and aid to develop. One estimate, nearly a year after reunification, pointed out that the flow of aid from the western part accounted for more than 50 percent of East Germany's GNP.[27] Strikes, increasing inflation, and the shifting population certainly left the former G.D.R. reeling; the cost of cleaning up industrial pollution will be extremely high, costing billions of marks.

Overall, one effect that reunification had and will have on Germany in the immediate term is a net loss in productive capacity and output per capita. This may mean, of course, that the engine of Europe will slow down as West Germans reeducate, train, and provide new equipment for the eastern work force. By West German standards most East Germans are simply unemployable except in the most basic of jobs. The OECD has estimated that it will take at least fifteen years to bring the East German economy up to the same standards as those of West Germany (and some estimates say this period will more likely be thirty years). While the overall German GNP had a growth rate of 3.2 percent in 1991, only 7 percent of this growth actually came from the East German economy. This figure is actually less than the overall flow of goods and services transferred from the western sector.

In 1991 the state transferred nearly $90 billion worth of financial assistance to the eastern part of Germany, raising fears of imminent recession. The question remains, Can state and industry afford to transfer such fast sums annually in order to subsidize the creation of jobs and municipal and regional finances, particularly in times of recession? Higher interest rates are one of the costs of reunification; in late January 1992 the vice-president of the German Bundesbank, Hans Tietmeyer, was claiming that this was the price to be paid for reunification: "If it is not paid for by necessary corrections in fiscal, social and pay policy, then it will be revealed all the more clearly in interest rates. . . . The problems of unification cannot be overcome for free."[28] Part of the problem, then, concerns the willingness of West Germans to sacrifice some of their living standards to finance the recovery of the former G.D.R. Heiner Geissler, the deputy chairman of the Christian Democratic Union, argued that the main issue was to persuade West Germans to accept that "the task of getting rid of the gap in living standards between the two parts of our country is the absolute priority."[29]

Psychological-Cultural Difficulties. Not only were major economic difficulties inherent in the unification of Germany; the psychological and cultural problems facing the new state have been just as traumatic in many senses. For one thing, eastern and western experiences of political culture were totally different from one another. And this has played a significant part in delineating the distinction between the "Ossis" (the East Germans) and the "Wessis" (West Germans). In a televised address in October 1991, the German president, Richard von Weizsäcker, declared that "We have difficulty in recognizing and comprehending how, under two quite opposite systems, completely different outlooks and life-styles have developed over the decades."[30] Changing the mentalities and attitudes of 16 million people who spent up to forty years under a Communist system is not an easy task.

Unification in its early stages had already claimed victims of the angst of finding a new identity or even just acquiring a new job after having taken employment for granted in the G.D.R. Statistics pointed to a rapid increase in psychological breakdowns, suicides, and divorces among Ossis.

The differences in organization of the East and West have major implications for the new German state. In the G.D.R., for instance, the Communist system maintained a rigid form of managerial supervision; the idea of democracy was virtually unknown. An Aliensbach Institute survey published in the German newspaper *Frankfurter Allegmeine Zeitung*, found that, among East Germans, the concept of democracy was extremely vague. In the army, officers were complaining about a breakdown in discipline among their soldiers. Clearly, however, the area where this is a real matter for concern is among the youth, many of whom have turned to expressing themselves in extreme right-wing terms. The "skinheads," for instance, espouse neo-Nazi ideologies and authoritarian values. And this is clearly in direct contrast to many of the West German youth influenced by "postmaterial" values such as greater freedom of speech and more participation in the Federal Republic. The racist attacks and xenophobia that observers witnessed in East Germany are clearly symptoms of a people who have a great deal to learn about democratic political culture and process. The clash of values is all too apparent. Thomas Kreuger, Berlin's senator for youth and family affairs, pointed this dilemma out: "After World War II, West Germans learned to live with lots of different cultures. In East Germany they couldn't do that at all. Now they are so overwhelmed by change and by new values that this eruption was bound to happen."

Recent Status of German Reunification

In his August 27, 1992, editorial, Jean Francois Kahn, the editor of the influential French centrist weekly *L'Evenement du Jeudi*, argued that

> The size of the xenophobic riots in Rostock in the former East Germany, and the shouts of "Germany for the Germans!" taken up in chorus by the witnesses of those pogroms, demonstrate how easy it is to spark an exalted wave of pan-German nationalism. . . . Only by placing Germany within the constraints of a dynamic and integrated Europe can these old demons be contained.[31]

It is clear now that the fears in the Western camp shortly before the reunification of Germany were mistaken. It was argued at the time that Germany's economy would be 50 percent larger than France's, and the addition of 17 million East Germans would transform productivity. Germany might begin to look to the east again, seeking a distinct role in shaping its own foreign policy freed of the constraints of NATO. European political union was seen as the anchor that would place Germany firmly within the Western camp and secure its allegiances and loyalty.

Four years later, Germany was suffering from economic trauma, military indecisiveness, and social malaise as well as an enormous refugee problem (how will it absorb 500,000 refugees?). The idea that a strong, united Germany posed a threat to European stability dissipated as a myth in the post–Cold War period. Germany, to some extent the model of corporate capitalism in the postwar period, is foundering in an economic mire midway through the 1990s.

A national poll by ZDF television in June 1993 found 96 percent of the persons surveyed were unhappy with their problems, while 46 percent saw "big problems"; 38 percent worried about a difficult crisis, while 12 percent were so upset they said that Germany faced a national catastrophe. After the honeymoon, Germans seem more and more willing to blame increasing public deficits, the confusion in the European monetary system, and even extreme right-wing violence on the entire process of reunification. In the rush to get together, the government created an economic disaster. The question that reappears after euphoria has dissipated is, How much is the democratic system based on a real democratic consciousness, and how much is it only a product of economic prosperity? From the creation of the Federal Republic through its birth in the 1950s to the present, German political stability and the adoption of democracy have been largely assessed through the success of the German auto and machine-tool industries and the strength of the deutschemark. In other words, performance is the most important criterion in measuring German success.

Furthermore, the strains of reunification, the collapse of the East German economy, and the attendant social problems have created a searching obsession with national identity. More than anything, reunification has created a national awareness of the difficulties and problems associated with what it actually means to be German. And a weakness in politics is in part a long-running affair in German history. In Thomas Mann's major political tract *The Reflections of an Un-Political Man*, he identifies politics with democracy and sees both as inimical to the German spirit. In a poll conducted in June 1993, only 22 percent of West Germans and 11 percent of East Germans said they shared a common identity—a sharp decline from previous surveys.

The question of identity is linked in part to the idea of a national dream. One senior German Social Democratic leader regards the lack of the latter a huge stumbling block. He argues:

> The problem is German politics cannot appeal to a national dream as [Americans] can. There is no German dream. There is only German nightmare. People talk about returning to normalcy now that the Wall is down. What does normalcy mean in German history? And what does return mean?[32]

Part of the problem is of course that Germany became reunited at the start of a deep worldwide recession. Industry in the East collapsed, with the result that the Bonn government increasingly had to subsidize its eastern areas. The decision to provide more than $65 billion a year for the east in the form of unemployment and welfare programs coupled with retraining programs has helped produce social acquiescence but also ultimately a dependency-type culture. On the eve of the third anniversary of unification in October 1993, the joy and euphoria seen in the early days had given way to a form of *Götterdämmerung*—a deep-seated pessimism. Even the German president, Richard von Weizsäcker, in admitting the degree of unhappiness prevalent, pointed out that "joy has given way to disillusion." In the long run, however, the sense of national crisis may lead to a strengthening of the character of German democracy and promote it as an intrinsic virtue, not just a good based on economic performance.

Conclusion: A Reassertive Germany

German reunification is representative of a dramatic political discontinuity in German political life. It is important to remember that Germany was only really united for a very short historical period, between 1870 and 1945. Prior to this and after (until 1990) it was mainly divided—politically, socially, and economically. And those divisions are highlighted in the distinct differences and attitudes of its citizens East and West and the distinctive learning experiences and patterns of socialization they experienced in the postwar period.

It is not an easy task to weather an abrupt transition from an authoritarian dictatorship to a democracy, from a rigid, centrally planned economy to a free-market structure, and from an ossified set of political values (which had less in common with liberal democracy than with totalitarianism) to a political culture that in part espouses a postmaterial and democratic set of values. The economic and political traumatization witnessed after the initial euphoria of reunification was the political angst of a society unprepared for discontinuity after having recently become used to the idea and reality of division. As Peter Schneider put it: "Faced with unification, West German society turns out to be morally and intellectually unprepared for the challenge. The problem is precisely not the new German nationalism some people fear but the almost total lack of it."[33]

It would be a mistake to think, however, that the institutions of democracy and economic strength developed in postwar Germany are insufficient to overcome the initial turmoil. After all, it could also be argued that West Germany was morally and intellectually unprepared in 1945 for the challenge of rebuilding German society. And yet it has passed the tests of democracy and economic vibrancy with flying colors. In short, unification will be problematic, will be a discontinuity, and will cause hardship and uncertainty in the initial stages. The benefits of having a strong democratic Germany at the center of Europe, however, will in the end be worth the price.

Race and Immigration

One of the most difficult issues that the newly unified German state had to deal with in 1990 is in many ways the issue that it is least well equipped to handle. This is the issue of race, which has had a long and troubled history in Germany. An essential truth about Nazism was its basis in racism. During the 1980s for instance, various television programs and books documented aspects of the atrocities committed by the Third Reich, the specific operation of death camps, and the people who worked in them. There is little doubt that in the period between 1933 and 1945 German Nazism attempted to create a new order based on a hierarchy of race. In attempting this it had few parallels before or since; it was a policy of fear and terrorism.

When West Germany came into being in 1949, its very existence prompted a mass exodus of refugees from the East to the West (in 1950–55 alone, 1.5 million people crossed the borders). This in itself created a crisis: with the threat of a G.D.R. that appeared to be in imminent collapse in 1958, the Soviets reacted by threatening to give East Berlin over to the G.D.R., thus trying to make the West negotiate with East Germany over control of access to West Berlin. Despite this maneuvering the West retained the concept of a four-power administration. By 1961, the leaky borders were being swamped; between 1949 and 1961 refugees leaving the G.D.R. totaled over 2.6 million; of these, nearly 300,000, or 8.6 percent, left in 1960–61. The Soviets and the G.D.R. decided to take drastic action to stem this exodus. On the thirteenth of August 1961, they closed the East-West border in Berlin except for specified crossing points. Four days later they erected what came to symbolize East-West division in the postwar era, the Berlin wall, in an effort to prevent people from leaving the East. This then was the basis for confrontation between 1961 and 1989, a stark symbol of the Cold War and ideological differences that in the near term proved unresolvable.

Old Agendas and New Problems

In the 1980s the Federal Republic of Germany faced a major challenge which is now faced by the reunited Germany in the 1990s. That challenge sprang from the assimilation of various ethnic groups from other societies into Germany. The 1980s saw a rapid influx of new groups into German territory unparalleled since the 1950s. Ethnic Germans from Poland, for instance, constituted two-thirds of the 78,500 settlers from Eastern Europe in 1987. The Soviet Union saw a 50 percent increase in the number of ethnic Germans exiting its state after 1986, and all in all by 1988 the numbers of ethnic Germans flooding into Germany reached 202,600.

Case Study: The Gastarbeiter—Guest Workers or Unwelcome Guests?

In the migration to Germany in the postwar period, there have been two distinct stages. First, between 1945 and 1962, there was the migration of Germans from Eastern Europe and the G.D.R., with fairly minor problems of assimilation and adjustment. Nine million came from Poland and 3 million from East Germany, for instance. The Berlin wall ended that influx from the beginning of the 1960s until 1989. But since 1987 almost 50 percent of migrants have been either ethnic Germans from Eastern Europe or Germans from the former G.D.R.

The second wave, between 1955 and 1973, comprised workers recruited under the guest-worker scheme by the German Bundesaushalt für Arbeit (BFA). Under this scheme, workers were recruited from southern countries and underdeveloped societies such as Turkey, Greece, Italy, and Yugoslavia. They were housed in special camps and meant to be only temporary workers. Many migrants, however, did not want to leave.

The largest and most salient minority group in Germany are the foreign workers who constitute almost 8 percent of the work force and nearly 15 percent of the unskilled labor pool.[34] The "economic miracle" that Germany experienced was due in no small part to the large influxes of refugees from regions annexed by the Soviet Union and Poland. Germany was in the same boat as other Western European nations in this period: the need for labor could not be met internally because of the large depletion of labor during the war. The West German government responded in much the same way as the British and French governments did when faced with labor shortages. They recruited workers from southern Europe by drawing up agreements with the governments of Turkey, Greece, Spain, Portugal, and Yugoslavia. Labor offices were established in each country in order to act as liaisons between local officials, potential workers, and the host government.

During the early 1970s, jumbo jets continually plied routes from southern Europe bringing workers to new jobs in West Germany. In 1957 there were 110,000 guest workers on German soil. By 1973, sixteen years later, this figure had increased to more than 2.5 million.[35]

During the 1970s and 1980s, as West Germany experienced some economic downturn, these numbers were reduced. However the remainder of the minority still formed a substantial number by any standards. Turks constituted the largest group of *Gastarbeiter*, with 23 percent of the total number; Yugoslavia accounted for 21 percent, and Italy, 17 percent. In the large urban conglomerations such as Frankfurt, Dortmund, Munich, and Stuttgart, the guest workers make up about 15 to 20 percent of the work force and between 30 and 40 percent of manual workers. These areas resemble immigrant ghettoes, with poor conditions and poor housing, different from the rest of West German society. As in Britain and France, the guest workers perform vital tasks and jobs that the natives are no longer willing to perform. They clean the streets, remove the garbage, and operate in the sewers. They undertake the lowest level of manual, unskilled work and suffer from discrimination because of their lack of the German language, limited training, and the prejudices of their employers. Wage discrimination by the smaller German firms against their minorities is a salient feature of employment in Germany.

In the 1980s, one book, *Ganz Unten (At the Very Bottom)*, caused controversy over the plight of the Gastarbeiter. It was written by a German who disguised himself as a guest worker and spent a year chronicling firsthand their experiences of discrimination and life in general in Germany; the book was an immediate best-seller.

Governmental Responses to the Gastarbeiter

Germany's law on immigration is a throwback to the Nazi legislation of 1939. It is called the "Foreigners' Law" (*Auslandergesetz*) and it allows foreign workers to live in Germany as long as they can show they are worth it.

During the economic crisis of 1972–73 and the related oil shocks, a clampdown was enforced, and recruitment of foreign workers ended. In response, many Turkish workers sent for their families. Some Christian Democrats in 1973 favored repatriating unemployed foreigners, but this was not done for fear of the political backlash, both domestically and from the countries of emigration. In 1978, a new commission was set up which a year later produced the Kuhn Memorandum arguing for more efforts to integrate migrants, increased authority of migrants over their residences, the right to citizenship for immigrant children, and the right for migrants to take part in local elections. The government at the time rejected all these proposals and simply continued to enforce the foreigners' policy.

In the new Germany, things haven't changed much. In spite of the fact that you may be a third-generation immigrant from Turkey, neither your children nor yourself will be considered German. On the other hand, if your family had lived in Poland or Czechoslovakia or other European states for several hundred years and could prove their roots in Germany, they would be eligible to qualify as Germans. This is clearly a racial policy devised to ensure a more "pure" German identity. Thus, only 2.9 percent of Italian, 2.89 percent of Spanish, and 0.75 percent of Turkish populations are naturalized. The rest remain under the threat of constant expulsion.

In Germany, nationals are defined by origin; one must be born a German. The German nation in that sense is a biological construct. Germany operates under the policy of *jus sanguinis* ("the law of blood"), which guarantees all ethnic Germans the right of return to their native land. In France, by contrast, the idea of the nation is a political construct: if one accepts French culture and assimilates, one can become a French citizen, while migrants' children born in France have a right to opt for citizenship.

Similarly, the strict laws on intake for political asylum indicate a Germany that is hostile to "outsiders," no matter how much they may have contributed to that society. About a hundred thousand people arrived in West Germany seeking asylum in 1980, the year the first visa restrictions were passed. Asylum seekers had to wait up to eight years for a decision on their application. By 1983, the influx was cut to under twenty thousand. The same process was going on in France and the United Kingdom with regard to asylum seekers. On the whole the percentage of asylum seekers among immigrants has gone down from 65 percent in 1980 to around 10 percent in 1990. And today Germany only accepts around 3 percent of those that apply. Whereas 90.6 percent of applicants seeking asylum in 1987 were not granted it, by 1990, this percentage had increased to 96.5. Refugees in Germany were also confined to camps and not allowed to travel far from them. They were not allowed to work for five years. Despite these restrictions, however, overall immigration has increased; many of the newcomers are ethnic Germans.

The major political development affecting immigration was the 1989 collapse of the Communist regimes and the accompanying re-unification. The new dimension of ethnic and East Germans actively seeking entrance led to a need to redraw the consensus over this issue. This development renders the claims of Third World workers and the rights of other asylum seekers even more peripheral and marginal than before.

The change in attitude from the period after the wall fell is dramatic in itself. Only a year later, in late 1990, the West Germans were feeling resentment towards the "Ossis." Efforts have been made to keep them in East Germany by offering them decreased social security in the West and replacing this in some cases with a lump sum (in other words, no real guaranteed income).

Response of the Extreme Right to the Gastarbeiter

References to a "revival" of the extreme right in Germany imply that the right had somehow gone away or disappeared, only to reappear in the late 1980s and 1990s. This implication is misleading, however. There have always been strands of the extreme right within German political life. Only ten years after the Federal Republic of Germany came into being, there were racial and anti-Semitic outbursts. In December 1959 and January 1960, for instance, right-wing elements desecrated a Jewish tomb and synagogue in Cologne. Despite the obvious negative publicity generated by such incidents, there were 170 similar occurrences in the following month throughout West Germany. There was also some remaining support for Nazism among the general public. Between 1949 and 1963, for instance, between 7 percent and 13 percent of the populace expressed admiration for Hitler and supported Nazi views concerning the Jews.[36] Even in the late 1960s, a sizable number of Germans appeared to identify with Nazi viewpoints. In 1953, a survey found that 13 percent of those interviewed would welcome the return of a new Nazi party, while roughly 5 percent offered active support.

The recent rise of the Republicans, or the radical right, in Germany after 1989 has given rise to new fears about the German past. This is particularly so because of the Republicans' xenophobia and racist hostility to the Gastarbeiter, providing a direct link with the Nazi doctrines in the 1930s. In June 1989, the Republicans won 7.1 percent of the national vote and representation in the European Parliament at the expense of the mainstream political parties. In any time of economic uncertainty and anxiety, such as the period after reunification, minority groups are generally seen as available scapegoats for economic problems. In this sense the Republicans are merely taking their cues from the mobilization of the Front National in France (and its positions against North African immigrants) in pursuing actively the relationship among race, immigration, and politics. The main target for hostility in Germany has been the Turkish immigrant groups, who represent a fairly visible contingent among the 4 million foreign residents. While anti-Semitism is strictly taboo (although this might change if the right makes some headway in the electoral process), given the political and social context of the past, the guest workers are vulnerable to resentment and its implications within Germany.

The revival of the extreme right is highly problematic; the shock troops of this movement are widely acknowledged to be the "skinheads"—or gangs of young men with shaven heads who are extremely violent, with nihilistic tendencies. The skinheads in Germany may appear more active than their counterparts in the rest of Europe, and this possibly has to do with their openly Nazi beliefs. The numbers of these people in Germany are estimated at about four thousand (perhaps 50 percent affiliated with the Nazis). They comprise mainly men from fourteen to twenty-five years of age. German intelligence argues that perhaps 36,000 youths belong to Nazi groups; other reports say there are roughly 50,000 to 60,000 Nazi sympathizers altogether in Germany.[37] The same source listed some of the kinds of attacks for which skinheads were responsible in 1991, including beating up a seven-month-pregnant Vietnamese woman and bringing on a miscarriage, burning a Ghanaian refugee to death, beating up a group of Romanian refugees, and firebombing a village where refugees were staying. In early October of the same year there were reports of over 70 attacks within the space of two days alone; over 600 attacks in total took place in 1991 (half of those in West Germany). Rising unemployment, the increase in refugees from Eastern Europe, and the ramifications of these developments provided the setting for a new rise in xenophobia, chauvinism, and racism. Not everyone was a victim; as one author notes:

> The targets were foreigners, Jews, homosexuals, the left, anyone considered different and "un-German"; the perpetrators were neo-Nazis, Republicans, skinheads, fascists. . . . The Republicans opened an office and began organizing in Prenzlauer Berg. On 20 April, Hitler's birthday, there were riots in East Berlin following a football game. . . . Skinheads attacked a house occupied by squatters. . . and in Alexanderplatz they attacked police, foreigners, and a cafe known as a meeting point for homosexuals.[38]

The reasons for the revival of such groups are to be found in the reunification process itself and the attendant economic, social, and political dislocations. Unemployment (a previously unknown phenomenon in East Germany) has, along with attitudes of despair over the future, become a common feature of life in the East.

One writer argued that this economic explanation for the attacks on immigrants and asylum seekers is problematic. The xenophobia sweeping Germany at present is not necessarily a temporary hiccup in the process of reunification but may be essentially symptomatic of a much larger crisis of identity in the new Germany. The issue of German identity has been revived. With the extension of West Germany to the east in a wholesale takeover, the leaders of West Germany were working on the premise that they could "spare themselves a nationwide examination of the new state, its composite heritage and its place in the world. Somewhat in the manner of the

West German leaders in the 1950s who repressed the past instead of coming to terms with it and overcoming it."[39] The problem of what constitutes Germany and the German has reemerged and refuses to be swept under the carpet. Coming to grips with this issue must be high on the political agenda of present and future German leaders and political parties.

Despite denouncing the violence of the skinheads, the extreme-right Republicans and the right-of-center Christian Democrats continue to play on the fears raised by the specter of uncontrolled immigration.

Skinheads in Germany

The increasing activity of Skinhead youths in Germany in the wake of German reunification is in part a symbol of the frustration of young Germans at the decline in job opportunities and the economic malaise that followed the joining of the two Germanies. The gangs of extreme-right-wing youth, however, are not all skinheads, and neither are all skinheads related to the extreme right wing of the spectrum constantly engaging in attacks against foreigners.

Right-wing racist youth have been mainly responsible for most of the attacks staged against refugee camps and immigrant houses throughout Germany. In 1993, for instance, at least eight Turkish nationals were killed in several arson attacks which are thought to have been carried out by these gangs. Typically the rampage consists of hurling abuse such as *"Deutschland den Deutschen, Auslander raus"* (Germany to the Germans, foreigners out). In particular asylum seekers are a target (especially ones from the former Yugoslavia seeking a temporary refuge). However, any non-German is vulnerable, especially darker skinned foreigners; Turks, Vietnamese, and gypsies among others have all been attacked in the past. In 1992, three people a day were seriously injured, for a total of eight hundred that year, and right-wing violence was responsible for the deaths of seventeen people. In May 1993 alone, there were over four hundred racist attacks with five left dead and ninety-six injured. According to the domestic German intelligence service, there are more than 40,000 right-wing extremists from the older Nazis to the skinheads; xenophobia and racist sentiments unite them.[40]

The skinheads distinguish themselves by attacking punks, the homeless, gays, and anti-Nazis as well. In eastern Germany, the main scene of their activity, they number roughly three hundred according to official reports. None of these groups has a clear leader however; there may be perhaps twenty national neo-Nazi figures throughout

Germany, but none of them has a major following in terms of their leadership. Attacks against foreigners on a Europe-wide basis are encouraged by economic malaise and by politicians who, in their inability to provide economic solutions, tend to pick on scapegoats. The immigrants become victims because of their supposed incompetence and failure. And nowhere else in Western Europe has the line of ethnic nation state been drawn more firmly than by the Germans in their immigration policy, designed to keep Germany free of ethnically un-German influences.

The apologists for the skinheads argue that these are little more than children who for years under communism in the G.D.R. were urged to show solidarity with East Europeans; the reaction now is simply their way of letting off steam and their frustrations.

One view on racism does not blame the economic difficulties. The argument, at least for racism in Western Germany, is that

> The racism of West Germany is not the racism of the defeated but of the victorious, the economically victorious. It is the racism of prosperity, not of poverty, the racism of those who define poverty itself as culpable, if not genetic, hereditary, racial.[41]

And even in this light, Chancellor Kohl in 1993 was accused of silent complicity with the right-wing violence taking place against foreigners.

The other side of the coin is of course that most Germans are not racist, but some are merely reacting to the large number of refugees and the difficulties in coping with them. In 1992, 450,000 people applied for asylum, and as one author argues

> Far from being racist, the distinguishing characteristic of today's Germany is precisely its openness to foreigners. More than 1 million refugees have been admitted since 1990, more than twice the total accepted by all other European countries combined.[42]

Despite its openness to refugees, it still appears that Germany has racist immigration laws. As has been seen, German citizenship is clearly defined in terms of blood, and the nation is seen in ethnic terms. Until institutional mechanisms designed to protect the purity of ethnicity are abandoned, it seems unlikely that the skinheads and other right-wing racist groups will abandon their virulent attacks on foreigners.

Conclusion

Although Germany is not the only society in Europe presented with the dilemma and contradictions of open borders, the new freedom of movement, along with restrictions already moving into place in conjunction with the new status of the European Community (EC 1992) places it in a problematic position. East Germany, for instance, has never had the experience of actually trying to accommodate a multicultural society. In turn we find that many right-wing groups have readily exploited old racist fears and sentiments over the question of immigrants.

The revival of extreme-right-wing groups in the wake of reunification poses a particular problem not just for Germany but also for the rest of Europe. Old fears of German nationalism and the consequences suffered by the rest of Europe are obviously reawakened when such groups grab headlines and win votes. And of course this question is more difficult in the German context precisely because of its history of authoritarianism. It is clear that Germany will be the most powerful economic and probably political force in the new Europe, but its neighbors are obviously hoping that this power will not revive the unrestrained ambitions Germany previously harbored. Moreover the fact that Germany will lie at the heart of the EC (with the European Monetary Union probably tied to the Deutschemark) provides Germany with a stake in Europe and vice versa, not potential rivalry of nation against nation.

Finally, the German economy readily attracts people searching for a better life and escape from the misery of poverty; this beacon of hope, however, appears ill-equipped in present circumstances to deal with these problems. Rather, it is beginning to represent the political language of intolerance. In 1991, 77 percent of a sample population in East Germany expressed sympathy for racism compared to 61 percent in the West. In addition nearly every German (96 percent) wanted to see fewer "economic refugees" allowed into the country, while more than two-thirds would refuse entry to German speakers living elsewhere in Europe.[43] Whether these problems can be resolved peacefully will be important not only for the sake of Germany but also for Europe as they move together into the twenty-first century.

An Economic Giant and a Political Dwarf?

Germany as an Economic Giant

It would be a mistake to classify Germany as an economic giant after the Second World War; that would ignore the reality of history. West Germany certainly became an economic giant; East Germany suffered from a centrally planned economy that effectively produced an economic dwarf. The division of Germany in the postwar period saw two separate economic and political systems develop side by side and with dramatically different results. While West Germany underwent a *Wirtschaftswunder*, or economic miracle, the G.D.R. was embarking upon economic disaster, a fact that was only fully revealed with the dismantling of the wall and its consequences, which are still unravelling.

All of Germany, in fact, like the other European nations that fought in World War II, was an economic nightmare directly after the end of the war. Its economy had collapsed, its infrastructure was in ruins and it was faced with the difficult problems of refugees. Still, with generous aid from the Western Allies the economy started a slow but sure process to recovery.

In the 1950s the government could boast a growth rate averaging 8 percent annually, only dropping to 5 percent in the 1960s. By the latter period the West Germans had the strongest economy in Western Europe, with virtually full employment and little or no inflation. The deutsche mark became one of the strongest currencies in the world, a marked contrast to its position in the Weimar Republic of the 1920s. Many Germans deferred demands for higher wages in order to give the economy the kick-start needed; Germany was plagued by few strikes like the ones in Britain and France throughout this period. With large amounts of investment and a fairly cheap labor force (wages could be kept down with such a large refugee population), Germany began to prosper. By the 1960s the government could loosen its rein, and real wages rose dramatically (two and a half times between 1950 and 1973), providing the workers with one of the highest incomes in Western Europe.

The strength of the West German economy continued to grow well into the mid-1980s. In 1989, it had the third-largest GDP in the world with an enormous trade surplus of DM 135 billion (this made it the biggest exporter in the world, ahead of Japan). The strength of this economic dynamo was rooted in solid foundations: 40 percent of employment was in industry in 1988, which was a higher average than that of other, weaker European economies (the average in the EC was 33 percent). Similarly it increased its GNP and industrial output, and halfway through 1989 it was the second-largest creditor nation in the world after Japan (in 1991 Western Germany's economy grew by 4.5 percent, second only to Japan's 5.6 percent). With such large assets it is not surprising that writers were quick to argue that it clearly had the financial ability to meet its ambitions.[44]

Emerging Problems in the German Economy

The West German economy ended the 1980s with an extremely healthy record. This meant low inflation, strong exports, and a budget deficit that was still manageable. After reunification this was all to change. Heavy taxes incurred as a result of the amalgamation of East and West, a worldwide recession, and the sheer underdevelopment of the eastern part of the economy meant that the West would probably have to sacrifice a good deal more than it had anticipated. The contrast between East and West could not have been more stark. After the reunification the economic collapse of the East was a severe blow to the optimists, with Ostmarks (the East German currency) being exchanged at very generous rates for the East Germans. Decreasing the level of wage differentials between eastern and western sections will further add to this burden of trying to bring the Ossis into line with the Wessis. The East German economy was also hampered by the sheer poor quality of goods and products; there was no market for these when finally Western goods started to fill the shelves. East Germany also lost a huge market when its trading arrangements with the Soviet Union and the Eastern European economies ceased to exist. These latter markets had accounted for almost 40 percent of East German exports but vanished in the wake of unity and the end of the Cold War.[45] In addition the problems facing East Germany in the early stages of reunification have to some extent spilled over into the West.

In 1990, the West Germans had a GNP per head of DM 38,000 ($23,500) in comparison to their eastern counterparts' meager DM 13,000. Huge transfers of capital were required and still are required to salvage the eastern German economy and attempt to bring it to the level of western Germany. In 1991, for instance, the government transfers to the five new länder in eastern Germany were roughly DM 170 billion, and nearly DM 30 billion were paid in taxes by Bundesbank estimates. This meant a net transfer to the East of DM 140 billion. In 1992 one estimate has the net transfer as DM 180 billion (or an increase of DM 40 billion over the previous year). This would be roughly the equivalent of more than 6 percent of GNP, or nearly 25 percent of total public spending.[46] If this spending on unity continues at the same rate, then the predictions are that it could increase to over 51 percent of GNP by 1995.[47] The risk of becoming increasingly indebted is real, not only for German elites but also for ordinary Germans.

The cost of unity has already begun to have negative effects in terms of industrial conflict within Germany. On April 27, 1992 much of western Germany went on strike primarily because of the expense incurred through the process of reunification and the problems of inflation and higher taxes which have resulted. These were the largest strikes in postwar history in western Germany and for at least a week placed the fledgling German state into complete chaos. The public-sector unions managed to cripple Germany's efficient transport system with 100,000 workers initially striking in support of a 9.5 percent pay increase; trains stopped running on time for the first time in twenty years, and many stopped running at all. Subways and buses, garbage collection, telephone exchanges, and mail deliveries were all affected, with 100 kilometer traffic blockages around the major cities. It appeared that the British "disease" was visiting Germany. The strikes finally ended on the seventh of May as Helmut Kohl's government capitulated and provided pay increases ranging from 4.02 percent to 6.2 percent.

After one and a half years of German reunification it is clear that western Germans are sick of the bill for the unification process. They are left with the belief that they have been cheated; aftertax wages, which had a healthy growth rate in 1989–90 of 4.8 percent, declined by 0.4 percent in 1991 as a result of the tax surcharges, the "user" fees, and inflation (inflation was built into the process of reunification). The majority of the reunification bill was financed by borrowing, which caused not only an increasing deficit (roughly 5 percent of GNP in 1992) but also high interest rates. In 1992 the federal budget deficit had reached DM 130 billion with the government paying DM 200 billion simply to keep the eastern economy afloat. It appears in some ways one of the classic problems of underdevelopment. With such a poor, underdeveloped state on the one hand and a rich, affluent postindustrial state on the other, the question of who bears the brunt of reunification is clearly problematic for the West Germans. The political elites failed to acknowledge in the euphoria of the initial unity that cost would have to be borne mainly by the West Germans. Inevitably this may mean some fall in living standards, which many "Wessis" seem reluctant to agree to. They voiced their discontent with crippling strikes and the threat of more. It is the classic case of the crises of distribution: How do you allocate goods and services and wealth to members of your community, and in this particular case, how does government redistribute wealth and resources evenly and with a minimum of suffering in the process? One report highlighted this dilemma:

> The new German buzzword is "verteilungskampf," the distribution battle. Imagine four people sitting around the table in front of opulently filled plates. They are joined by a fifth person who has only a dry cheese sandwich. The only decent thing to do is share.[48]

For the Federal Republic this will be a crucial issue which Germans will have to face for at least the next ten years: whether or not to share. If Germany is to retain its stature as an economic giant, it will have to develop ways of resolving this distribution battle in a manner that caters to both populations, and this dilemma will be at the forefront of the political elites' agenda in the near future.

Germany as a Political Dwarf

Just as Germany cannot be fully made out to be an economic giant in the light of the recent problems and costs of unification (although many optimists are confident that Germany will regain this title very quickly), the assertion that the Federal Republic is a political dwarf is equally a misnomer in the present context. It is difficult to use this term because Germany is still constrained in many ways by its past, by internal politics and external constraints.

Germany's Role in the Gulf Crisis. Germany in many ways is one of the most difficult nations to understand in terms of its response to the threat of security in the Persian Gulf in 1990–91. Despite its obvious economic stature, West Germany in the beginning stages of the crisis played a very minor role, content to relegate the military burden to the United States, Britain, and France. In fact this caused a certain amount of political frustration in the Western camp, particularly among the nine-member Western European Union (WEU). One German expert on the Middle East expressed a general feeling of criticism in the following terms: "West Germany has been called an economic giant and a political dwarf, and this statement is still valid as far as its behavior in the gulf is concerned." Germany was constrained by its post–1945 political status. The main argument revolved around whether the 1949 Basic Law expressly forbids the deployment of the Bundeswehr as part of a United Nation peace-keeping mission. The confusion over this issue was accentuated by the election campaigns in a reunited Germany. In the end, German troops never took part in "Operation Desert Storm."

One area in which Germany did become involved was in economic support of the United States during the Gulf crisis. Helmut Kohl, the German chancellor, informed James Baker, the American secretary of state, that Germany would pay DM 3.3 billion ($2.1 billion) in total. Nearly DM 1.6 billion of this contribution went to the American military effort and the rest to help Egypt, Turkey, and Jordan. Kohl, who was in favor of sending German armed forces to the gulf without amending the constitution, was and is politically hampered by the nature of the West German coalitional system in which the junior partner can effectively veto any such moves.

The issue is more problematic however; the Germans are clearly in a position of being "damned if they do and damned if they don't." If they had sent troops to the gulf they would have been accused of being too assertive and would have reinvoked old fears of German ambitions among the Western Allies. On the other hand, if not acting they could just as easily be accused of not playing any role and failing to perform their responsibilities. When Germany lobbied for European recognition of Croatia and Slovenia as independent states, they were seen as too intrusive into other countries' affairs. External constraints to German use of national power show that the West is cautious regarding German exertion of political power and yet realizes that such action is inevitable. The hope is to anchor Germany firmly within the context of European union in order to ameliorate national appetites. Internally, political parties squabble about the use of German forces abroad. Some favor peacekeeping, while others support the notion of a more direct military role for such forces under the supervision of the United Nations. Whatever role Germany eventually settles into, one thing is clear: Germany will be a major actor on the stage of European politics, and even if the other members of the European Community do not take their cue from the German political scenario, they will be forced to pay attention and respond to a resurgent German economy.

The German Question Revisited

Much of the history of Germany has been acutely located around the concept of the "**German question.**" In a historical sense, at least since the nineteenth century, this question has revolved around the unity of the country and therefore its borders (and the claims made concerning these) and, in turn, the actual nature of the German state. With the peaceful reunification of Germany on October 3, 1990, and the recognition of the Oder-Neisse border with Poland, Germany was for the first time in its history a united democratic state with no territorial claims or ambitions, and it was thought that the German question had finally been laid to rest. However, other "German questions" have started to arise, as can be seen in the gulf crisis and the Yugoslav crisis—issues that extend beyond but are related to Germany and its role in the world. The situation for Germany, however, is clearly different from the one in 1918 or even 1945. The western half of Germany has enjoyed over forty years of continuous democracy and substantial successful economic growth. As Germany overcomes the burden of its past, it would seem unfair to then announce the German state as a pygmy on the political landscape. Whatever role Germany assumes in the wake of the Cold War, it will be an important one.

Conclusion: Germany at the Crossroads

Germany stands at a crossroads in terms of political continuity. In its history, democracy still remains a somewhat unknown quantity, in particular for the inhabitants of East Germany, who endured communism for over forty years in the postwar period. With the collapse of the Communist system and its rigid structures in the workplace, industry, and the political arena, many are finding it hard to adjust to their newfound democracy. Nowhere is this more evident than in the attitudes of East Germans themselves who, according to opinion polls, equate democracy with permissiveness.

The fact that German political culture is in a state of flux is hardly surprising. For forty years and more, West Germans have enjoyed an open democratic political system with a healthy and vibrant economy, in comparison to a rigid authoritarian system with an essentially pathetic economy in which fear ruled. After reunification, we did not witness the symbiosis of East and West but rather the culture shock and confusion of two peoples who had experienced different patterns of political socialization. And in turn, more and more youths in the eastern section turned to authoritarian ideology, neofascism, and anarchism. Support for extreme right-wing groups developed overnight and had a major impact as political violence and race hatred were directed against immigrant groups. Many of the pent-up frustrations that East Germans felt under their regime were now being laid bare for the world to see, much to the embarrassment of their western countrymen (the *Wessis*).

German reunification enhanced these extremist factors. The gulf between East and West in economic, political, social, and psychological terms is clearly a dramatic one requiring years of patience and understanding on the part of both communities. In the short term, resentment, deep-seated frustrations, and hostilities are bound to be prevalent. Germany, however, has been through far worse scenarios, as we noted in the historical overview. The end of two world wars and the discontinuities experienced as a result have strengthened the German state; over forty years of democracy in the West have produced a polity that seems likely to weather and cope with the challenges of politics in a democratic sense rather than be swept under in a tide of authoritarianism. In this sense the German state, having emerged from discontinuity in the postwar period by coming together, appears to stand a good chance of enjoying the continuity of the democracy the Federal Republic received and experienced after the Second World War.

Key Terms and Concepts

Each term appears in the text in boldface type.

Der Alte (Adenauer)
Basic Law
Berlin Wall
Bismarck
Diffuse support
Gastarbeiter
German Democratic Republic
  (G.D.R.)
German Federal Republic (F.R.G.)
"German question"
Die Grünen (the Greens)
Holocaust
Junker classes
Jus sanguinis
Länder

Marshall Plan
National Socialist party
  (Nazis)
Obrigkeit
Ossis
Ostpolitik
Schonwetterdemokratie
Sinatra Doctrine
Specific support
Third Reich
Treaty of Westphalia
War guilt
Weimar Republic
Wirtschaftswunder
  (economic miracle)

5
Italy

Italy invites hyperbole. Almost everything about it appears monumental. . . . Italian politics seems a chaotic, unmitigated fight to the finish. Indeed the picture we have of Italy is that of an ideologically polarized country in an unremitting political war of all against all and on the verge of total disintegration.[1]

Historical Overview

Italy, like Germany, was a collection of smaller states, many of them controlled by the jurisdiction of the Roman Catholic Church and the papacy. It emerged as a patchwork of various different states fueled by a developing sense of nationalism in the wake of Napoleonic invasions in the nineteenth century. Similar to Germany, it underwent a fairly long struggle over who should control power, and in part this was also problematic for the country in the sense that Italy also experienced various invasions and occupations from the eighteenth century onwards. It was in response to these incursions on Italian territorial integrity that nationalism as a political force increased in scope and ability in the nineteenth century. The pattern exhibited by the French and the subsequent invasion by Napoleon laid the groundwork for unification in the sense that it provided for innovations at every level and encouraged middle-class Italians to adopt a nationalist position.

Despite the failure of revolutions on the Continental mainland (especially in France and Germany) to substantially alter political structures, Italy gained enough nationalist momentum to continue its struggle. A national resurgence (the **risorgimento**) led by a motley

159

crew of intellectuals, revolutionaries, and politicians, supported these moves.[2] In turn the ideological impetus had practical consequences as the various disparate territories such as Piedmont managed in the 1860s to secure victory in the conflict against Austria (an occupying power) and further extend this power over central Italy. The country took more than sixty years to settle into its final form. Like Germany, Italy had its Prussia, the dynamic Kingdom of Piedmont and Sardinia, and like the Prussian state under Bismarck it also had a dynamic and ambitious prime minister, Cavour, who acted as a major driving force in the process of unification. Eventually, with the gradual extension of control, Italy became united in 1870 and established the republican form of government while retaining the monarchy. Italian political history has clear parallels with the German experience; it had a divided and underdeveloped group of principalities, a weak middle class, and a landed aristocracy that were slow to change. Nationalist revolutions in 1848 failed, but the movement towards unification came gradually to fruition with the risorgimento ensuring that the routes towards unification and integration were similar in both countries.

In these terms Italy was a relatively new member of the system of European states parallel to the German experience, and so the sense of national identity was initially weaker than in the other states. And of course this lack was to have major consequences in the period of constitutional democracy in the aftermath of World War I.[3] Italians include several ethnic and tribal strains and are not in any sense a homogeneous people. This diversity may provide a clue to the separate patterns of development in different regions that has given Italy major problems. Institutionally and culturally Italy has similar features to the mainstream in Western Europe; it has had more in common with France, for instance, than Spain from the nineteenth century onwards. Italy's drive towards modernization, while an effort to emulate the cases of Britain and France, also produced strains within a society that was acutely conscious of the models for development in Western Europe. Such strains were indicated by various patterns in an emerging political culture: many people consistently rejected the system of governance, intellectuals were discontented, politics were instable. These conditions served to produce in some ways the idea and reality of an Italian political system prone to endemic crises.

Few states in Western Europe faced as many simultaneous challenges to their continuity in such a short period of time as Italy. And in some ways this tumult has produced a legacy that even the present Italian state has problems in trying to solve. The problem of a late political unification based around a collection of diverse, heterogeneous areas and the difficulties in engaging in industrial revolution for which resources were sorely lacking were only two of the difficulties faced in the 1870s. The further imposition of a king, constitution, economic policy, and elite class structure by the North on the South also proved to be contentious issues in the eyes of the Roman Catholic church and the South. These issues were to have lasting repercussions throughout the political history of Italy.

Initially, progress toward the ideal of liberal democracy was a slow and haphazard affair which only really "took off" after 1918 with the end of the First World War. The period thereafter saw several changes crucial to what we understand now as the contemporary government in Italy.

First, there was a shift to constitutional monarchy following the war and the introduction of parliamentary democracy. The sudden introduction of such change into Italian society had dislocating results and provided some discontinuity. Italy was beset by increasing nationalism in the aftermath of the war and became divided ideologically and politically over what should be done. The failure of democratic institutions to take root among the populace caused severe dislocations within the political process. As in the attempt at democracy under Germany's Weimar Republic, many parties were involved in the competition for power. The split between left and right became a major fixture of the Italian political landscape in this period as the political community suffered severe schisms. And economic and social problems ensured the fragmentation and violence of politics in this period, undermining the stability of the country. The resort to political violence, in turn, allowed the Fascist party led by Mussolini to exploit the situation.

Fascism in Italy (1922–1943)

In 1922 Mussolini led extreme right-wing members and followers of his Fascist doctrines to Rome (the "march on Rome"), where he successfully challenged the government. While democracy broke down and a political crisis emerged, the fascists blamed democracy for the breakdown of law and order, which ironically they had helped to create. In the event, the king, Victor Emmanuel II, was persuaded to appoint Benito **Mussolini** as prime minister in an effort to restore some semblance of law and order amidst the political turmoil. Mussolini and the blackshirts preempted the accession to power of the other fascist party, the Nazis in Germany, and quickly moved to consolidate power mainly by murdering, intimidating, and assuming dictatorial powers for themselves. Fascism was less of an ideology or a coherent system of thought and practice than it was a political myth, in some views. Clearly it varied from country to country; it was a European phenomenon but with country-specific attributes. It was filled with contradictions, as Hamilton has pointed out:

> In substance Fascism was a "myth" in the Sorelian sense of the word, a "system of images" defying logical definition or rational analysis, filled, if submitted to either, with contradictions. From myth to reality, from theory to practice, the gulf, as is often the case, was exceedingly wide. If examined with any degree of objectivity, if its course was traced and its achievements compared with its principles, Fascism was less than a myth: it was a hoax.[4]

One of the goals of the Italian Fascist party was to eliminate competition and individualism; in this sense the ideas of liberal democracy were to be abandoned. A united Italy based on cooperation and self-sacrifice for the goals of the state was emphasized; the state was put on a pedestal, and everyone was to be in the service of the state, joined in one collective purpose.

In practice the Fascists controlled political office, political mobilization, and political representation. The opposition was abolished and public opinion controlled through the media and other aspects of socialization such as education.

It would be a mistake, however, to understand the rule of Mussolini and the Fascists as an exercise in total control. Mussolini's rule cannot be compared to the dictatorships of Hitler and Stalin, who exerted fuller control over their societies. The Fascists in Italy were always faced with sections of society that resisted and resented the intrusion of fascism in their lives. In the final analysis, Mussolini was inept—a classic bungler who delighted in violence and strutting around the arena of politics but who was ill fitted for the management and development of the modern Italian state.[5]

It came as no surprise that he linked his fortunes with the German Fascist dictator, Hitler, to form the Axis pact in an alliance against the other major European powers. It also came as no surprise that he was overthrown by the Italian military in 1943 and executed in public on April 28, 1945, by partisans. To the end, Mussolini was incompetent and disorganized, creating a politics of chaos in the Italian state.

Postwar Developments

Postwar Italy represents a unique combination of the old and the new in the European context. It is old in the sense that parts of the

South (notably the **mezzogiorno**) are underdeveloped and primarily agricultural. It is new in the sense that it has become the world's fifth-leading industrial power, with a high standard of living and per capita income. Italy is clearly a society of contrasts and extremes, reinforced, not dissipated, by a major postwar economic transformation. The comparative scale of migration from the rural countryside to the city has been the largest in Italy; its annual rate of economic growth is one of the highest in Europe in this period.

Postwar reconstruction in Europe proceeded with a great deal of intensity and in the main was beneficial, at least in the early stages, with rapid industrialization helping to create better economic conditions and increasingly higher living standards. Italy's "economic miracle," however, was not all a bed of roses. Glaring gaps in distribution of income and social inequalities were blamed on a lack of direction in the planning process: "Apart from the expansion of the state enterprises and the programs for the South, there was no overall concept, much less developed program, for economic advance."[6] More and more, such disparities gave way to social and political unrest; researchers attributed the unrest to a sense of disharmony stemming from the fact that Italy at this time was basically "out of sync" with other industrial democracies.[7]

It is common to analyze the postwar developments in Italy by focusing on two major characteristics. One was the cleavage between the left and right sides of the political spectrum. In parliamentary and party activities the cleavage was seen in the conflict between the Communist working-class bloc and the Christian Democratic conservative group. (At times, however, the two acted in coalition, with the Christian Democrats the dominant partner.) The cleavage resulted at times in violence from extremist groups that portrayed deep seated ideological predispositions (the Red Brigade and the MSI for instance). The other major characteristic was the fact that Italy (perhaps as a consequence) had weak and ineffective political institutions. A general overview of the post–1945 period reveals these fundamental characteristics.

Following the war, in June 1946, Italy held a referendum to decide its new constitutional arrangements. A republican regime was the preferred option to monarchy, and at the beginning of January 1948 a new constitution went into effect. It would be a mistake to conclude that fascism died with Mussolini. Italy is the only country in Europe apart from France at the moment where the extreme right has maintained a fairly secure position in the established party system. The neo-Fascist **Movimento Sociale Italiano** (**MSI**) has survived with its extreme-right credential intact within the Italian polity even if it has secured minority support; in 1972 it had nearly 9 percent of the vote and in 1987 just under 6 percent, with strong support in Rome and Sicily. The persistence of right-wing tendencies is almost certainly carried over from the period of Mussolini, but the MSI does not represent a dynamic force within Italian society. It is in fact a leftover from a bygone period. It would be difficult to consider the MSI a real contender for power even though it has a core of ideologically committed support. Rather, the MSI serves as a conduit for various social grievances, exploiting issues and ultimately threatening the fabric of the republican political system. Even though the party has failed totally in this latter objective, it has succeeded in causing some disruption in confronting the extreme left and thus has left its mark on Italian society. In general it would be difficult to classify such a group as anything more than a marginal force, albeit a force for violence and extremism. However, the Allied coalition never really succeeded in delegitimizing communism and fascism in Italy with the same effect as in Germany. The polarizing tendencies of such different extremes had a substantial effect on the direction of Italian political life.

Despite the failure of fascism to retain a strong grip on Italian political life after 1945, the democracy that Italy has opted for has created as many problems as it has solved because of the special behavioral difficulties in Italian society. Compared to the rest of Europe it is a society of marked extremes. There is a marked contrast in economic development in the North and the South; the former is industrial and economically developed, and the latter, agrarian and underdeveloped. Compared to neighbors like France and Germany, Italy represents a poor relation in the sense that it has to some extent failed to modernize its economy and social structures. Furthermore Italian society suffers endemic crisis: while dominated by one party, the Christian Democrats, it has had over fifty coalition governments in the postwar period. Extreme violence has resulted from antagonisms between the far right and far left. The active left-wing political terrorist organization, the Red Brigade, was throughout the 1960s, 1970s, and early 1980s complemented by its counterpart on the other end of the spectrum, MSI, the largest Fascist party in Europe, which was formed as early as 1946.

Many political scientists attribute the instability in Italian politics to the constant high turnover in cabinets. Few of the numerous coalition governments in the postwar period have lasted as long as twelve months. Some analysts have concluded that the multiparty system and provision for proportional representation in elections is to blame for the situation. However, other systems in Europe, such as Germany and the Scandinavian states, have multiple parties and proportional representation, and they have proved to be stable. The failure to build lasting and binding coalitions is related to a failure to value consensus and compromise as positive virtues within the system. Consensus has never had much grounding within Italian politics, and it would be a mistake to attribute blame to any one type of electoral or party system. These may of course compound the problem, but they are certainly not at the root of the political instability.

Consensus is often lacking even within a party, and the lack of party discipline, particularly in comparison to the British case, further highlights the problem. Intraparty factionalism muddies major political and social questions such as divorce, abortion, and differences between regions. Another continuing issue is the distribution of "spoils," particularly at the political elite level. To understand this situation, it seems more useful to analyze the behavioral context of Italian politics rather than the institutional formulas.

Some would argue that the Italian system is not unstable at all—that the fact that Italy has produced so many coalitions over the years has ensured its stability. In other words we know and we can predict that Italy will change its government every year, and this allows us some certainty in regard to Italian politics. The instability in the Italian system is therefore more of an illusion than a reality. For instance, one party, the Christian Democrats (DC), has managed to dominate all postwar governments; between the end of 1945 and 1981 every Italian prime minister was from the same party, the Christian Democrats, not a feat that we can attribute to the "stable" British system.[8] In fact it would be very difficult to imagine government formation in Italy without the Christian Democrats. The political system survives regardless of cabinet turnover; policies get passed and things get done. In spite of weak political institutions and a debilitated executive one could argue that the real success story of the 1948 constitutional settlement and postwar development was the strengthening of the party system. In the postwar years the party became a crucial element in mobilization and representation. So, in effect, the party system and the dominance of politics in this period provided a discontinuity within the Italian political system; even today major decisions are not effected by executive politics but by intra-party and inter party discussions and compromises well before the issue comes before the cabinet. These paradoxes are at the root of political analysis concerning Italy. With over seventy parties taking part in elections and usually ten groups sitting in parliament, the question of importance would be how and why one party has managed to maintain the reins of power throughout the entire post-war period.

Contemporary Issues in Italian Politics

Several issues predominate in Italian political life; these are of course not unique to Italy. Economic problems are a constant preoccupation of the government.

Economically, Italy has gone through various stages from economic reconstruction to economic slowdown to recovery and a greater dynamism in the 1980s. In fact, in this period, Italy's economy grew at a faster rate than any of the other European economies discussed. People who have heard of Italy's reputation as the "sick man" of Europe would be surprised to know that the Italian state experienced two decades of major growth between 1950 and 1970. Like all of the European economies under discussion, Italy's economy was virtually transformed in these years. In 1946, for instance, nearly 45 percent of the work force was involved in agriculture, forestry, and fishing; only since the 1950s have more people been employed in industry than in agriculture. By 1981, this agricultural work force had decreased to around 12 percent, and at the end of the 1980s the majority of the work force was employed in the service sector, following the general economic trends of the postindustrial societies.

Beginning in 1970 the slowdown that in turn affected all of the advanced industrial nations had a major effect on Italy. In 1973, with the beginning of the oil shocks, Italian inflation started to run out of control. By 1980 it reached 21.2 percent, but it has since been gotten under control by successive governments. In the 1980s, Italy had a higher growth rate than the so-called model of parliamentary stability and liberal democracy, the United Kingdom. In 1987, for instance, it was reported that Britain had been demoted to sixth place in the ranking of the world's industrial democracies, while Italy had achieved fifth place in terms of the size of the economy, the GDP, and per capita income. The stereotype that Italy endured as the "sick man of Europe" and the weak link in NATO's chain of command appears to have lost much of its descriptive value. Given the backwardness of the *mezzogiorno*, this level of economic performance is all the more impressive.

Discontinuity and Change

There are some parallels between the history of Italian political development and the German case. In its early stages Italy was also characterized by a set of backward, divided smaller states, a struggling bourgeoisie, and a conservative landed class. In both Italy and Germany, revolutions in 1848 failed to establish liberal republics, and similarly, in the 1870s unification was finally achieved under the conservative regimes of Victor Emmanuel II, king of Piedmont, and Chancellor Otto von Bismarck and the Prussian junkers, respectively. Both societies experienced forms of fascism that brought them closer together. And both societies pursued different variants of the liberal democratic route after the Second World War. Finally, both exhibited (with some modification of course) similar continuities and discontinuities in the process of development.

It would be safe to say that since 1948 the Italian political system has remained fairly stable and has not broken down. The crisis view of Italian politics would of course argue that its politics are symptomatic of breakdown. But one would have to ask whether this was really the case. Italy has not capitulated to anarchy and chaos; governments may change but the system survives. In this respect Italy has experienced a change to the continuity of liberal democracy in the postwar period.

There is no doubt that Italy has undergone remarkable changes since the end of the Second World War; there have been large-scale shifts in population from South to North, from rural areas to urban conglomerates. Secularization and education have increased dramatically across society. Divorce and abortion have been allowed; traditional values embodied in the Roman Catholic church have not fared so well. At the same time, gross inefficiency, scandals, and wide-scale incompetence remain hallmarks of government and politics. Terrorism was a major problem in the 1960s and 1970s. While we have seen some degree of continuity within the political system, we have seen discontinuities at the level of society.

In the preface to their work *Italy: A Difficult Democracy*, Spotts and Weiser make an argument about continuity in Italian political life. They argue that descriptions of the political system in the late nineteenth century bear a striking resemblance to the contemporary situation. They cite the important work of Giuseppe Tomasi Di Lampedusa ("The Leopard"), who argued that "if we want everything to remain as it is, it will be necessary for everything to change."[9] This seeming paradox pervades Italian politics and ensures it some degree of continuity and change at the same time. Italy did not disintegrate or fall apart in the post-1945 period; it displayed some degree of continuity despite the failure of the Axis powers to secure victory.

The fact is that the Italian system of government has survived in the post–Second World War period, and this fact alone has guaranteed it some legitimacy, at least enough to sustain it in the immediate future. Some would argue that politics in Italy has been at least as stable as in most other democracies, if not more so. Italian governments resemble the **commedia del l'arte**: the masks may change but the actors remain the same. For instance in 1988 the *Economist* passed this judgment on Italy's leadership turnover:

> In a world where the British Prime Minister has been in office for nine years, the American president for eight, the West German chancellor for six and France's president may stay for fourteen, the brief life expectancy of an Italian prime minister leaves Italy back with the countries that grow coconuts.[10]

Leaving aside the usual political sarcasm of the *Economist*, we can argue that, yes, it is true that Italy has had a rapid turnover of leadership, and yet in the same period of the 1980s it has experienced the fastest rate of economic growth among the "big four" economies of Western Europe. Such comments only serve to belie the real social and economic progress that Italy has achieved.

Problems exist in Italy as in every other system. They revolve around the crises of distribution, the allocation of resources and wealth in the Italian system, and the ability of government to deliver goods and services efficiently. But the issues of identity, legitimacy, penetration, and participation have been resolved, at least to the extent that they do not pose a major threat to the functioning of the Italian political system. Over the years, acceptance of government has increased, and participation in elections and in political parties has risen substantially. In all of these senses, Italian democracy appears to be on a much surer footing than before, when the system experienced major discontinuities. Pessimists could argue, of course, that one of the major continuities of the Italian political system in the postwar period, the Communist party, is breaking down with the collapse of communism in Eastern Europe and the general discrediting of communist ideology as a blueprint for society just about everywhere. The Italian version now calls itself the democratic left; it is split into several factions and has lost many of its voters. This change may in itself be enough to provoke more political and social change in the overall Italian political system.

Towards Change?

Italian politics appears in a contemporary sense to be heading towards change, signified by electoral developments and an evolving party structure. In the postwar period more than 30 percent of parliamentary seats remained frozen in opposition, acting as a constraint on political turnover and therefore a reinforcement of the status quo. After the general election on April 6 and 7, 1992, this political mold appeared to be breaking. Several factors are important. At the end of the 1980s, the crisis of communism in Eastern Europe meant that the support for Communist parties in Western Europe was also severely diminished, as mentioned. For forty years the Communist party was kept out of power thus ensuring Christian Democrat predominance. Ironically, in the last election not only did the Communists lose votes, but so did the Christian Democrats (who were reduced to their lowest percentage of the vote since the end of the war). And this has gone some way to breaking the stranglehold they exerted on the coalitional governments. Second, a series of protest movements and regional groupings has begun to make an impact on Italian politics, which in turn reflects that people want change and are willing to cast their ballot for it. Groups such as the Northern League increased their vote substantially, as did other regional parties and single-issue groups. This minor earthquake is not only a landmark event for Italian politics but also threatens to shake the foundations of the Italian power structure in the postwar era, thus introducing discontinuity into a system that, despite being coalitional and fragmented in nature, had the virtue of providing continuity and political stability. It remains to be seen what the consequences of this change may be.

Political Culture: Change and Continuity

To a large extent, the Italian political system is by nature discontinuous, significantly different from that of the other European states involved in our discussion. However that distinction cannot be attributed to political institutions; Italy's parliamentary system is very similar to that of other West European democracies. Rather, it is important to look at the distinct political culture and social behavior of the Italians, which have been shaped by history as much as by anything else.

A Question of Trust

An attitude of trust or, conversely, distrust is an extremely important element in any society's political culture. The ability of people within society to feel confident in the motives and behavior of the state and of their fellow citizens constitutes a crucial element in the maintenance of legitimacy within the political system. In the following section the emphasis will be on the level of trust, first in the state and then in terms of interpersonal relationships.

One striking feature that stands out in Italian political development is the deep division between the society and the state. Public alienation towards the state goes back several centuries in Italy; after unification in 1871, government ineffectiveness and later on twenty years of Fascist rule simply served to increase this sense of distrust and antipathy. In the late nineteenth century, Roman Catholic and Marxist groups specifically rallied against the "liberal oligarchy" which they regarded as the source of Italy's problems. The state was regarded as the source of Italy's problems. The state was regarded as a hostile entity. In the postwar period the new constitution established no clear center of power, thus allowing for clashes between the left and the right; scandals and corruption were endemic in the early years. Patronage and privilege were rife, and inefficiency throughout state organizations was the norm. The Italian public developed a strong sense of contempt for the state and its agents, the parties, which ironically comprised the Catholics and the Marxists—groups that once opposed the state. And of course the extreme opposition to state institutions and parties now rested in the hands of various terrorist groups, such as the Red Brigade. There existed a general feeling that only institutions outside of state authority could achieve things effectively. The state and its apparent wider connections to crime and corruption have long been a source of animosity for the Italian public.

Historically, there has been a "distrust of government, indifference to politics, a lack of belief in the honesty and capacity of bureaucrats and politicians, and, on the other [hand], instrumental participation for personal benefit, and gross pragmatism."[11] Giacomo Sani cited survey evidence in 1974, for instance, which detailed public distrust of the state. Just over a fifth of the respondents thought that the state apparatus was "fine as is," while 43 percent decided it was "in need of major reforms," and 35 percent declared it was in need of "radical change."[12] Measures of public opinion such as the Eurobarometers (annual social surveys) also provide some indication of dissatisfaction and frustration with Italian democracy. Between 1987 to 1988, an average of 75 percent of those polled replied that they were "not at all satisfied" or "not very satisfied" with the way democracy worked in Italy, which was a far higher proportion than that of the other major European countries polled.[13] The combination of distrust for both state and political system is clearly a crisis that will continue to affect legitimacy for some time to come. The failure of both to some extent to resolve crucial questions of democracy will be a factor in producing political change in the republic.

Other writers have noted the absence of a strong sense of national identity, which supports the view that Italians have been less than enchanted with the state and the system. One author goes so far as to argue that few Italians would actually die for Italy, and while they may identify with other Italians, they seem incapable of identifying with Italy.[14]

There can be little doubt that attitudes like this have changed over time. The Italian state has managed to accomplish some major achievements in the postwar era, providing its citizens with security and prosperity. In the 1970s the Italian state went to great lengths to extend welfare services and aid in an effort to alleviate the gaps in the distribution of goods and services. The state has been the only player able to mount a counterattack against terrorism and the economic crises that threaten to engulf and destroy Italian society. Therefore, Italians are somewhat ambivalent about the state today; it is viewed as a necessary evil, and this is complicated by their attitudes towards other aspects of politics and government. It is to these attitudes and how they have changed over time that we now turn in order to gain a fuller picture of the Italian political culture. It is the combination of attitudes towards the state, society, and the individual, in other words, that provides a more detailed assessment of the Italian citizen.

Political Attitudes

A great deal of the information that we have on Italian political culture derives from two Almond and Verba studies, *The Civic Culture* (1963) and *The Civic Culture Revisited* (1980).[15] Although the former is somewhat outdated, the two books still provide a benchmark from which we can examine change within the Italian political culture.

To a large extent Almond and Verba were concerned with the perceptions of the masses towards the elites in society. How well is the country being run? Do they feel positive towards the institutional structure in their society? Do they feel allegiance or alienation toward their system? And as we have seen, the use of the survey instrument was developed in order to gauge the feelings of Italian citizens in these respects. When they took their polls in 1959 they found that Italians in general—like Germans at the time—had a fairly low degree of allegiance to the political system compared to residents of the United Kingdom.[16]

Almond and Verba's general findings showed that Italians were alienated and cynical concerning their political system in the late 1950s. Indeed, they characterized it as a political culture of "unrelieved political alienation and of social isolation and distrust."[17] This finding might be explained by the weakness of the economy and by the short tenure of the regime. It had gained power only in 1948, and they had still to acknowledge it as a legitimate political entity. In the 1960s, the economy picked up, and attitude surveys revealed more positive pictures of the system, just as they did in France and West Germany. It is altogether possible that attitudes towards the political system have a great deal to do with its perceived economic performance. A slump, however, followed in the 1970s, and increasing numbers of Italians began to blame the social and political system for Italy's problems. Governments were evaluated negatively. There was little diffuse support for the overall political system, and citizens displayed a general distrust of democracy. Nor was there specific support for the particular government in power at the time. It appeared that most Italians felt alienated rather than allegiant to their political system, and this was experienced over time.[18]

Clearly these apparently negative evaluations of government and the system do not explain very much. Why were Italians cynical and distrustful of elites and still did nothing about the situation? In their 1963 survey, Almond and Verba used questions designed to tap what they called "civic competence," meaning the extent to which ordinary citizens felt that they had the capacity or ability to influence the decisions of government at local and national levels. They came to the conclusion that not only did Italians display distrust towards the system, but they also distrusted one another. In *The Italians* by Luigi Barzini, such personal distrust is linked with a high degree of perception that life is a constant struggle for survival. As he argues, "An Italian learns from childhood that he must keep his mouth shut and think twice before doing anything at all. Everything he touches may be a booby-trap, the next step he takes may lead him over a mine-field; every word he pronounces may be used against him someday."[19] These general attitudes may of course be reflective of Italian historical experience, particularly during the period of fascism, and of the prevalence of patron-clientelism within the rural areas of the peninsula. In general these beliefs are reflected at the larger level: to the Italian democracy seems to be an illusion that simply serves the interest of the few, so why bother about politics? Apathy keeps the system going. Moreover, survey evidence shows that Italians are less willing to discuss politics or even reveal their voting behavior than other citizens. In other words, civic competence at the national level was particularly low in Italy, especially in comparison to the United Kingdom or even West Germany.[20] There is a pervading sense of cynicism within the system; idealism is not a characteristic of the Italian people when it comes to evaluating their institutions or political system.

Another perspective is offered by a 1975 survey showing that fewer Italians were willing to take part in illegal activities or unconventional political behavior than their counterparts in the United Kingdom or West Germany.[21] In part this finding might be attributed to the conservative influence of the Roman Catholic church, which claims 95 percent of the Italian citizenry, and its role in Italian society as a social and political force. The Catholic church possesses a very tightly organized network of institutions that provide a reference point and a framework for the masses and the party that predominates, in this case the Christian Democratic party, the traditional Catholic party in the twentieth century in Italy and the one that enjoys the church's sanction and blessing. We have seen that traditionally the Italian political leadership has always had close ties with the Vatican. The fact that there is a distinct Catholic subculture in Italy is reflected in the intensely partisan loyalties of sections of the Italian citizenry.

The Christian Democrats (DC) look to the church to secure their support. In particular the votes of women, farmers, and people in the northeast regions are important and responsive to clerical influence. Christian Democracy as an ideology has its roots in the resistance of the church to fascism in the 1940s and 1950s and wields a great deal of power among the Catholic citizenry and the other Christian groups, not only in Italy, but also in Germany. The other major parties in Italy, the PCI (Italian Communist party) and the PSI (Socialist party) (which have been renamed) do not receive equivalent support compared to the DC, which along with the church espouses anticommunism and respect for papal authority and the Catholic church in general. Given the nature of the links between Catholicism and politics in Italy and the conservative nature of the church, it should perhaps come as no surprise that Italians do not appear to be interested in unconventional forms of political participation like these displayed by their French, German, and British counterparts.

Voting Behavior

Even though protest activities do not attract the levels of participation in Italy that they do in other European societies, the same cannot be said when Italians take to the polls. Italy relies on a long urban tradition of voter participation, which has provided Italians with a prime source of legitimacy ever since 1848, substantially earlier than many states in Western Europe. The vote was gradually extended to the masses much as in England; by 1919 all men over the age of twenty-one were given the vote, and women received the same right in 1948, resulting in major increases in the numbers of eligible voters. The year 1948 also marked the advent in general of the dominance of organized mass parties and in specific of the Christian Democrats and the Communists; it was specifically the turning point of the postwar period for valuation of political participation. The demise of Mussolini, the ignominious failure of fascism, and the final postwar settlement prompted mass mobilization of the population through the new vehicle of the organized political party. Moreover, to some extent, the high turn-out rates can be attributed to cultural and social roots engrained in the different secular and Roman Catholic subcultures. Strong party loyalties ensure that Italy maintains one of the highest rates for electoral participation among Western democracies, close to 90 percent in general (national) elections.[22] Regional and local elections also tend to attract a high turn-out. This is a clear indication of a degree of civic-mindedness within the Italian political system; if political alienation and distrust are comparatively high at the level of political culture, they certainly cannot be seen from the perspective of the most conventional form of political participation, voting. In comparison to their American counterparts, for instance, Italians represent models of democratic citizens in terms of going to the polls (although in 1979 and 1983 there were drops in the voting rates). In addition, young Italians are highly partisan and politicized. This is particularly interesting given the fact that the rate of cabinet turnover in Italy has been the highest of any Western European democracy in the postwar period. A legitimate question would be, Why would people bother to vote in such a climate of instability and alienation? And the answer again draws on the strength of the subcultures that lend support to the maintenance of the overall political system. If the specific formation of governments is a difficult, fragmented, and messy business, resulting in rapid changes in coalitions, at the diffuse or general level of the political system, stability is maintained by the endurance of the traditional subcultures that underwrite party politics.

Scandals and Corruption in Modern Italy

Another source of cynicism and reason for disbelief in state and politics is a constant barrage of scandals that never fail to be exploited by the Italian media. In the late 1970s the Italian president and two former cabinet ministers were implicated in a bribery scandal involving the Lockheed Aircraft Company. The president resigned to avoid being charged; the ministers were indicted, with one convicted and jailed. In the 1980s the trail of scandals led to even more high profiles.

In one case a secret Masonic lodge (illegal in Italy) called Propaganda 2 was found to have cabinet ministers, members of parliament, businessmen, bureaucrats, and senior members of the armed forces amongst its membership. The president of the Lodge, Licio Gelli, was actually found to be conspiring to overthrow the parliamentary regime. When the membership lists were made public, the cabinet was dissolved and this weakened the Christian Democrats.

In another case, the Banco Ambrosiano, the largest private bank in Italy, was linked to the Catholic church and the Vatican. The bank's collapse in 1982 caused major economic harm to Italian depositors and to foreign banks that had invested large sums of money in it. Its bank president, Roberto Calvi, who was also a member of Propaganda 2, was found dead shortly before the crisis emerged, hung under a railway bridge in London in 1982. The bank had made loans of a dubious nature to various Central American dummy companies, and they were defaulted upon. When Italian officials demanded the money from Vatican coffers, the scandal seriously affected the Christian Democrats, who were strongly affiliated with the church. The Vatican has been accused at various levels of funding illicit operations, but it is difficult to prosecute because in Italy it enjoys sovereign status as an institution.

The connections of established political parties (indeed, the party that forms the government) with Sicilian **Mafia** figures has also rocked Italian politics in recent years. In March 1992, the Mafia was involved in the shooting of Salvo Lima, a prominent Sicilian member of the European Parliament (Euro-MP), who had delivered many hundreds of thousands of votes for the Christian Democratic prime minister, Giulio Andreotti, and was rumored to have had connections with Mafia members. In the aftermath of the killing, the Italian government issued a somber warning about an obscure "plot to destabilize the country."[23] Shortly after this, on May 23, 1992, the leading anti-Mafia judge, Giovanni Scalfaro, was brutally murdered in Sicily. The political message that the Mafia were announcing was one that is engrained into the antistate culture of Italy—that is, that the state can be defied with impunity. The Mafia followed this on Sunday, July 19, with another spectacular bomb attack, killing another major anti-Mafia judge, Paolo Borsellini, and five police escorts in Sicily.

In addition the system of *lottizzazione* (allotment), in which jobs are distributed according to the parties' electoral strengths, has, despite producing a very weak form of democratic consensus, damaged the system because it is inherently corrupt. Through this system, embezzlement and fraud are perpetuated in the south in the awarding of public contracts, one-party domination of government is accepted, and a highly inefficient public sector has been maintained. Party loyalists in such positions command enormous patronage. In turn the development of patron-clientelism, particularly in southern Italy, perpetuates corruption and, as we can see in the mezzogiorno, underdevelopment.

To some extent the system reflects a culture of cheating, one in which taxes are avoided, regulations are bypassed, a black economy succeeds. Contracts for public works are given in the full knowledge that organized crime will benefit. The example of Mario Chiesa, the Socialist head of a Milan charity group, is illustrative of this cheating. In February 1992, Chiesa was arrested with 7 million lire ($5,700) in his pocket, which was a kickback for a cleaning contract; such kickbacks, known as ***tangenti***, are integral to the system throughout Italy. Initially twenty-four people were arrested, including fourteen businessmen and nine officials from political parties, but more were to follow on corruption charges. The case is interesting because it highlights the networks of corruption between political parties and business. And it was not just confined to one political party: three members of the Democratic party (the renamed Communist party) were also involved.[24] Again it shows how the state manages to be both complacent and ubiquitous in such matters; political corruption and patronage permeate the system. And scandals appeared to invade the entire political system in 1993 and 1994. One analyst noted that the implications were staggering, with decades of pork-barrel politics contributing to a national debt exceeding $1 trillion. The reform-minded Christian Democrat Mario Segni argued that every Italian born today "begins life $20,000 in the hole."[25] In this period at least eight hundred people, including a quarter of the parliament's 630 members, were under investigation for corruption and illegal activities. A report issued by the Luigi Einaudi Institute in Turin estimated that between $10 billion and $20 billion had been drained from the economy in the previous twelve years of corrupt activity.[26]

No one, not even the president, appears immune to the culture of corruption that permeates Italian society. Perhaps the real difference that has emerged recently is that this has become more explicit, and we can detect how engrained it is in the national fabric of Italian society. Italians always knew that there was a great deal of corruption; what they didn't know until recently is the extent to which it penetrated society and politics.

It is clear that scandals and corruption are important elements; that while they may not shape overall voting behavior, they at least shape political attitudes, and this may in turn be a determining factor in the vote.

Changing Patterns of Politics

In the late 1960s an increasingly activist section of the Italian public began to make its presence felt. The traditional organizations through which they voiced their grievances—political parties, student groups, and labor organizations, and others—appeared inadequate for this discontented minority within Italian society. The waves of protest that affected other European and Western democracies were beginning to affect Italian politics. Peaceful demonstrations gained more widespread acceptance, protest activities increased, and unconventional behavior was seen as less of an aberration. There is, of course, some history of this form of activity at various levels throughout Italian politics. Voting was not the only form of participation; during the risorgimento of the nineteenth century, for example, citizens withheld taxes and organized demonstrations against various policies. In the years before World War I, strikes were commonplace as a form of economic as well as political protest. The Catholic Action Movement, which developed in the 1880s, served several functions in terms of attempting to influence the established authorities. Plebiscites were also conducted during the risorgimento (over unification for instance) but were typically more symbolic than real. However the extent of atypical participation should not be exaggerated, particularly during the post-1945 period when, as we have seen, there were new and important channels for participation via the party system. In the immediate aftermath of the war the majority of the Italian population clearly eschewed such unconventional activities.[27]

Recent political participation has seen, however, the innovation of a particular (and previously unused) constitutional tool to effect changes in political decisions. Officially, if 500,000 citizens sign a petition asking for a specific law to be repealed, then a national referendum on the issue must be held. The invoking of the referendum procedure by the population is in direct contrast to the practice in the United Kingdom or France, where the procedure is evoked by the government. The procedure was never used in Italy until 1974, when the first referendum was held; since then another four have taken place, for a total of five. The first four (in 1974, 1978, 1981, and 1985) failed to change the laws proposed, but in 1987 large majorities of voters overturned five proposed laws on nuclear energy and legal immunity for judges. Interestingly, the high turnouts that observers had come to expect in these referendums decreased or leveled off by the late 1980s. However the change to direct democracy as a form of political action is indicative of a subtle change in the politics of participation among Italian voters. If parliamentary supremacy is an unwritten law in many liberal democracies, the use of referendums must constitute a threat to such supremacy. The popular will, on the other hand, may strengthen and reinforce the democratic process within the Italian state.

A number of interesting societal changes have occurred in the past twenty-five or thirty years. The two main political subcultures, socialist and Roman Catholic, are not the dominant forces they once were, due in part to a growing secularization of values. The linkage between politics and religion is no longer an automatic assumption, and religious feelings are not necessarily the strong predictors of voting behavior they once were. The Catholic church's support for the Christian Democrats is weaker now than in the past, and the younger generation's orientation towards both has declined, as they are less religious.

Similarly, support for socialism as a subculture has decreased in Italy and is in steady decline for a number of reasons: Italy has modernized to a large extent, and this has called into question the viability of the Socialist model. In a crucial sense, the startling developments in Eastern Europe and the now ex-Soviet Union have catalyzed a fundamental reexamination of the practice and ideology of communism. The left has been discredited as outmoded, and this has been an explicit political development forcing the Communists to change their name if not their practice. Nothing has really appeared to take the place of Communists ideology in the wake of the left's demise.

The decline of these two important subcultures which guided and shaped Italian politics in the postwar years has gone hand in hand with the depolarization of society. Ideological views have softened; the intensity that characterized the debates has been watered down; and confrontational politics have increasingly diminished.

In addition, the traditional ingredients underlying politics, such as religion and class, have been reduced in importance; this change has led, as noted, to the introduction of other political actors to Italian politics, such as environmental groups. The old institutional channels reflecting traditional interests can no longer accommodate new demands as citizens in Italy increasingly organize outside established channels and experiment with new modes of participation.

The recent Italian election in April 1992 registered this change, with protest movements and over one hundred different political parties putting forward candidates for the election. The Greens, the Housewives' League (the *Lega Casalinghe*) and Anybody's Party were among the groups offering different choices to an electorate that was clearly tired of established parties and conspicuous levels of corruption.

Apart from these factors in the trend towards a different political culture, there are several others. The antiincumbency vote seems to constitute a general pattern in Europe on the whole. Economic difficulties, worries over immigration, and the decreasing salience of the old politics based on class and ideological cleavages all meant that the marginal or fringe parties benefited. Overall, choices have become less clear and voters more willing to defect to parties like the far right and to regional parties such as the Lombard League. One report noted that "Italians are fed up with the shabby politics of the ruling parties in Rome, and they are no longer afraid to vote for alternatives."[28] The idea that Italy is a *partitocrazia* (a system run by parties, not government) may be in for some real change as the traditional cleavages wane in influence. Clearly the traditional dominance of the Christian Democrats and left-wing parties are under attack, and therefore the rules of the game are in for a period of flux and change and in fact subject to discontinuity.

Internal Wounds: The Problem of Political Violence

Threats to the Italian State

It would be difficult to compare Italy to the other Western European states we have discussed in terms of threats or dangers to their very existence. We would need to discuss the major differences, because Italy, unlike any other country discussed here, faces such a plethora of difficulties that they defy the imagination. A weak and divided party system, instability in government, and inefficiency in public administration are only a few of the problems the modern state faces. In Italy, however, there are several more that threaten the root and fabric of the state. These include various conspiracies, terrorism from the left and the right, organized crime in the form of the Mafia, and in general a long tradition of political violence.

In this section we will assess and probe some of these threats and dangers that Italy faces and the different kinds of responses that have been adopted to deal with them.

Political Violence and Organized Crime: A Family Affair

Chi parla muore, chi tace campa.
(Who talks dies; who is silent lives.)

—Sicilian proverb

The subject of hundreds of books and articles, and many films is one of Italy's most famous social and cultural phenomena: the Mafia. An organization and network of families drenched in blood and rooted in organized crime involving everything from prostitution to drug running to construction industries, the Mafia first and foremost has its roots in the nineteenth century and the rural island of Sicily. Mafioso and bandit chiefs that prevailed in this part of the world tended in the past to be revered as Robin Hood figures who would defy the political authorities and what was regarded as the illegitimate state; it was a rural oligarchy. The special role of the family in the history of the Mafia is synonymous with the role of client-patron relations in southern Italy, and nowhere was this more pronounced than in Sicily. The entire system is based on the exchange of favors and rewards. As one author notes, the "Mafioso literally goes through life doing 'favours' for his 'friends' and expecting favours in return"[29] (the code name for the Mafia in Sicily is the "**friends of the friends**") Today some contend that the Mafia is a far greater threat to the established legal order than the various terrorist groups such as the Red Brigade. The three main criminal organizations of the Mafia, in Sicily, Calabria, and Naples, play a major role.

Prior to the 1960s the Mafia (at least in Italian perceptions) did not pose a serious threat to the state's legitimacy; it appeared quaint with its strict rules and unusual antiquated code of honor. In fact it appeared no more than a relic of feudalism, an interesting anachronism that would have difficulty finding a role in a modern state. This misperception received a rude awakening in the 1960s when, during the period of the Italian construction boom, the Mafia moved into industrial areas and developed into a modern, urban, and sophisticated crime syndicate.

Thereafter the Mafia's interests became refined in various ways. When two big Mafia trials resulted in mass acquittals in the 1960s, the findings of a parliamentary commission of enquiry, which included potentially damaging evidence, were quietly ignored by legislators. The Mafia expanded into kidnapping and gambling on the mainland. In the 1970s drugs became big business as the Sicilian families sought to exploit their family ties with their American counterparts. Most of the heroin on the streets of New York City by the end of the 1970s had been refined by the Sicilian connection; Palermo by the beginning of the 1980s was the world center for the sale and production of heroin. While drugs and the mafia went hand in hand, so did the upsurge in violent gang wars in the 1980s.

The Mafia's main activities revolve around the control of wholesale agricultural markets, protection rackets in large and small-scale businesses, and the construction of public works projects. Prostitution, smuggling, and drugs are all part of their normal activities today. Blackmail, extortion, and rake-offs are the common means of extracting payment; murder, assassination, and simple terror serve to silence people who oppose them or will not cooperate. While the rate of assassination in the period after the war was nearly fifty persons per year, since the end of the 1970s the activity has taken on bloodbath proportions with the killing of five hundred people a year.[30] Although many of these people were victims of Mafia gang wars, others were important administrative and political figures, including a number of police and judicial officials. The *Godfather* trilogy of movies by Francis Ford Coppola, based on the book by Mario Puzo, has given widespread global exposure to Mafia activities and the methods by which they carry them out. As a result, Mafia trials have become controversial, Hollywood-like affairs. In 1991, the movie *Goodfellas* by Martin Scorcese provided a fascinating sociological and psychological insight into the lives of Mafia members in the United States.

A Resurgent Mafia. At the beginning of the 1980s, major Mafia trials opened in the capital of Sicily, Palermo. Several politicians predicted that they would be the end of organized crime on the island. The predictions were wrong; the Mafia not only did not give up, but they actually expanded their operations on the Italian mainland and in particular in the north. In July 1991, ISTAT, the Italian Statistical Office, published figures that testified to the resurgence of Mafia activity and violence. The figures pointed to the sharp rise in murders; the Mafia, the Camorra (the Neapolitan section), and the **'Ndrangheta** (the Calabrian Section) were responsible for the deaths of 189 people in the first three months of 1991, compared to 122 killed in the same period in 1990.[31] Furthermore, the gangs that carry out such killings are increasingly able to operate with impunity. According to the central statistical office of Italy, only 13 percent of murders went unpunished in 1971; by 1987, the proportion of reported murders that went unpunished had risen to 50 percent, and by 1989 this figure had increased to over 70 percent.[32]

More recently, the links between organized crime and organized Italian politics have become increasingly explicit. Indeed, the difference between the two appears difficult to ascertain at times. Most Italians have known for years that there has been a pact between the southern Mafia and the Christian Democrats. The former would deliver the southern vote to keep the latter in power. The latter would deliver public works, contracts and development aid to ensure that the criminal families maintained their grip on the south. However, the startling revelations in the first few months of 1993, which illustrated the reach of the Mafia, certainly came as a surprise for most Italians. Giulio Andreotti, seven times an Italian prime minister, was under investigation for helping the Mafia. Government ministers were widely implicated in collusion and corruption involving hundreds of politicians, the Mafia, and billions of dollars.[33] A new study on the Italian Mafia in 1993 provided insights into their workings. Oxford sociologist Diego Gambetta argued in *The Sicilian Mafia: The Business of Private Protection* that the Mafia is a "specific economic enterprise, an industry which produces, promotes and sells private protection"; in essence the organization in this light need not be seen as a gang of criminals but a coterie of enterpreneurs.[34] If this hypothesis is valid, it may be even more difficult than expected to solve the problem of organized crime, not only in Italy but Europe in general.

The undermining of democracy is caused not only by the Mafia in Italian society. The fact that such an organized crime group exists and acts with a large degree of impunity suggests that the problem is larger than simply a criminal one. The Mafia appears to be part and parcel of Italian political culture in its operations and in its connections with top government officials and the political establishment. Where such groups appear to be tolerated, democracy can make only limited inroads, and Italian political life appears to be a long way from the political cleansing that many of its citizens demand.

According to Italian Prime Minister Carlo Aglezio Campi, in November 1993, the "fight against the Mafia is at a turning point."[35] New groups are now channelling their frustrations against the Mafia, including the party La Rete (the Network Party), formed in 1991 to fight the regional elections in Sicily, the heartland of the Mafia. It remains to be seen whether rhetoric will have an impact in producing "cleaner" government and politics in the republic. And it is clear that the threat to democracy in Italy will not subside until the state takes such a task upon itself.

Terrorism in Italian Politics. In the 1970s and 1980s, there was a sudden upsurge in the number of terrorist incidents within Italian society. The weakness of the Italian state was further exacerbated and increasingly put to the test by these problems. In addition to a party system that was uncohesive and fragmented, a highly inefficient public administration, and a politicized judiciary, Italians were now subjected to violent terrorism and political violence within their society. The group that was most prominent and received the most media attention was the **Red Brigade** (*Brigatte Rosse*), who were characterized by their notorious headlining attempts to disrupt and damage the credibility of the democratic political system. In 1978 the *New York Times* described the group as having "established itself as an effective military and political power in Italy, transfixing and intimidating the country and paralyzing its political leadership in an attempt to create a climate of civil war."[36]

Political terror is not simply representative of drama; to ignore the consequences and implications is to turn a blind eye to innocent victims and to forget the disabling and disintegrative effects such strategies have on democratic societies. Terrorism threatens to uproot the moral fabric of society in the sense that it is a pervading challenge to the commitment of the masses and elites to democratic principles. In the view of the political terrorist in Italy, democracy is the obstacle and therefore must be humiliated, demoralized, and ended.

One example was the Bologna railway station bombing in 1978. Other left-wing groups also played a role in sustaining political terrorism, including the Armed Proletarian Nuclei and the Front Line. The agenda of domestic politics was also under pressure from the right-wing or neofascist terrorists, despite the lack of coherence in their programs and their inability to formulate a successful strategy. Extreme-right-wing bodies often resorted to simply detonating bombs in public places for no apparent reason except to gain publicity (the oxygen of terrorists). In some ways this is a more dangerous threat because the options for disruption are much more widely spread.

Explanations for Terrorism. The reasons for terrorist activity in Italy contrast sharply with the situation in other European nations, such as the United Kingdom, France, and Spain. There, terrorism has been linked with ethnic, separatist, and nationalist movements such as the Irish Republican Army in the United Kingdom, the Breton groups in France, and the Basque nationalists (the ETA) in Spain. These groups use political violence at least in part to draw attention to their demands for autonomy. In Italy, however, the problem was that terrorists on both the right and left had much more fundamental demands than simply ethnic separatism. Such groups desired and still desire an overthrow of the existing political state structure, however vague and ill-defined is their expression of this goal. Their grievance is similar to that of the extreme right and left wings in Germany, in the sense that their goal was to remove and replace the existing regime and possibly the system. On the other hand, in the 1970s and 1980s Italian terrorists were providing a more important challenge to democracy than achieved by their German counterparts. The fact that the Italian state has always been seen as a less stable institution within the European context of nation states enabled the terrorists to have a greater psychological effect on society at large. Between

1968 and 1983 they managed to kill 296 civilians and 92 policemen through their various actions, with a loss of 42 on their side. The threat of domestic terror has not disappeared from Italian politics. It lurks beneath the surface seeking opportunities to disrupt and harm the political process within liberal democracy.

Some authors contend that terrorism was in large part an extension of such protest movements as the student demonstrations of the late 1960s. In the beginning, these groups simply engaged in dialogue and verbal expressions of protest; later some turned to more serious activities, including kidnapping and finally murder.[37]

In his seminal work *Democracy Italian Style,* Joseph LaPalombara provides a list of twenty-one issues that many Italians themselves believe are the causes of political terror. Here I will cite what I regard as the most important ones. According to Italians, political terror exists because:

1. Society is unjust.
2. The political system is a fraud; nothing ever really changes in Italy.
3. The growth of the tertiary, or service, sector in the economy has weakened the control the unions have over workers.
4. People have improved their economic conditions too fast, and so they have "rising expectations" and want even more.
5. Italy's governmental institutions do not function as they should.
6. The state is impotent against organized crime and political corruption, against the rape of the environment and rampant tax evasion.
7. The "true believers" of the Catholic and "Marxist" "churches" are angry because first principles of these organizations have been neglected or abandoned.
8. Modern industrial society produces "alienated" persons.
9. Liberal democracies are a disillusionment.
10. The state itself is essentially violent, and its laws inflict injustice, pain, suffering, and death on others.[38]

As noted in the historical overview, a sense of growing resentment in the late 1960s culminated in student revolts in 1968. There was a general sense of malaise at the societal level; the system expressed disharmony. This malaise, coupled with a lack of faith in institutions, a sense of alienation from the state, and the perception that the means of political articulation was closed to many, produced a real feeling of marginalization and discontent. In terms of social psychology, the argument can be made that the social frustration that students felt led them to adopt violent methods and join terrorist organizations in an effort to produce change.[39] Structural factors also help to explain why terrorism emerged in Italian society, as noted by the list offered by LaPalombara. Two authors stress the role of economic development in marginalizing workers in industrial societies; the fact that young people were unable to find appropriate jobs for which they had been trained is an indication of the fact that the Italian economic system and political system were "out of sync" with the processes of economic modernization. Moreover, change in traditional industries left many other people displaced and ultimately marginalized, in turn creating breeding grounds for unrest and political violence.[40]

The Abduction and Death of Aldo Moro: A Case in Terror

The terrorism that had its birth in the ideology of student revolt in the late 1960s, its subsequent expression in the "hot autumn" of 1968, when labor unrest was at its height, and its continuance into the 1970s clearly reached a climax with the death of Aldo **Moro**, a former prime minister, in March of 1978. The mid-1970s saw a revival of "executions" of political opponents; twice as many cases of terrorism were reported in 1977 as in the previous year. But it was not until the brutal execution of Aldo Moro in 1978 that terrorism so dramatically occupied the attention of government and other leaders. Aldo Moro was an influential leader in the Christian Democratic party. His kidnapping in Rome on March 16, 1978, and subsequent death at the hands of the Red Brigade left not only Italy but the world shocked by the brutality of the violence. For fifty-four days, Moro was held hostage, given a so-called proletarian trial, declared "guilty," and finally murdered, his body found on the ninth of May in the trunk of an abandoned car.

The case of Moro is instructive; it symbolizes the crisis nature of Italian politics, particularly in terms of the acute levels of political violence inherent in and directed against the political system. Moro, who was actively attempting at the time to negotiate a compromise between the Christian Democrats and the Communists, was deliberately killed by an organization that eschewed the idea of political compromise. The stance of the Italian government, which refused to enter into negotiations or bargaining with the terrorists, was a courageous act under the circumstances, but it almost certainly cost Moro his life. And this situation represents a major problem and dilemma for liberal democracy. How does a democracy deal with acts of terrorism? Should it capitulate to the demands? Should it take a hard-line stance regardless of the fact that its citizens' lives (as in the case of Moro) may be severely endangered?

In Italy the Moro kidnapping signified at the very least a temporarily destructive event in the process of Italian democracy. When such events have this kind of impact on the day-to-day running of liberal democracies, when they produce a "general curtailment of freedom, months of power instability, and, worst of all, a state of mind characterised by fear, intolerance, and a desire to cover up the truth, any claim of victory for democracy would in the most generous instance be cause to ask what kind of democracy the claimant has in mind."[41]

To a large extent violence has succeeded in disrupting the democratic process because it has become part of the political agenda. In such circumstances compromise is ruled out. The government of a democratic society is forced to meet force with the idea that there can be no compromise, resulting to some extent in a further increase in the no-compromise position of the protagonists in the conflict. Irreparable psychological damage to the cause of democracy and ultimate success to the men of violence are to a certain extent guaranteed. This is the dilemma that liberal democracy faces against terrorism.

The Red Brigades and their violent strategies represent a threat and a challenge to the concept and practice of Italian democracy.

Conclusion

Political violence remains a continuing problem in contemporary Italy. The state appears weak and ineffectual in dealing with such challenges. Between 1969 and 1983, for instance, there were more than 14,000 acts of violence committed by terrorists from the left and the right, causing the deaths of 409 persons and injuring 1,366 people.[42] Italy thus has witnessed terrorist violence at a level and magnitude unseen in most Western liberal democracies. Terrorism of the right and the left have produced deep scars on the Italian body politic, and it is unlikely that the survivors and the families of those dead and those who have suffered will forget in the near future.

Terrorism since the end of the 1970s has been reined in by the authorities. In 1978 the left and rightist political parties came together to endorse a common front in the proposal of antiterrorist laws. They provided the police with major new powers in dealing with terrorism, including rights to arrest suspects, to search private property, and to carry weapons. Sentences were increased and more punitive measures introduced to deal with the terrorists. By the beginning of 1982, much of the terrorist threat to the state had subsided.

As one author notes, "After 1980, terrorist incidents dropped sharply in Italy: from over 2,500 in 1978, to 217 in 1983, 310 in 1984, and fewer than 100 in 1985, 1986, and 1987."[43] Despite the fact that terrorism will not fully go away, the Italian state has successfully managed and contained the threat. There is no doubt that such a problem continually remains a dilemma for liberal democracies in the effort to maintain openness and at the same time protect the citizenry. At the same time, however, the fact that Italian institutions, social cohesion, and democracy were not seriously damaged in light of these problems suggests that democracy in Italy is more capable of standing up to pressure and handling serious threats than the pessimists would argue.

If terrorism of the ideological brand has subsided within the Italian state, then a more insidious one has emerged. The Mafia is a serious threat because it appears to be part of the political culture itself. In 1983 a Sicilian journalist stated on national television that "Mafia members are in parliament, they are sometimes ministers, they are bankers, and they are those who are at the top of the nation." A few days later the journalist was murdered.[44] The murders of anti-Mafia judges in 1992 as the state appeared to begin stronger action against organized crime merely served to increase the prominence of the Mafia and highlight the fact that it can act with impunity. To a large extent the problem is not one of inventing new laws to deal with this menace but actually to put existing laws into practice. And despite some successful actions in the mid 1980s, the Italian state appears a long way from curing this particular Italian illness and breaking the hold of long-standing traditions. The Mafia appears as a threat to the notion and practice of liberal democracy, operating as it does by its own rules. In this context it remains a pressing challenge to political continuity in the Italian republic.

Race, Ethnicity, and Immigration

Immigration

Italy has traditionally been an exporter of labor to other parts of the world and in particular to northwestern Europe. Only in the 1970s did the Italian state become an importer of labor, and only after 1986 did immigration become an issue that commanded media attention and debate within Italian society. As in the United Kingdom, the immigrants are typically not European Community passport holders; they are Third Worlders who come to Italy in search of employment and a better standard of life for themselves and their families. These economic immigrants are different from the refugees seeking political asylum, who are given a different name: the *"immigrati extracommunitari."*

The immigrants appeared on Italian soil in two waves: the first between 1970 and 1985, and the second after 1985. The first wave comprised mainly African workers, Iranian political refugees, and some Filipino domestic servants. In the post-1985 period, Senegalese migrants as well as Tunisians, Ghanaians, and some Asians entered the country. Two forms of work are generally available to these people. In the first case they are similar to Third World immigrants in the other European countries: they perform jobs that the native population will not do. They work at bringing in the agricultural harvests in both North and South; they receive no legal protection and low wages. At the industrial level they perform unskilled work in small and medium sized firms, again in positions that native Italians refuse to accept. The urban centers attract the most immigrants, and one can find concentrations of them in Milan, Turin, Bologna, Florence, and Naples. Many were recruited illegally, further forcing down their wages.

A second group of immigrants have to some extent created their area or market where previously a market did not exist. As one author points out, "In traveling sales, in particular, there is no explicit demand for immigrant labour, and yet this is often the point of entry into employment for many immigrants. . . . It appears that the more or less legal zones of the market economy which control such activities have rapidly created a demand for immigrant labour."[45] Unlike other European countries, however, the recruitment of labor was not a specific undertaking by the state and the private sector with trade union cooperation; it was a much more haphazard arrangement.

Figures on immigration are derived from the National Institute of Statistics (ISTAT) which provided a recent estimate that Italy harbors approximately 800,000 to 1 million Third World immigrants from outside the EC borders. This total accounts for just over 1 percent of the Italian population.

Responses to Immigration

The fact that Italy has had comparatively less immigration than the other European societies has meant that there has been less overt reaction than that which we have seen in the United Kingdom, France, or even Germany. Italy simply never had overseas colonies on the same scale as other major European powers and therefore not as many people would and could simply arrive there on the grounds of colonial obligation. Prior to the Second World War, the Italian state had acquired some territories in North and East Africa, such as Eritrea, Libya, and Italian Somaliland, in an attempt to keep up with and emulate Britain and France. In the 1930s it seized Ethiopia. These acquisitions, however, were relatively unimportant in comparison to the British and French empires, which claimed far larger areas and maintained more control. After losing the Second World War, Italy was stripped of all possessions and renounced claims to them. The impact of losing such colonies actually decreased Italy's economic burden and allowed for investments to be transferred to the south. An additional benefit was relatively light immigration, in part because of Italy's weak history of colonialism and in part because Italy offered less economic opportunity to Third World people seeking a better life, in comparison to Germany for instance.

In addition, immigrants have maintained a low profile in society. Italy's population has been relatively homogeneous in comparison to other European societies since it did not experience the labor shortages in the 1960s that the rest of Western Europe did. However, recent events, such as the case of the **Albanian boat people** and the racist murder of a young black South African in Naples in 1989, and an anti-immigrant raid at the Florence carnival in March 1990, have raised the issue of race as an increasingly significant problem in Italian society. Outbreaks of violence at soccer matches, once directed at opposition supporters, have increasingly become directed at immigrant workers. Leagues have developed to mobilize anti-immigrant sentiments, such as the Lega Lombarda and Liga Veneta; these present new developments in Italian society. One explanation of this phenomenon revolves around the idea that Italy is undergoing an identity crisis in a way not too far removed from the situation of contemporary France. This argument is based in the erosion of the twin pillars of Italian social structure, the Catholic church and the Communist party. Both are no longer fulfilling their traditional role as socializing agents and identity markers for the younger generation.[46] And in turn this erosion of traditional values has prompted a sense of malaise and insecurity among youth and promoted intolerant attitudes.

The government has set up various mechanisms to deal with problems of race and immigration. The Martelli law, issued in February 1990, and Law 943 of 1986 represent the basic points of reference for Italian migration policy. The more recent law is an attempt to control the entry of immigrants by joint cooperation from the ministries of foreign affairs, interior, planning, and employment. Beginning the end of June 1990, illegal immigrants were not to be granted legal status, and frontiers were to be tightly controlled. In October 1990,

Italy signed the Schengen Agreement, designed to provide a common policy on migration for the European Community, thus lining itself up with the EC in general on the issue. It is within this context that the issue of the Albanian boat people became an important test case in the immigrant and migration policy of Italy.

Case Study: The Albanian Boat People

Albania represents an interesting case study in terms of the people who left to seek refuge in Italy. It offers an explicit comparison with efforts of other Third World refugees and migrants to seek asylum and economic prospects—for example the Vietnamese boat people in the 1970s and 1980s who went to Hong Kong, Malaysia, and other ports of call. Albania is important in terms of the Italian immigrant calculation because, of all the former Communist states, Albania provides perhaps the strongest motivation to emigrate, given the extremely weak state of the Albanian economy and the almost total failure of the regime to provide any basic standards of living for the populace.

In the summer of 1990, nearly 3,000 Albanians who arrived in Italy were welcomed as political refugees fleeing a repressive hard-line Communist government. A year later the definition had changed substantially. In March 1991, 24,000 Albanians crossed the Adriatic to southern Italian ports. Previously boat people had been seen as a specifically Third World phenomenon, particularly because of their concentration in Southeast Asia. Could it be possible that Europe was now faced with the same kinds of problems? The answer was and is, of course, yes. The authorities resorted to the same solutions as the governments of Hong Kong and Malaysia had done: simply label the boat people "economic migrants" to take care of the problem. In fact the Malaysian deputy prime minister in August 1991 noted the double standards of the West in Italy's expulsion and forcible repatriation of its boat people. Since 1989 the Malaysian policy of dealing harshly with Vietnamese refugees has been criticized widely by the Western press and establishment, but in 1991 the Malaysians could counter the criticism by pointing to the harsh treatment of the Albanians, many of whom were offered 50,000 lire (about $40) and some new clothes to pack up and leave.[47]

Changing Events in 1991

In March 1991, 25,000 Albanians turned up on the Adriatic coast of Italy, the second of three waves in the period between 1990 and 1991. The scenes of hungry Albanians in Italian ports was a shock to the Italian government, which was simply unprepared to handle the influx, politically or logistically. Almost half the refugees agreed to go home, prodded on by Italian aid, money and clothes. Of the remainder who stayed, only 1,200 had found jobs by August 1991. The Albanian state was on the road to collapse, suffering the same fate as many other Communist dictatorships in the aftermath of the end of the Cold War in Eastern Europe. With the disintegration of the Communist government in June the circumstances appeared to be pushing Albania in the direction of democracy, and the 17,000 additional Albanians who appeared in Italy in August 1991 experienced some difficulty describing themselves as political refugees fleeing oppression. More plausible explanations registered the fact that Albania was the poorest country in Europe, that its economy was a disaster, and that young Albanians had witnessed a better quality of life on Italian television programs beamed to Tirana, Albania's capital. The food queues, unemployment, and severe shortages had only served to prompt them to escape across the Adriatic.[48] What appears most likely is that the boat people left Albania for a combination of economic and political reasons and that to separate refugees and migrants into different categories is in itself a political attempt to control and manipulate the situation in the interests of the state.

The arrival of the 18,000 boat people in August, however, was significant in that it received enormous media attention and highlighted the dilemma that European states faced in particular over the disintegration of the Eastern Communist bloc and the implications of immigration from this region to the more prosperous nations of Western Europe. What Italy shares with the rest of Europe is the fact that it welcomes the movement to democracy on the part of these former dictatorships but does not welcome the free movement of their populations across open borders, particularly when that means major disruptions in their own internal affairs. The hypocrisy of Western Europe, which on the one hand pushed for and welcomed reform in Eastern Europe and on the other seeks to stem the tide of immigrants and refugees leaving their erstwhile Communist states has proven to be a difficult contradiction in individual state and European policy which will not disappear overnight. And this will remain on not only the Italian but also the European agenda for the 1990s and into the next century. The events of August 1991 as they unfolded in Bari, Italy, and the problems they raised, morally, politically, and economically, have major implications for immigration and freedom of movement in Europe. The situation was summed up accurately in a newspaper report at the time:

It was simply a shocking sight; hundreds of Albanians left desolate to camp on the quayside of the Italian port of Bari for four days. Amid litter, ankle deep and saturated in urine and sweat, they fought Italian police using tear gas and rubber batons. Welcome to the West! The Rome Government insisted that most of the 10,000 who drove through the naval blockades on a rusty freighter would be going home immediately. It is an ugly illustration of the old order; a collapse which the West encouraged and celebrated without considering that, as a sponsor, it was taking some responsibility for a new order.[49]

Policy Responses

Given the fact that there are few precedents in Western Europe to deal with the difficulties raised by the likes of the Albanian boat people, it is not surprising that the Italian authorities were short on real solutions to the dilemma.[50] The first response, as seen, was to approach the problem with a lenient policy. Cases were reviewed to determine whether they were worthy of political asylum; millions of dollars worth of food and medical supplies were given to Albania, and Italian ministers flew to Tirana for discussions with Albanian authorities in an attempt to stem the influx. The Italian authorities also pressured the EC to provide aid to Albania to defuse the situation. The community responded by offering 50,000 tons of wheat and several million dollars in economic aid.

The situation changed, however, when many of the boat people refused to leave, even though they had been kept for four days in an outdoor soccer stadium with excessive heat, poor conditions and little food and water. The Italian authorities adopted a hard-line policy in rounding up Albanians and forcibly repatriating them by either sea or air. Tear gas, baton charges, and riots followed on the dockside of Bari when the police tried to send back the last of the refugees.

The Albanian refugee situation provided the Italian authorities with a political quandary. In September 1991, Guido Bolaffi, an expert on immigration, pointed out that "Italy is the only industrialized country to be overtaken by the mass immigration problem before it ever reached full employment. In other cases, generally, immigration comes to fill in. Here immigrants overlap with 2 million unemployed."[51] An interesting irony of the situation, of course, lies in the fact that Italians were in a similar position in the not-too-distant past. Even today, more than 5 million Italians live abroad, having left their own society in order to improve their economic position.

Conclusion

The case of immigration in Italy is clearly a complicated one. As we have seen, even boatloads of Albanians have been turned back in recent years, the threat being seen as an implicit economic one and not necessarily a cultural or religious one. An unemployment rate of approximately 11 percent in 1992 has sharpened people's awareness of relative economic deprivation in a job market where opportunities are decreasing. For politicians and masses alike, scapegoats are increasingly available in immigrants. The right-wing parties have gained a great deal of political ground in manipulating such sentiments. The Northern League, which has campaigned on these positions, for instance, had eighty deputies and senators in parliament after the 1992 general election, a significant increase from its position five years earlier. In addition the granddaughter of Mussolini, the Fascist dictator of the 1920s and 1930s, was elected to parliament representing the neofascist MSI in April 1992. On the immigrant question it is clear where priorities lie: Alessandra Mussolini has stated that "in Naples there are plenty of black immigrants, but we have to look after the interests of our own young people first."[52]

For the time being, then, it appears that the immigration issue, a new discontinuity on the landscape of Italian politics, will prove explosive in the Italian political agenda.

The North-South Divide

Italy is plagued by the problem of uneven development in the sense that it has a developed rich, urban, industrialized North and an underdeveloped, poor, mainly agricultural South. The division of the Italian state into separate regions appears more pronounced than in the other Western European societies studied. Other European states examined have of course divisions between north and south; in Britain it is common to talk of the more prosperous South (specifically the south of England) and the poorer North, the North and South in France and in Germany; however, none of these divisions represent such a stark economic, social, and cultural contrast as is the case in Italy. Cities in the North, such as Milan and Turin, maintain living standards on an equal footing with those of northwestern Europe, whereas in the southern reaches, in the regions of Calabria and the interior of Sicily, the picture is one of a preindustrial peasantry struggling to survive, an anachronism in a postindustrial society.

Geographical factors have contributed to the continuation of the divide. The northern Alps and the smaller southern Apennines have had a dividing effect which has encouraged disintegration in the South. Whereas the Po valley in the North has a degree of continuity in rich, fertile farmland which stretches from near Turin to the Adriatic, the plains of the South are small, fragmented, and isolated by the Appennines chain, which also acts as a barrier to ease of transport and communication between the urban populations of the South. Climate, combined with the smaller Apennine mountains, contributes to a lack of water for irrigation (this is exacerbated by drought) and to a less plentiful supply of energy in the South (unlike the North, which has major reserves of hydroelectric power). Moreover, the higher levels of deforestation and poor-quality soil in the South merely tend to reinforce the problems of water supply and fertility.

Political and cultural factors have also played their part in separate patterns of development for the North and the South. Historically, since the ninth century, the North and the South fell under different forms of political control. For several hundred years after the fall of the Roman Empire, the North was under the control of Germanic political domination, whereas the Moors were in control in the South. Different attitudes, cultures, and forms of rule developed as a result. This was reinforced, not abandoned, when the Normans defeated the Moors and their allies in the eleventh century, establishing the Kingdom of the Two Sicilies. At a time when northern and central Italy was expanding in terms of wealth and power and developing autonomy, the area south of Rome was experiencing a different political pattern, a centralized but mainly inefficient autocracy. Autocratic government in turn had negative consequences for the growth of the Southern economy and the development of urban commerce.

The division between North and South is to some extent a historical one. When Italian unification was achieved in the nineteenth century, neither region was economically developed, but the natural economic advantages and rich resources of the North ensured that its development would proceed at a more advanced speed. Socially, the South had a higher birth rate, higher infant mortality, widespread illiteracy, and a largely unskilled labor force, many of the skilled people having emigrated to the richer industrial North and the urban conurbations. It was only with the unification of Italy towards the end of the nineteenth century that Northerners sat up and actually paid attention to the unequal pattern of development seen in the South. However, if the North paid attention to the South it wasn't exactly with the South's best interests at heart. The Northern elites pursued policies that favored Northern agricultural and industrial production at the expense of nearly every other region of the country.

With unification, the **Sardinian Tariff** was extended to all Italy, decreasing the protection previously enjoyed by struggling industries in the South and backward areas. This tariff was not intended to help young industries in this region but merely to open up new markets for the North; Northern industrialists were unconcerned with the detrimental effects that such a policy would have on the rest of the country.

The continuation of the dominant agricultural sector in the Italian South, and concomitantly a powerful landowning elite and large peasantry, is an extension of traditional values in this region into the twentieth century. The 1950s saw the beginning of major investment on the part of the Italian state in the backward region known as the *mezzogiorno*.

The South, or *mezzogiorno*, has some contrasting statistics in terms of wealth and resource disparities, comprising 38 percent of Italy's population, 40 percent of its land area, but a mere 25 percent of its gross national product (GNP). Average per capita income stands at only half the national average.[53] Migration has been a major factor in the postwar economic development of Italy. At the beginning of the 1950s, nearly 42 percent of the employed population worked in agriculture; by the mid 1980s only 10 percent remained in these rural occupations. Southern farmers and peasants had clearly moved in droves to urban conglomerations. However, despite these major internal movements, the actual nature of landholding in the North and South saw relatively small changes. Whereas mechanized farms and agribusiness constitute the main agricultural sector in the North, the South continues to be controlled by small farmers and sharecroppers who tend the land for absentee landowners.[54] Preindustrial patterns of land use continue to dominate the pattern of agriculture in the South.

The Government's Response

In the 1950s the Italian government decided on a program of active state intervention to resolve some of these disparities. It initiated the *Cassa Per il Mezzogiorno* (Fund for the South) in 1950 to develop an infrastructure for agriculture and communications. A law was passed in 1957 obliging national corporations to locate 40 percent of their total investment in the South. Heavy industry was encouraged along with the development of commercial agriculture; in the case of the former a major effort was initiated by the public sector, particularly in the petrochemical industries.

Despite these programs the gap between North and South has

not substantially narrowed. Several reasons have been suggested for this failure:

1. *A poor industrial policy.* Despite the fact that investment has shifted towards the South in an effort to reduce the unemployment problem by setting up new industries, these ventures have turned out to be highly capital-intensive rather than labor-intensive. For instance in the 1960s one petrochemical plant in Sicily and a steelworks in Taranto employed only 6,500 workers, and the average capital outlay per worker came to 50 million lire. Similarly a ten-year plan to build a steel plant in Calabria during the 1970s, when steel plants in Italy were operating at 65 percent capacity due to low demand, managed to destroy relatively wealthy farms in the area. In 1979, the plant was closed without ever realizing its potential or even making a profit.[55]

2. *Capital disinvestment.* When rich Southern landowners were compensated for the loss of their land, financial capital was actually drained from the South (rather than reinvested) to support property speculation in the rich North.

3. *Patron-clientelism.* A system of patronage was introduced to the mezzogiorno by the Christian Democrats. The intention of the *Fanfani* system was to create a network of patron-client relationships which would obligate the people to support the party in return for rewards and favors. This meant that future development would be more closely controlled in the arena of party politics.

   In turn the economic and social structures of the South fostered and reinforced **patron-clientelism**; a smaller electorate and lack of competition between political parties meant that political-machine parties could manipulate voters in exchange for political favors. Jobs, subsidies, and contracts emerged as key goods to exchange for political support.

4. *The Mafia.* These "progressive" moves posed a threat to private and business interests. The Mafia had many strongholds in the South and were active in forcibly sabotaging industrial developments that competed with their interests. Moreover, they possessed the relevant political clout to divert funds for their own objectives.

Thus, we have what is in some ways the dilemma of most Third World societies: modernization without development. In turn, this has to some extent increased the gap between North and South. Plans to industrialize the South did bring new factories, but development did not occur. The new plants failed because they were isolated, not only from labor, but also from sufficient markets.

Clearly, the failure of attempts to bridge the gap between North and South has implications for a rich, strong, core North and a poor, weak, peripheral South. And, for Adrian Carello, the consequences of the *mezzogiorno's* inferior position within the Italian economy share a common element, that is, that the *mezzogiono's* underdevelopment manifests itself as economic development without sufficient employment opportunities for its population."[56]

The comparison of Southern Italy to the semi-industrialized nations of the Third World that maintain a dependent relationship with the core developed states is fairly accurate. Investment may come from the North, but the profits are returned to the North also. When workers travel to the North, many learn new skills and talents which could be of use to the South, but they tend to remain in the North and the South loses the benefit of a skilled work force.

Disparities continue; in the middle of the 1970s average per capita income in the South was only just over half that of the national average for Italy as a whole. In terms of per capita GDP, the South delivered 7.4 million lire in comparison to the North's 12.6 million lire, and unemployment levels were double the national estimates.[57] And the problems do not end there. There are several types of inequities in patterns of Italian economic development. In the first place there is the dual economy on a national scale—the contrast between the industrial North and the underdeveloped South. Second there is a dualism between the sector of the economy that has a modern industrial structure and the sector rooted in fairly unproductive and traditional industries. Finally we can see a dual economy in terms of the labor force: those in stable, well-paid positions and others who work in marginal, poorly paid occupations.[58] Despite the argument that these kinds of dualisms are present in many countries, we can see quite clearly that such patterns of uneven development are more pronounced within the Italian economic system.

The 1980s did not produce much important change in this relationship. Certainly the South increased its prosperity over this period, but not at the same rate as the Center or the North. While unemployment fell to some extent in cities it rose in the South—again a classic case of relative deprivation. It is clear that the expectations of the Southerners do not reflect their actual situation. This, as one writer has argued, has led to "accumulating frustrations" such as "youth unemployment, economic distortions, imbalances between resources consumed and resources produced. The southern question is more open than ever; indeed economic growth has accentuated its importance."[59]

The gap clearly remains in Italy—the gap between a developed country and an underdeveloped one still exists despite the attempts to change the situation. It can be seen at all levels: unemployment, gross domestic product, income levels, and quality of life, to name a few. Patronage and corruption are endemic in Third World countries, but they also appear endemic in southern Italy. Indeed several studies have been done on patron-clientelism using this region as a case study. Changes have taken place, however, and the South no longer appears as isolated as it once was. Ultimately, growing appreciation of these divisions will help to ameliorate them and eventually, perhaps, overcome them.

Conclusion

Italy appears to be a political system consumed with paradox—a system that has experienced continuity in the postwar period despite crises that have often threatened to plunge it into disintegration and chaos. Two authors, Spotts and Weiser, have argued that despite the crises that plague the system, it still manages to move. They borrow the description from Galileo who of course pointed out that the earth does not stand still, but revolves around the sun, announcing "***Eppur si muove***" (But it does move). As we have seen, politics in Italy does not stand still. In the space of more than forty years, the Italians have moved a great deal—from the position of "sick man of Europe" to the world's fifth richest industrial country. This is no mean achievement for a country plagued by grave internal threats and challenges.

This is a nation-state where terrorism raged in the 1970s, with ideological warfare and discontent expressed in often violent outcomes. The kidnapping and brutal murders of politicians and judges like Aldo Moro, who worked for compromise within the system, produced and reinforced a bitterness in politics that continues and is underlined by the importance of the Mafia. Having dealt with the challenge of terrorism, Italy is still faced with the threat that this organization poses to the liberal democratic state. With a highly secretive network and code of honor based upon family ties, it clearly exerts tremendous influence in government, business, and society. The murder of two major anti-Mafia judges in June and July 1992 illustrates the problems the Italian state still has in defeating this threat. As one European Community official stated in the aftermath of the bombings, "It showed the emperor really has no clothes," meaning that the Mafia can and does act with impunity. The corruption scandal involving political elites noted in the section on political culture suggests that this phenomenon is not an aberrant one; indeed it follows from a long and violent historical tradition. If we were to consider whether the Mafia represents a form of continuity in Italian politics, then we would have to answer in the affirmative. We would qualify that answer by arguing that this type of continuity is particularly dangerous because it poses a threat to the idea and practice of liberal democracy in the Italian republic in the postwar period. The existence of the Mafia suggests that there is an alternative government, an invisible one which we cannot measure or quantify but which exerts a highly insidious influence anyway. Secret networks, privileges, and patronage; methods of fear, blackmail, extortion, and the use of threats and favors in the end can only serve to undermine, not reinforce, liberal democracy in Italy.

Italy has many other problems to deal with: a distrust of the state and its institutions as a result of political alienation is a disturbing facet of political life. One should remember that, like Germany, Italy is a relatively new democracy. It does not have the long tradition of constitutional continuity and political stability of the United Kingdom. The influence of the Mafia in politics remains a testament to this fact. In addition, Italy still retains a sophisticated underground economy in which thousands of small businesses pay no taxes, have no official records, and produce income that is not calculated into statistics such as GDP or GNP. Some figures put this black economy at 25 to 30 percent of Italy's total GDP. Many economists can only estimate such activity but argue that it has powered economic growth in a highly substantive way. It is factored into the calculation that Italy is the fifth-richest industrial power. There still remain deep divisions between the southern region known as the mezzogiorno and the rich industrial north, and the strong emergence of regional parties in the 1992 election attests to the growing influence of regional politics in the Italian political system. And as we have seen, the immigration question has clearly spilled over in the light of the breakdown of the Eastern European Communist regimes.

Italy may invite hyperbole, it may appear monumental, and its politics may seem a chaotic, unmitigated fight to the finish, as LaPalombara suggests at the beginning of this chapter, but Italy has also developed a real resiliency in response to the crises it has encountered. It has become adept at weathering and dealing with crises that have threatened to overwhelm it. If paradox is at the heart of Italian politics, then many Italians seem content to live within that state of paradox. The republic has survived, it has not disintegrated, and this in itself provides continuity amidst discontinuity.

Key Terms and Concepts

Each term appears in the text in boldface type.

Albanian boat people
Cassa Per il Mezzogiorno
Commedia del l'arte
Eppur si muove
Friends of the friends
Immigrati extracommunitari
Lottizzazione (allotment)
Mafia
Mezzogiorno
Moro

Movimento Sociale Italiano
   (MSI)
Mussolini
'Ndrangheta
Patron-clientelism
Partitocrazia
Red Brigade
Risorgimento
Sardinian tariff
Tangenti

6

The European Community: Beyond the Nation-State

Historical Overview

> Europe has never existed. It is not the addition of national sovereignties in conclave which creates an entity. One must genuinely create Europe.—Jean Monnet[1]

Most people think that the idea of European unification is a relatively modern phenomenon. In particular the period of the 1980s and 1990s has seen a major outpouring of literature on Europe, the European Economic Community (EEC), prospects concerning the economic union of 1992, and the implications of a political union. Terms like *"Europe des Patries,"* a **"United States of Europe,"** and "federal Europe" have been widely used and abused in journals, newspapers, books, and the mass media as a whole. The idea of a united Europe, however, has been around since the first century A.D.

In the first two centuries A.D., the Roman Empire extended to all societies in North Africa, Asia Minor, and Europe that bordered on the Mediterranean. By A.D. 800 the Emperor Charlemagne ruled over most of Western Christendom, but it was not until the beginning of the twelfth century that we see the attempted extension of European control in the spreading of ideas.

At the beginning of this century, Saint-Gilles invaded Turkish territory in an effort to rescue a fellow Christian crusader. The crusaders were slaughtered by the Turkish Muslims (except for Saint-Gilles, who managed to escape). It was an instructive episode in European history; the crusades were a primitive effort to construct a united European foreign policy based on shared Western values at the time (predominantly white and Christian). They were inevitably a failure. Of course, Europe was much more divided in this period than the present time. And the problem stemmed from a lack of ability to define their external enemy; the Muslims in the East were the obvious choice; the difficulty was that the white Christian Europeans were too busy fighting and murdering each other to construct a unified policy. Territory, religion, and the spoils of war kept Europe more divided and disunited than coherent and organized, and so the Ottoman Empire could count on a divided and fragmented enemy. The Ottoman Empire had achieved a higher degree of religious coherence, military capability, and effective organization of society than its counterpart in Western Europe. It was not until the end of the seventeenth century, 1683 to be precise, when the Ottoman rulers decided to march on Vienna, that the Europeans achieved partial unity. The Austrians, Poles, and Germans managed to repel the attack and send the Turkish armies back. A common agreement that Turkey had effectively no place in Christian Europe emerged after this period. This consensus still prevails among Western European members of the **European Community (EC)** more than three hundred years later.

The idea of European unification was still a long way off. But it was getting closer, and in particular the transition from feudal monarchic regimes to nation-states helped the process along. Britain first, France, Germany, and Italy later—all began to bear some resemblance to the modern nation-state. In 1814, Henri de St. Simon stressed the advantages of a united Europe in his work, *On the Organisation of European Society, or on the Need to Bring the Peoples of Europe in a Single Body Politic While Conserving the National Independence of Each of Them*. The rise of nationalism no doubt exacerbated internal divisions and tensions between European countries, but it did provide a very basic common point of agreement. That was that Europe had a special role in spreading "Western civilization" through the colonization of other (usually poor, underdeveloped) societies. When not fighting each other they could be free to conquer, exploit, and control the rest of the globe. The "Age of Empire," with its need to expand territorial boundaries, was a direct consequence of the rise of the nation-state and the need to find new markets for domestic consumption.

Some notable attempts to impose a unity among European states were pursued by Napoleon and Hitler. Napoleon was interested in a united continent under French rule in the nineteenth century; in 1810 his empire stretched from Spain in the west to the borders of Russia and the Ottoman Empire in the east. Hitler, of course, tried to subjugate the continent under the fascist dictatorship of the German Third Reich in the late 1930s and early 1940s. He succeeded in extending the boundaries of Germany to include large sections of Russia, the Scandinavian countries, and regions of southern Europe. Both attempts to unify through military conquest failed in their objectives and were succeeded by attempts to achieve unity in one form or another by peaceful methods involving consent and cooperation.

After the First World War the development of a pan-European movement found expression in calls for a "United States of Europe" by the Austrian leader of the movement, Count Coudenhove Kalergi. He argued that the rationale for this objective was based on the struggle of the Swiss to unite in 1648, the foundation of a unified Germany in 1871, but more than these, in the achievement of independence for the United States of America in 1783. These ideas were given a significant boost when on September 29, 1929, the French foreign minister, Aristide Briand, called for the creation of a European Union within the framework of the League of Nations. Such a proposal, it was argued, would create closer cooperation among European societies while maintaining national sovereignty; the failure to unite Europe would probably result in another war. (Nine years later Hitler marched into Poland and the Second World War began.)[2] Briand followed this up with a memorandum on May 17, 1930, which made a strong case for the linkage between economics and security, which he regarded as inevitably related to each other. Thus it was necessary to consider an economic union in political terms, with members sharing a common set of political and institutional structures, "a common market."

Unification was desired in order to prevent the outbreak of another "Great" war in Europe. The forces of nationalism and imperialism were still stronger than the forces of unification, however. Fascism in Italy and Germany led to another devastating and disastrous war for Europe, which superseded supranational visions. After 1945, the imperatives of unification were raised again, this time by the British leader Winston Churchill. He argued like Briand for the building of a united Europe. In 1946, in a speech in Zurich, he advocated a "United States of Europe."[3]

After 1945 there were three main factors in the impetus towards union:

1. The internal weakness of Europe in this period after being displaced on the world stage by the rise of two new superpowers, the United States and the Soviet Union.

2. The belief that Europe should never again enter into the disastrous sort of conflict that it had experienced in the previous two wars. Europe as a whole had been the main victim of these conflicts, and the prevailing view was that more strife should be avoided at any cost.
3. The conclusion that closer integration would create the peace that Europe needed to resume its rightful place and would provide mutual benefits for each member of a common European home.

In the early stages there was a great deal of rhetoric regarding ideas of European union. But in the event, the ideas and views of two men, Jean Monnet and Robert Schumann, were to prove crucial in the drive for integration. Monnet, a French civil servant, had been interested in furthering European integration even before the end of the Second World War, when he proposed the merger of French and British governments. Despite support for these ideas, the Monnet initiative failed due to the disinterest of the puppet Vichy Regime, which had reached the stage of complete defeatism in the war against Germany and become subservient to Nazi interests. Later Monnet wrote that peace would not occur in Europe while states still worked on the principle of national sovereignty and urged that the European states should form a federation or "European entity" which would constitute a joint economic union.

After the war the urgency in moving towards union increased. The political and economic reconstruction of Western Europe was undertaken by the United States, which responded to the economic crisis with the Marshall Plan offering crucial financial and economic assistance to aid recovery. When the Soviets rejected the offer and moved to establish control over Eastern Europe, the Cold War was initiated. This move inadvertently accelerated the process of integration.

In 1948 the Congress of Europe met for the first time in an effort to push union a little further. Its recommendations established the **Council of Europe** in 1948 along with some other European associations. In August 1949, the Belgian prime minister, Paul-Henri Spaak, was elected as its leader. Yet the organization failed to live up to its promising start. It had no real legislative powers; recommendations to member states were as much as it could achieve. Meanwhile events began to overtake preparations for integration but subsequently increased the need for it at the same time. The Cold War, the Berlin blockade, and the antagonisms between East and West provided Western Europe with the drive to unify. Jean Monnet (who was to be the founder of the Action Committee for the United States of Europe and was described as the "father of Europe") submitted another plan to establish a common program of coal and steel production under Franco-German auspices. On May 9, 1950, Robert Schumann, the French foreign minister, proposed the creation of the **European Coal and Steel Community (ECSC)** on the principle of supranationalism (that a common institution would be independent of the control of its member states), and this was established in the Treaty of Paris, 1951. Schumann clearly recognized the difference between **supranationalism** and the powers of a full-fledged federal state. While the latter was an ultimate goal, he argued that supranationalism is

> situated at equal distances between, on the one hand, international individualism which considers national sovereignty untouchable and accepts only limited sovereignty in the form of occasional, temporary treaty clauses: and, on the other hand, the federalism of states which are subordinated to a super state with complete territorial sovereignty.[4]

Little did he realize that this issue would become a major bone of contention among the various states in the drive towards European unity nearly forty years later.

The ECSC lived up to the functional role envisaged by its primary architects. Inevitably the aim was to accomplish general political goals in the future; in the immediate term, it was to foster integration within the coal and steel industries of Europe, a move that would ultimately facilitate the political vision of Monnet and Schumann, that of a federal Europe. The aims of the ECSC were fairly ambitious: to set up a common market through a free trade area. However it was provided with enormous powers to achieve such measures. Two new institutions, the High Authority and the Council of Ministers, were to oversee the abolition and prohibition of internal tariff barriers and the establishment of levies on coal and steel production in the various member states.[5]

With the formation of the ECSC, the movement for integration shifted to a higher level. Two new communities followed on its heels: the **European Defense Community (EDC)** in 1952 and the **European Political Community (EPC)** to complement the former. Defense proved to be a stumbling point for European unity, however, particularly around the implications of German participation in a European army. Economic integration in effect was seen as a far less controversial area, and so the defense mechanism was in effect left in the hands of the **North Atlantic Treaty Organization (NATO)**. The consequence of the increased economic emphasis was the signing of the Treaty of Rome in 1957 by France, West Germany, Italy, and the Benelux countries (Belgium, the Netherlands, and Luxembourg). This treaty signalled the advent of the **European Economic Community (EEC)** or **Common Market** and another development, the European Atomic Energy Community (EAEC). The goal of the common market was to secure closer and closer economic union in Europe.

Expansion of the EEC

Despite many countries' initial hesitancy to join the community, it eventually became more and more widely accepted as an attractive option. On January 1, 1973, the United Kingdom finally joined, mainly out of economic necessity, along with Ireland and Denmark. The U.K. route to membership was a difficult one with many problems. France under de Gaulle was specifically hostile to British membership and vetoed the admission of the United Kingdom twice, under both the Conservative government of Harold Macmillan and the Labour government of Harold Wilson. Eight years after Britain's eventual entry, on January 1, 1981, Greece became the tenth member to join. Exactly five years later, in 1986, Spain and Portugal acquired membership, making the community into a Common Market of twelve. The expansion has not only been in terms of members, of course; the community has acquired new resources and increased its population from almost 265 million to 320 million inhabitants.

Recent Events and the Movement toward European Union

During the period 1958–72, the economies of the European Community members grew at a much higher rate than that of the United States. Living standards reached an unprecedented level as the modernization of all members and the application of new technologies accelerated the development of their societies and pushed them towards the postindustrial age. With the oil crisis of 1973, however, this age of plenty came to an end, and Europeans found themselves on the receiving end of recession, inflation, unemployment, and general economic malaise.

To understand the problems and seek solutions, the European Parliament initiated a series of reports and studies drawing on the expertise of business leaders, academics, and governmental officials within the European Community. One of these reports, the Albert-Ball Report, published in 1983, argued that the major problem lay in the fact that the EC had been shortsighted in its approach. Instead of pooling its resources, it had installed other types of barriers to growth. Consumption had preceded investment, and each member had acted as an autonomous unit regardless of the fact that the EC represented a community of supposedly common interests. The report detailed the failure of the EC after 1973 to grow economically in comparison to the United States; with unemployment rising, investment falling, and inflation rising, the community seemed caught in the grip of economic malaise.

It argued that national, individual solutions were not feasible, as the economies of Europe were now increasingly tied to one another; European interdependence, not to mention global interdependence, had already arrived. As the report argued:

> Any country wishing to go it alone in pursuit of growth is bound to lose. Any country which, having put its house in order, agrees to go for growth with the others and according to the rules reflecting the collective interest, is sure to gain by this action.[6]

Other reports increased awareness about the costs of divisions between members of the EC. There were many diverse interests that could not be reconciled under the Common Market, as the obstacles to free trade and the free movement of goods and services had not been achieved with the operation of a customs union. For instance there were widely differing rates of value added tax (VAT); there was a tremendous diversity in national standards of products and technical regulations. The bureaucracy was enmeshed in red tape, which made a great deal of trade costly, and internal borders slowed down the growth of the community with long and again costly delays.

Many of these problems in the EC were summed up in the 1988 European Community report *The Cost of Non-Europe*, by Paolo Cecchini. The conclusion was that the overall cost of maintaining the barriers was roughly 5 percent of the community's GDP, equivalent to £130 billion. The report highlighted the costs of massive delays in border crossings. A comparison of two truck trips of 1,200 kilometers each, one in the United Kingdom and the other between London and Milan, made the differences obvious. The former was accomplished in thirty-six hours, whereas the latter (not counting the time crossing the channel) was completed in fifty-six hours, resulting in a 50 percent difference in the costs of the trips.[7]

These reports and views did not go unheeded within community policy-making circles. The challenge of reducing barriers and integrating the community more fully and efficiently gave rise to a 1985 white paper which proposed the removal of all internal barriers within the community. The "free movement of people, goods, services, and capital" by 1992 would create an economic area not subject to national frontiers. The paper proposed approximately three hundred measures to be set in motion to achieve this end, ranging from removing immigration and passport controls (EC members now have a single European passport) to abolishing national transport controls to fixing minimum standards for goods and services and more. For example, certain British beers which were not available in Germany before 1992 because of national standards will now be available. The 1992 changes mean *free* movement of goods and services rather than *restricted* movement.

The proposals in the white paper were approved by the members of the European Council at a meeting in June 1985. At the end of 1985 the **Single European Act** (SEA) was formulated and, after ratification, it came into force in 1987. The SEA was a crucial development in bringing about the reality of European integration in 1992; it not only laid the groundwork for a full economic union but also provided the basis for the development of a political union with common cooperation in foreign and security policy.

The Legacy of Maastricht

Despite all of the problems and disagreements between the various members over the shape of EC 1992, a major turning point comprised the two European Union Treaties constructed at Maastricht in the second week of December 1991. **Maastricht** was a historic event because it provided the key basis for the union to proceed.

Several major steps in the movement towards political and economic union were achieved at the Maastricht summit. These were:

1. The decision to create a European Central Bank between 1997 and 1999.
2. The adoption of a single currency to eventually replace the national currencies of the nations that are willing to accept it.
3. The special concession to Britain to opt out of monetary union if politically necessary.
4. The decision to create a joint security, defense and foreign policy using the **Western European Union** (with a link to NATO) but without the formation of a common European army. Any major decision would require unanimity.
5. Adoption of a common, cooperative policy on immigration and drugs, utilizing cross-national policing.
6. Extension of EC authority over internal national affairs in areas such as industry, health, education, trade, energy and the environment, tourism and culture, and consumer protection.
7. Harmonization of social policy (inclusive of labor laws) throughout the EC, with the exception of Britain.

8. The award to the European Parliament of more authority to determine some aspects of EC legislation and to provide more money for underdeveloped members of the EC, such as Spain, Greece, Portugal, and Ireland.

Many of these issues were contested enthusiastically by such "reluctant Europeans" as the British. Britain was the stumbling block in many ways to European Union; it had great difficulty in acceding to any dilution of sovereignty and in applying a European social policy to the United Kingdom. Maastricht provided the go-ahead for a social-policy pact without British participation. The United Kingdom is totally exempted from the Protocol on Social Policy and its accompanying rules, and this is possible because the social-policy agreement will work outside of the formal EC treaty. For the formation of legislation in this area, the EC Commission will make a series of proposals, and thereafter the Council of Ministers will vote by either unanimity or a weighted majority, depending on the specific measure, as is usual by EC procedure. In turn, weighted majority voting rules will be adjusted to account for the absence of the United Kingdom. One of the reasons that Britain was so adamantly opposed to this measure and wanted exemption was that major changes in social policy had been initiated during Margaret Thatcher's term in office: the power of trade unions and their ability to strike were reduced significantly. As John Major, her successor, who was broadly responsible for giving Britain a more moderate image in the EC, argued, this exemption would probably give the United Kingdom a more competitive edge, attracting more foreign investment. He cited the statistic that Britain had reduced the number of workdays lost to strikes from 29 million in 1979 to 2 million in 1990.[8]

Conclusion

The long history of European integration and the processes, events, and landmarks that are part and parcel of this history have been essentially a stop-and-go effort. We have seen by tracing briefly the major points of interest along the way that Europe has invested a large amount of effort and trouble in such a venture, one that many think is culminating in some specific end or final scenario. This is far from the truth, however, for integration is essentially an ongoing development with hiccups and periods of frustration and tension between the various nations involved. The idea that Europe is transforming smoothly into a single political and economic entity is by and large a convenient myth used for political purposes of one sort or another.

For instance, no sooner were the Maastricht treaties on political and economic union signed when they appeared to have stalled. In the beginning of 1992, there were few initiatives emanating from Europe on the General Agreement on Tariffs and Trade (GATT) talks. Farm policy appeared incapable of reform, and even ratification of the actual treaties appeared problematic for certain states such as Denmark, which decisively rejected them in a referendum.

The attainment of a "United States of Europe" seems difficult in an age when many states are undergoing disintegration (such as the ex–Soviet Union). To argue that the idea and reality of European union is fraught with inherent difficulties would be an understatement on many different levels.

However, at the same time, it is clear that there is an underlying process, which has gathered more and more momentum in recent years, that points to a strengthening and clearly deliberate movement toward a much more unified Europe. While divisions become exacerbated and tensions flare between nations because of such a movement toward union, it is also apparent that integration has played a special role in making Europeans and their leaders more aware of what they share in common rather than how they differ from one another. And this should be borne in mind when one is assessing some of the more specific contemporary problems of this European question.

Problems with Economic Union

There have been many problems in the European Community over economic matters, and before we discuss the details of the immediate economic union of 1992, it is helpful to understand some of its previous and still present economic issues.

The idea of the **European Monetary Union (EMU)** derives from a supra-national approach towards policy making in the EC, one rooted in the internal market and the increasingly close coordination of economic policies. Economic and monetary power would in effect be transferred to the main seats of the EC's institutions in Brussels, Luxembourg, and Strasbourg.

It is hoped that EMU and the EC's project 1992 will produce various worthwhile economic changes including:

1. The removal of thousands of barriers to trade that exist within the EC, including delays in frontiers, red tape and paperwork jams, and restrictions in freight hauling.
2. More freedom of capital flows so that money can circulate freely among the twelve members.

3. Allowing European workers and labor to practice trades and professions anywhere in the community.
4. Bringing a greater uniformity and standardization to various countries' valued added taxes and excise duties.

Removing Barriers to Trade

There have been tremendous changes in the ideas and practice behind the movement of goods and services in the European community. The rules have changed dramatically in a very short space of time. In 1983, the European Commission was in the process of assessing 770 different cases of protectionist blocking of the flow of goods across the internal borders of the EC. Similarly, in the same year, the German chambers of commerce were suggesting that tariffs on goods should be installed among member states.[9] Ten years later, in 1993, dramatic differences will be in force. Trucks or lorries carrying cargo across the borders between EC members will not have to show papers or documents of any kind. A vast majority of goods will be sold on a cross-national basis under European regulations without recourse to internal national standards. Customs controls at internal European frontier posts will be removed, and national tax collection systems will be responsible for gathering revenues. Clearly one of the main beneficiaries is the consumer who desires choice:

> The man in the street will be able to buy all that he could reasonably need—with the glaring exception of motor cars—anywhere in Europe, paying the local taxes and duties and carrying his buys across frontiers with no more ado.[10]

Governments have introduced a minimum rate of 15 percent value added tax. Removing frontier controls will make delay at customs posts a thing of the past, and resources can be put to more useful tasks than the bureaucratic administration of trade.

In the service industries, the sectors that have most successfully fulfilled criteria laid down by the European project 1992 are the banking and road transport sectors. Previously, as we have seen, such businesses were separated into national markets with barriers to outside competition. On January 1, 1993, however, banks could start up branches in any other member country of the EC. Road transport, which at the beginning of the 1980s was under a bureaucratic cloud of quotas and national permits, will be free to move goods across the EC without restrictions. Insurance, telecommunications, and airlines still have some problems, but just ten years ago such movement would have seemed unthinkable. Again, the ultimate aim in lifting barriers to competition in areas such as retail banking and insurance is to force down the costs of financial services, including the costs of borrowing throughout the EC.

In terms of finance and capital movement, by the beginning of the 1980s there were exchange controls in place throughout the EC. Only Greece and Portugal (two of the "southern" members of the EC) retain these controls at present. And they have promised to give them up by 1995. Maastricht in a formal sense prohibits such controls; internally and externally the EC allows, therefore, for the free movement and flow of capital.

A Common Agriculture?

One of the major issues that has plagued the EC from inception has been the question of the budget and in particular the problem of the **Common Agricultural Policy (CAP)**, which accounts for the largest slice of the community resources. Some authors go so far as to argue that this is already a supranational element in the EC. At least three different times this issue has occasioned a situation of crisis over the net contributions made by the United Kingdom, which is similar to Germany in that it pays the EC far more than it receives for agricultural subsidies, inevitably subsidizing other European farmers. Ireland, for instance, receives six times the subsidies that it contributes to the EC—perhaps one reason for its acceptance of the Maastricht treaty in a referendum in comparison to the Danish rejection in 1992. Several calls have been made for the revision of the CAP, which has a policy of subsidizing production of agricultural commodities and then is required to pay to store the unsold, overproduced surpluses of butter, milk powder, cereals, and wine. This policy has increased agricultural costs, giving rise to the often noted metaphor of mountains of butter and lakes of wine as a description of the problem. The governments that endorse this policy are doing so in order to appease their own farmers, who provide crucial political support. This is especially so in France, Italy, Germany, and Ireland, where reliance on these constituents has rendered policymakers unwilling to accept a less costly system of price supports. France does particularly well out of the CAP, while the United Kingdom does not; the complaint that Britain did not get its fair returns from its contribution to the community budget resulted in Margaret Thatcher's demanding Britain's "money back" in 1979. The question of whether EC money should flow to the poorer members is also an issue: Should the richer societies of the EC transfer community resources to their poorer cousins in the south, such as Spain, Portugal, and Greece? The cost of the CAP is enormous. To fix EC prices in 1989 required 42 billion pounds sterling. The poor in Europe were and are paying for this policy disproportionately. One source pointed out that in 1989, the poorest 25 percent of households spent 29 percent of their disposable income on food, in contrast to the top 25 percent, who spent only 14 percent on foodstuffs. Similarly it was pointed out that the rich Germans spent only 14 percent, whereas the poor Greeks were contributing 36 percent.[11]

Since 1984 the EC has tried to work towards CAP reform, the main objective being reducing surpluses and therefore controlling and diminishing costs. Guaranteed prices have fallen in real value, and at the same time production quotas and ceilings have been enforced on farmers in order to reduce the wasted surplus and the money spent on storage. In 1991, for instance, ten out of the twelve members wanted to break out of the cash limit that restricted the CAP.

In terms of the community's budget, the CAP is clearly disproportionate; 60 percent of the budget is for agriculture. This sector accounted for 34 billion **European Currency Units (ECU)** out of a total of 64 billion in the 1993 draft budget, and half of the budgetary cost simply goes for storing and disposing of the surplus food. In 1987, this resource loss roughly equalled the annual spending on regional and social policy.[12]

Agriculture, not surprisingly, turned out to be one of the main items blocking the stalled GATT negotiations in the 1980s and early 1990s. Subsidies of EC exports, the critics maintained, were one of the main bones of contention. As a result, a new set of negotiations for CAP reforms was formulated between June 1991 and May 1992, and set in motion in July 1992. The criteria for reform were designed to produce a major reduction in the price of agricultural products and compensation for the consequent reduction in farming income. Specifically there were reductions in the overall quotas for milk (the volume of production for which farmers can obtain price supports) and encouragement for other farmers to take early retirements, among other measures. However, it remains to be seen whether such measures will really make a difference in the overall problem of agriculture in the EC, a problem which creates inequality of treatment for farmers and consumers not only in Europe but also in large parts of the underdeveloped world.

The EMU and ECU

The European Monetary Union (EMU) is an integral part of the plan for a genuine common market of goods and services. The EMU's ultimate purpose is to see most (if not all) of the community members give up their national currency and use instead a single European currency (known as the ECU). Proponents of this scheme argue that different national currencies are in themselves effective barriers and handicaps to trade and competition. In the mid-1980s, the idea of a European currency would have been easily dismissed as naive and idealistic; now its detractors are on the defensive as it has seemed more and more an inevitable part of the increasing integration of the EC.

Such trends are in line with the dramatic growth in trade on a global scale since 1945 and the corresponding increase in intraregional trade within the EC. And the fact that trade has increased relative to output has served as an important stimulus. In the 1960s, for instance, 45 percent of West German trade was with the other eleven members of the European Community; by the end of the 1980s this percentage had increased to 62 percent.[13] Furthermore such trends seem to suggest that, with the addition of new members, intraregional trade figures increase and thus promote integration—the classic case of spillover. In this line of thought, as economies converge the need for a common monetary unit and currency becomes apparent. And in March 1979, the first step in this process was embarked upon when the EC established the European Monetary System (EMS). The intention was to create a mechanism of stability in Europe in order to regulate exchange rates. Two goals were specifically aimed for: the promotion of intraregional trade in Europe and the reduction of inflation, a problem that had plagued all European governments after the collapse of the Bretton Woods fixed currency system and the oil shocks of the 1970s.

In practice the EMS is fairly complex. European governments are supposed to limit the movement of their currencies against each other within certain boundaries through the **Exchange Rate Mechanism (ERM)**. It is a way of enforcing discipline among the different economies. And in addition to stabilizing currencies, inflation rates are pushed downwards across the board toward the lowest common denominator (in the postwar period this would be the German standard). It was a flexible system that allowed, however, for some leeway and possible devaluation of a currency. (Such a combination finally prompted the United Kingdom to join the ERM in 1990.) The early results were significant. The eight members of the EC that had enrolled in the program saw average inflation fall from 12 percent in

1979 to less than 3 percent in the late 1980s, just ten years later. Moreover, differences between countries' individual inflation rates narrowed.

The idea of a single market does not go far enough, according to "Euro-optimists"; a single currency would be much more effective. Transaction costs involved in the conversion of currencies would be drastically reduced. Less resources would be necessary to deal with accounting and treasury management. Consumers would benefit as travelers would have more money to spend with less going to middlemen. The EC commission has estimated that such gains would account for around 0.4 percent of the EC's GDP—a substantial sum. Economic risk would also be dramatically reduced if European business structures with a single currency would fix intra-European exchange rates once and for all. This in turn would provide government and business with a more stable and secure environment. The cost of capital could be reduced, and in turn investment and output would consequently rise (perhaps as much as 10 percent). One argument put many of these pro-EMU positions in perspective:

> A common, non-inflationary money would be a huge asset to an expanding Community. It would complement the EC's framework of commercial law, and recreate the conditions of the late 19th century, when wealth creating investment flowed so generously relative to the GNP's of the time. This happened because investors could have confidence in the denomination and in the political security of their business risks. The gold standard took care of the first; the colonial system, the second. Monetary union and the rules of the EC could now be their worthier successors across all of Europe.[14]

Regarding these schemes, pessimists argue that national governments would be disallowed the "privilege" of choosing their own inflation rate (again seen by some to be a loss of sovereignty). Instead, one monetary policy and the inflation rate would apply cross-nationally. For some the problem is, Exactly who would be running such an arrangement? The German Bundesbank has, for instance, been much touted as the model for a European Bank. This, however, has caused problems, particularly with the British authorities, and it is also a problem given the high cost of German reunification, which in 1992 had produced a budget deficit and inflation rate of nearly 5 percent. Pessimists and detractors also argue that when national governments give away the right to devalue their currency they lose an important policy instrument. If they have to resort to other mechanisms to absorb economic shocks, such as reducing or restraining wages, a recession might follow. However, devaluation is a poor tool of policy. By reducing real wages in an effort to decrease costs, it can lead to even higher inflation.

One of America's most respected economists has gone further in arguing the case against the EMU. He argues that the EMU is basically sought by those who argue in favor of a political union in Europe and who see the EMU as strengthening this position. However, he points out that such a move may not benefit Europe economically: "Monetary union is not needed to achieve the advantages of a free trade zone. On the contrary an artificially contrived economic and monetary union might actually reduce the volume of trade among the member countries and would almost certainly increase the average level of unemployment over time."[15] The argument is made here that Europe should abandon the EMU because a single currency would cause economic damage and the political benefits of increased integration and closer union would fail to outweigh the economic costs of the EMU. In terms of a disciplined fiscal policy, it seems clear that all the EC countries except the United Kingdom are in favor of fiscal rules and penalties. But once the exchange rates were fixed, the main punishment against public overborrowing—a run on the currency—would disappear. One national government's excess would tend to increase interest rates across the board. The argument is made that rules should be introduced to prevent such problems. The question remains, How is the best way to achieve this? Under fiscal discipline, finance ministers may lose control over budget deficits, but they will be able to tell other countries how big their deficits should be. As one article put it, the countries that use the common currency will depend on which "survive a macroeconomic fitness regime designed by the martinets of the Bundesbank."[16]

The EMU is certainly an elaborate piece of work; the program accepted in 1992 will put into place a common European currency by the end of the century. The third and final phase of the EMU will start in 1997 and gradually provide a single currency to those of its members deemed ready. The United Kingdom, however, has decided to opt out of the plans for a single European currency as well as common social regulations.

Conclusion

Despite its early foundations, the real "common market" was not emphasized until 1968, when a customs union took shape. A customs union has a common external tariff and no internal customs. In theory, barriers were to be dropped at this point; however nontariff types of barriers, such as regulations over technical standards, have always stood in the way of putting the ideal into practice. Furthermore this union was supposed to allow for the free movement of workers, but again in practice the national differences in commercial law served as an obstacle. And clearly, the nations of Europe by the early 1980s were still some way from establishing a common system of commercial law that allowed for freedom of movement of goods, services, capital and labor within the EC.

As was noted, the Common Agricultural Policy (CAP), intended to provide fair measures for farmers in stabilizing markets, only served to promote overproduction, metaphorically characterized as "lakes of wine" and "mountains of butter," causing even higher prices for consumers. Attempted reforms in 1988 again met with resistance from nations such as France who clearly benefit disproportionately from CAP.

In 1987, the more ambitious task of fully implementing a single European market was embarked upon as national governments consented to consciously promote a program that would allow free movement of capital, goods, services, and people. It was a design for a Europe free of the complex regulations that had only served to hinder the EC's development. To this end a common bank and currency were proposed to supplement the European monetary system established in 1979 to promote currency stability and prevent large-scale fluctuations. In October 1990, the United Kingdom finally agreed to join the Exchange Rate Mechanism, signaling the end of major opposition to control over currency.

Increasingly large-scale European economic policy will be controlled and coordinated in meetings of EC finance ministers. In the end, despite the problems we have seen, the idea of European economic union has a certain dynamic of its own given the macro-level trends towards trade blocs around the world—in North America and the Asia-Pacific region, for instance. And only time will tell what kind of impact such a grouping of advanced industrialized nations will have on the global economy.

Political Integration: A Federal Europe?

Often the image of Europe presented in the media in the late 1980s and early 1990s gave the impression that Europe had no difficulties— that Europe was just heading unproblematically towards European union and political integration.[17] Many of these illusions were shattered with the breakdown of the Soviet Union and the Eastern bloc, with the problems of cooperation over the Gulf crisis in 1990–91, with the crisis in the former Yugoslavia, and with the difficulties created by immigration and racial tensions in European capitals. It should be borne in mind that the EC is to some extent a "political compromise which stems from strong differences of opinion about just what form the European idea should take—and specifically over the place of the nation state in an integrated Europe."[18] There is another problem, however, a specifically political one that poses a dilemma for Europe, and that stems from the divergence in views as to what Europe should be. One view sees Europe as a federal entity with a common currency, social arrangements, and economic structure as well as common political and defense institutions. The other view sees Europe as a loose but practical confederation of individual nation-states, A *Europe des Patries*. Or more bluntly, the differences are exemplified by the respective visions of the erstwhile commissioner of the EC, Jacques Delors, and of the ex–British prime minister, Margaret Thatcher. That is, if there was a political compromise over what shape the EC and its institutions and policies should take, then clearly that compromise has been eroded in recent years and developed into a debate that has divided and even polarized crucial players in the European Community.

A Europe des Patries? Thatcher's Case against Federalism

When academics, journalists, politicians, and others concerned with the agenda facing Europe discuss the topic of unification, one of the most pressing questions is, Does Europe have a choice? Is there an alternative to the proposed "United States of Europe"? For one politician in the 1980s the answer was quite clear—that is, Europe did have a choice and should pursue the alternative to a federal solution.

The alternative was of course the conception of Margaret Thatcher, the British prime minister between 1979 and 1991. It was Thatcher who most explicitly outlined the case for an alternative to the apparent steamroller of integration that was occurring throughout Europe. Her vision of the Continent ruled out a United States of Europe and instead argued for a European Community rooted in the active cooperation between independent sovereign states. These views were explicitly stated in a now-famous speech in Bruges, Belgium, in September 1988. Her views on European union were clearly articulated:

> Willing and active co-operation between independent sovereign states is the best way to build a successful European Community. To try to suppress nationhood and concentrate power at the centre of a European

218

conglomerate would be highly damaging and would jeopardise the objectives we seek to achieve. Europe will be stronger precisely because it has France as France, Spain as Spain, Britain as Britain, each with its own customs, traditions and identity. It would be folly to try to fit them into some sort of identikit European personality.[19]

Thatcher was clearly worried by the arrival of a supranational state in which national **sovereignty** would be lost and the U.K.'s governmental institutions directed by bodies outside of territorial boundaries. For Britain to give up its parliamentary supremacy would entail the loss of a major part of the identity of the British people, and therefore the idea is anathema to a nationalist like Thatcher. In this view, power should not be centralized in Brussels, nor should bureaucratic decisions be taken far from British territory that have a political impact on Britain. The essence of this argument is that the European Community is fine and suitable to the goal of integrating economies but should not interfere in the internal politics of member states.

There is agreement between Thatcher's position and the one taken by Charles de Gaulle. The concept of a *Europe des Patries* in which Europe is composed of different individual nation-states that working together without diluting or compromising their independence and sovereignty was also the perspective of the French president. Nicholas Ridley, former British cabinet minister, also warned of the dangers of **federalism** in terms of damaging the nation's identity. He argued that to try to give up or destroy the sense of purpose and loyalty that binds people to their individual nation "would only weaken the cohesion of society, not . . . strengthen it. It would negate so much that is good in British life: our political stability, our effective democracy, our traditions and ceremony, and our independent role in foreign policy." And in line with that he is against the idea of a single currency and a common European monetary system, which federalists support; he cites British economist John Maynard Keynes's argument that "whoever controls the currency controls the government."[19] And it is clearly the Germans, with their strong economy and low inflation, who will eventually come to control the economy in a federal Europe, as far as Ridley is concerned—an event he believes should be avoided at all costs.[20]

Critics of Thatcher argued that the alternative to a federal union could lead to dangerous nationalism and xenophobic tendencies. In such a situation, a reunified Germany would predominate, not necessarily in a threatening repeat of the past but certainly economically, and this would be enough to cause resentment from neighboring countries. Such a predominance could be avoided, muted, or ameliorated within a common federal structure in which each member would have a stake.

For Thatcher there was no real evidence that most Europeans were ready to commit themselves to a federal United States of Europe. As a federation such an entity would have a common army, a common foreign policy, and a central government from which the individual state could not reclaim power once ceded. British suspicions of federalism reflected fears that sovereignty would be ceded in such a structure: "Britain equates sovereignty with Westminster, and has built its national identity on an historical antagonism towards France. No wonder that Britain pales at federalism with a French flavour," explained one commentator.[21] The fear that outsiders such as the French and the Germans might determine key aspects of British policy was and is clearly too much for the antifederalists. Thatcher, the bete noire of the EC, and her supporters stoutly opposed the vision of the main proponent of federalism at the time, the European president, Jacques Delors.

A Federal Europe: The Case of Jacques Delors

Supporting and encouraging the drive for a federal Europe, Jacques Delors has presented the profederal movement clearly and passionately in the 1980s and 1990s. Delors was the president of the European commission in this period of hectic debate over European union and is the intellectual heir to Jean Monnet's vision of a federal Europe that would quell nationalist passions. Thatcher was responding in her Bruges speech to a speech he had made in July 1988, in which he declared that, because of the Single European Act of 1987, within ten years as much as 80 percent of economic legislation and perhaps the same amount of social legislation would emanate from the community.

For Delors, monetary union inevitably entails the transfer of major economic functions from one arena to another, from the national to the supranational. A single currency would be controlled by a European Community federal bank, not by national governments; but even so, individual states would exercise considerable powers, such as internal revenue collection. Interestingly enough, the idea of basing federalism on a single European market would allow for some transfer of wealth from the richer to the poorer EC countries, and thus federalism would provide an equalizing function.

The official English-language guide to the topic, *European Unification: The Origins and Growth of the European Community* (1990), describes the federalist approach as the "right" way to proceed in unifying Europe:

> The federalist approach, on the other hand, aims to dissolve the traditional distinctions between nation states. The outdated notion of inviolable and indivisible national sovereignty gives way to the view that the imperfections of social and international coexistence, the specific shortcomings of the nation state system, and the dangers of the predominance of one state over others (so frequent a phenomenon in European history) can only be overcome by individual states pooling their sovereignty under a supranational community. The result is a European federation in which the common destiny of its peoples—still retaining their individual identities—is guided, and their future assured, by common (federal) authorities.[22]

Supporters of Delors and the concept of a supranational European federalism argued that the solution to xenophobia and destructive nationalism in Europe was a genuinely supranational state. Frontier quarrels would be prevented if frontiers were irrelevant, wrote political scientist David Marquand.[23] Furthermore federalists would not ask that national sovereignty be simply given up overnight, as the likes of Margaret Thatcher would argue is the case:

> The European Community is a product of this federalist approach, though in a somewhat modified form owing to the Member states' reluctance simply to abandon altogether their sovereignty [sic] and the old nation state structure which they had only just regained and consolidated after the Second World War in favour of a European federation. Once again a compromise had to be found which, without necessarily establishing a federal structure, would provide more than mere cooperation along confederal lines. The solution, both brilliant and simple, was to seek to bridge the gap between national autonomy and European federation in a gradual process. Rather than relinquish sovereignty overnight, the Member states were asked merely to abandon the dogma of indivisibility.[24]

Clearly the Delors version of federalism is in line with the idea of **subsidiarity**, which has emerged as an important counterpoint to the antifederalists' rhetoric. Subsidiarity specifically refers to leaving decisions to the most appropriate level of government in Europe or the one that is best suited to deal with certain issues in economic and social life. It reflects the conclusion that Delors is not as ambitious a federalist as his opponents claim. In a recent interview, he categorically stated, "It is not our job to investigate every stone on the beach in the community to see whether they are clean enough. . . . We must lay down some general environmental principles in these areas and leave the national states to implement the details in good faith."[25]

In this sense then, the institutions of the community should in turn only be vested with the power to decide matters that they are best equipped to decide.

Conclusion

In 1951, when Ernest Bevin, the British foreign secretary, was asked about his future vision of Europe, his reply was succinct: "To be able to take a ticket at Victoria Station and go anywhere I damn well please," he answered. With the removal of internal frontier controls in 1992 and the 1985 introduction of a European passport to replace the national version, Bevin's wishes will be greatly facilitated. Of course the federalist version of a "Europe without frontiers" has been modified by the reluctance of nations to cede political sovereignty to supranational institutions. Thatcher's alternative, as we have seen, is designed to provide for a loose federation of states, a *Europe des Patries*. Others have claimed that the issue of sovereignty is a problematic one; in a world of increasing economic interdependence, can any nation claim to be truly sovereign? The issue is difficult, to say the least. The camp of Jacques Delors is firmly adamant that federalism is not about giving up sovereignty; the principle of subsidiarity works as a counterpoint against nation-states' giving up their privileged rights. Britain anyway has usually been seen as the anomaly in European politics, outside the mainstream of European history and politics, joining the EC late and the ERM even later.

There is an element of continuity in the development of ideas of federalism from Monnet and Schuman to Delors in the 1990s. All desire a strong European union in which the threat of war and insecurity will be removed on a permanent basis. In this sense it would be useful for the community in time to extend its arms to include Eastern Europe in a federal arrangement. The appeal of federalism and integration lies, not in an exclusive, inflexible club, but in a desire for genuine supranationalism. Recently it has become commonplace to argue that Warsaw, Prague, and Budapest are as essentially European as Paris, Bonn, and Rome. With the dissolution of the Soviet empire, the time is ripe to envisage plans to deal with these important changes. In this sense the EC should seek to be federal in an inclusive, not exclusive, manner. Thatcher is only half right when she caricatures federalism, as she did in speeches in Bruges, Belgium, and Aspen, Colorado, in the late 1980s, arguing that it provides for a homogeneous Europe. To a large extent the federal solution is designed to create organizations that allow diverse cultures, languages, and religions to coexist harmoniously. It is an integral aim of the federal solution to accommodate diversity, not suppress it.

European Security: Defense Issues

One of the most pressing problems and controversial issues within the European Community has surfaced over the problem of European defense. It is instructive that, as the institutions of European security were settled on after the Second World War in an atmosphere of Cold War tensions and ideological rivalries between East and West, so too are the institutions of European security being reevaluated and settled on in the atmosphere of the dissipation of the Cold War, largely as a result of the changes in the Soviet Union under Gorbachev in the late 1980s and early 1990s. The argument is that much of the North Atlantic Treaty Organization (NATO), which was set up to counter the Warsaw Pact, has lost its purpose as the enemy has disappeared. The need to reinvent a new "enemy" therefore is a priority of European defense institutions, some of which now appear as historical anachronisms. At the height of the Gulf crisis in 1990–91, the Belgian foreign minister, Mark Eysens, commented that the image of the EC was that of "an economic giant, a political pygmy, and a military larva."[26]

It is also interesting that to some extent the issue of security is a stumbling block to European integration, in much the same way that it was a difficulty in the 1950s when the French National Assembly refused to ratify the European Defense Community initiative that provided for the integration of a common European army because of fears of German rearmament. The debate continues, and it is an important one because it lies in the crucial area of security and political cooperation.

Within the initial months of the Gulf crisis, for instance, several European countries were already moving towards negotiations that would allow the EC a defense and security policy for the first time in history. Italy's foreign minister, Gianni de Michelis, had already pressed a plan for the EC to take over the defense coordination role of the WEU, suggesting that member states should make specific commitments to coordinate defense policies and guarantee mutual security. France and Germany are also interested in creating a more tightly integrated Europe with regard to security concerns. The dissenter in this regard is Britain, which seeks to maintain its distance over the issue of a common European defense policy. Douglas Hurd, the British foreign secretary, has stated, "For us NATO will remain the prime forum for collective security policy."[27]

It is clear that there is a potential division developing between, on the one hand, the EC and, on the other, NATO over the security issues. In September 1990, there were reports of U.S. officials pointing out that the Europeans did not want to be committed by the military actions of the United States. NATO Secretary-General Manfred Woerner has stated publicly that the EC should not attempt to usurp or overtake the alliance's military role. The secretary general of the WEU countered this view by arguing that the crisis had shown that "for want of a foreign and security policy, there is a genuine risk of the community becoming a spectator on the sidelines of history." The differences on what to do and how to do it suggest that the two groupings may be on a collision course.

When analyzing the response of the EC in this light, we have to be aware of the context. At the most basic level the community is not a federation because of the simple fact that federations prohibit individual member states from running their own foreign policy. Despite the federalization of a great deal of economic policy, foreign relations still remain in the hands of the members. The Political Cooperation body, for instance, which attempts to coordinate the views of twelve foreign ministries, tends to operate outside of the institutions of the EC, having virtually no power because decisions at present have to be unanimous. Roland Dumas, the French foreign minister, was interested in establishing a European Council consisting of all the foreign ministers, but such a body would be weak without some system of majority voting.

The crisis in the Gulf has stimulated new thinking about the role of the European Community in world affairs, particularly in light of the swift response of the United States and the simultaneous lack of response by the EC, which exposed a degree of disorganization and lack of strategic planning. As integration proceeds at all levels within the European Community, it appears that the resolution of these problems will come sooner rather than later, issuing in a major transformation and reformulation of the role of Western Europe in the future.

New Concepts of Security

Conceptually, security became much more prominent in the 1980s, and this was mainly due to the influence of the idea and reality of interdependence on both realist and idealist versions of international relations. With this new development both versions were forced to broaden the debate for fear of becoming irrelevant and redundant. This also forced them to elevate security to the center of the debate as a conceptual underpinning rather than place it on the sidelines while elevating concepts such as power and peace. The debate increasingly emphasized the interdependence of relationships of security rather than the traditional and limited views of security on a national level.[28]

Interdependent security also became a much more important concept with the decline in the Cold War, the subsequent collapse of Eastern European communism, and the apparent disintegration taking place in the Soviet Union. Not only were traditional concepts of security rapidly becoming redundant, but also new conceptual thinking about security was being swept along by the tide of events in Eastern Europe and the dramatic changes being played out there. Research on security, think tanks, and analysts all share a similar difficulty in the post–Cold War period, that of what Michael Howard has called "shooting at a moving target."[29]

Post-1945 Conceptions of Security

In the period between the end of the Second World War and the end of the 1980s, the East-West conflict or Cold War was central to the structure and notion of European security. Indeed these terms were synonymous with one another. Even as the Western Allies were finishing campaigns against Nazi Germany, they were already planning to deal with the perceived threat of the Soviet Union. For forty-five years this tension, which fomented, produced, and maintained much conflict and violent strife in the Third World, ironically managed to produce a relatively stable security scenario within European borders.

In the immediate postwar period, two organizations developed in the context of the new security problem. The first was the West European Union (WEU), established in 1948 by most of the major European powers after a Soviet-inspired coup in Czechoslovakia. At this point the Western Europeans began to realize that they would nevertheless still be weaker than the U.S.S.R. without the support of the United States. In April 1949, this problem was rectified with the formation of NATO based on the concept of **collective security**; that is, if any member were attacked then the rest would provide assistance against a common enemy (at least in theory). The alliance was reinforced as the pillar of postwar European security by various Cold War developments that followed, including the Berlin blockade (1948–49) and the Korean War beginning in 1950. These events cemented the security relationship with a shared perception that the common threat to Europe lay in the military power of the Soviet Union and that the United States was an integral and necessary component of European defense. One author recently went slightly further in this analysis, arguing clearly that what counted (and still counts) is not the "North Atlantic Treaty Organization but rather the North Atlantic Alliance. Whilst NATO is its military manifestation, the political substance resides in the Alliance itself."[30]

In fact the concept of collective security has recently undergone a revival as a central concept in security perspectives because it played a major role in the Gulf war and the U.S.-led military intervention against Iraq. The opportunity for such cooperation was in part stimulated by rapidly changing pressures in the Soviet Union, which brought about political change at a remarkable speed. At the European level of affairs the term has changed but its substantive meaning has remained intact. As one author notes, collective security has been seen in terms of an "overarching security system," "pan-European security," "cooperative security," or "expanded CSCE" (Conference on Security and Cooperation in Europe).[31]

Collective security in Europe was appropriate when there was something that resembled or was made to resemble a clear and unambiguous threat (the Soviet Union and the Warsaw Pact) or, in the case of "out of area" scenarios, the cutting off of Middle East oil supplies. This motivation, however, ran out of steam with the dramatic changes in world politics in the late 1980s. In short, not only had the West seen the disappearance of a tangible enemy with the end of the Cold War, but in addition it was claimed that "Western foreign policy . . . is losing the sextant by which its ship has been guided since 1945."[32]

Ironically in his famous effort to deprive the West of "an enemy" Mikhail Gorbachev succeeded in depriving himself of a country and deprived many American conservatives of an enemy they loved to hate. If stability characterized the postwar European security arrangements, then the visible disappearance of the "threat" to those arrangements ironically created uncertainty and confusion as to how to proceed in the new context. Previous definitions no longer applied, new ones were still to be worked out, and this left the notion and practical working of security in a virtual state of anarchy. Having achieved first prize in the Cold War, the West felt uncomfortable in delineating a new role for itself.

Confused Institutions

If a particular year can be attached to the demise of the Cold War and the confusion engendered in European security concerns, then that year would be 1989, when Eastern European states were given the opportunity to choose their own governments and East and West Germany were reunified. Despite the political flux and change this was to generate, few would question the monumental significance of this period for the structure of security in Europe and the Soviet Union. In 1991 the military role of the Warsaw Treaty organization (NATO's counterpart) was effectively terminated. The immediate agenda of the security apparatus was, of course, to mop up any final remnants of Cold War hostility and ensure that Eastern Europe made a successful transition to democracy. Apart from the crisis in Yugoslavia this proceeded fairly smoothly, with organizations such as NATO playing a passive role.

This left a question that begged (and still begs) to be answered. If the threat from the East had all but vanished (and the subsequent collapse of the Soviet Union confirmed this), then what would be the role in European security of NATO, a body whose effective raison d'etre was predicated on a threat that had ceased to exist by the end of the 1980s?

New Roles for NATO and CSCE

The view that the terms *East* and *West* were no longer justified as part of a security agenda was not simply a perception on the part of observers of international affairs or political scientists; such views had a material effect upon the actual NATO security establishment. At a meeting of the International Security Council in Belgium in March 1991, NATO's associate secretary general for political affairs, Henning Wegener, argued that the idea of the common enemy was a thing of the past. He argued quite clearly that in terms of security, "the source of that threat is now being reconstructed [and that NATO was operating] in a much newer environment" because there was no longer an "apparent enemy." Europeans were now "dealing with a new concept of security." Whereas previously such thinking was "impoverished by its exclusive focus on the Soviet Union," the new concept of security was seen as more expansive than simply providing a military response to any specific threat. Security was seen as shifting in emphasis to situations of crisis and how to deal with them, with the assumption that there is no longer an "apparent" enemy.[33] In fact, there is an enemy, but it is difficult to locate.

Not only is the military role of NATO unclear but its political agenda is uncertain in the new context of European security. As the *Economist* put it,

> NATO's generals must now plan for something they dread perhaps more than the actual enemy: Uncertainty. In future, NATO's re-

maining soldiers can expect to do their fighting, if at all, less in defence of NATO territory than in defence of Western interests in the wider world. It would be foolish to think that military threats to Europe had disappeared. The trouble is identifying them.[34]

As an organization, NATO had had problems to contend with ever since the 1960s, as the economic affluence of Western Europe and its sense of self-confidence had increased in the postwar decades. In 1966, France withdrew from the military command of NATO, illustrating that the alliance itself had internal difficulties in terms of its political balance. Western Europe and its citizens were beginning to demand more say in their own security. Many West Germans, for instance, adamantly demanded that nuclear weapons be removed from German soil, taking to the streets to vent their feelings over such important issues. West Germans were also more interested in making contact with their Eastern counterparts over issues such as the reunification of Germany and detente, a process instigated by Willy Brandt.

The idea that NATO operates in a traditional context, providing Western Europe with an Atlantic alliance against a Soviet threat, is clearly outmoded; reliance on nuclear weapons is being reduced significantly. Already in 1990, the British minister for defence procurement had declared NATO obsolete, its purpose achieved with the winning of the Cold War.[35] However, this may be a fallacious argument, particularly within the context of Serbian aggression against Bosnia in May and June of 1992. In this instance it was argued that NATO's military role was far from obsolete, that NATO was perhaps the only organization with the military capacity capable of ending Serbian aggression and imposing a solution on the Serbs, Croats, and Muslims. Moreover most analysts would still point out that there still exists in the ex–Soviet Union tremendous military capacity that still has not been fully resolved or discarded.

If some are willing to posit that NATO risks irrelevance, and then atrophy, then others are equally willing to counter that it provides a continuing security guarantee in uncertain times.[36]

Other developments in the 1970s already pointed to the emergence of new security arrangements to deal with changing circumstances. The **Conference on Security and Cooperation in Europe (CSCE)**, for instance, was in part an attempt to produce detente between the superpowers. It had several principles that sought to ease the dilemma posed by the two archrivals. On the one hand, it stated that borders could not be changed by force, thus giving the Soviet Union reassurance in its sphere of security. On the other, it provided some commitment to human rights, seizing the moral high ground in dealing with the Communist societies, whether rhetorical or not. Initially set up to improve East-West contacts in the areas of security, trade, and human rights, it rapidly expanded to a grouping of fifty-two nations in the wake of the Cold War, comprising all the European states including countries of the ex–Soviet Union as well as the United States and Canada. Recently, it has widened its scope, holding more meetings and summits. It is important to realize that the CSCE has virtually no military role in comparison to NATO and the emerging European defense community. In the case of the former Yugoslavia, for instance, NATO offered to place peacekeeping forces at the disposal of the CSCE. The difficulty, of course, is getting fifty-two governments to agree on military intervention. It seems difficult to be optimistic about the role of such a large and unwieldy body as a conflict-resolution mechanism, despite the optimism of some observers. Zielonka argues that the CSCE responds to the differentiation of security images and simultaneously is pushed forward by these images.[37] Brock and Holm argue that this development implies that "the CSCE will be better able to cope with the internal tensions arising in the USSR or Yugoslavia than any other international body."[38] However with the process of reform in the ex–Soviet Union itself in a state of constant flux, it remains puzzling how the CSCE could be very effective.

The "new security architecture" developing in Western Europe certainly gained more attention and import with the end of the Cold War. Just exactly what this new "security architecture" is appears at the moment to be more a matter for speculation than anything else. What is clear is that there is a continuing debate over the value, relevance, and utility of all existing European security institutions, whether NATO, WEU, or the CSCE.

If European images of security were dominated by the scenario of Cold War and East-West conflict, this ended with the collapse of Eastern Europe's Communist regimes and the breakup of the Soviet Union. Images of security required and require redefinition. National and supranational security must be defined at the policy level. Specific solutions should be sought for problems of ethnic and racial tension, immigrants, refugees, and such subnational issues as the revival of tribalism in Europe that previously were considered to be in the category of low politics.[39]

In the wake of the Cold War the problem of what constitutes security is undergoing fragmentation and redefinition (or reinvention) as policymakers scramble to invent and construct new versions of security in the evident absence of old ones.[40] In a recent article, Barry Buzan speculates on the nature of some of the new patterns of global security, several of which have come to be increasingly important to the European agenda. These include (but are not limited to) the development of what he argues is a "civilizational cold war" between North and South as a result of resistance to the hegemony of the West. At the forefront of the resistance will be Islam, which with the apparent breakdown of communism in ideology and practice will assume this role by default. This will be a great clash around identity and culture and the "threats and vulnerabilities that affect patterns of communal identity and culture."[41] It represents a threat from the periphery to the center and revolves around such issues as migration, religion, and identity. Buzan identifies other areas where security will become much more important, such as the environment, and more specifically the issue of boundaries and where they are drawn. This latter issue of course has been given special significance by the breakup of the Soviet Union and the crisis in the former Yugoslavia. Other writers such as Stuart Hall discuss the relationship between boundaries and identity. He notes that Eastern Europe is a boundary that has always been problematic for Western Europe: where does Europe stop and Asia begin? This for Hall is a critical question, because of its relationship to economic prosperity but also in terms of identity and the question of "others." As he notes,

> Now that a new Europe is taking shape, the same contradictory process of marking symbolic frontiers between inside and outside, interior and exterior, belonging and otherness, is providing a silent accompaniment to the march of 1992.[42]

And clearly it is the ideas of migration, race, and fundamentalism that are encouraging the development of symbolic and not-so-symbolic frontiers.

Another version of this redefinition of security involves the support of democratic reforms. The idea of course is to further influence the behavior of erstwhile enemies, changing them into staunch allies: "security policy has not only an antagonistic element but also a cooperative one in terms of attempting to influence the behavior of a potential enemy."[43] Political rhetoric about rewards for good behavior and punishment for human rights abuses is apparent in elite statements and throughout the media in the West.

If we regard the relationship of the state to security in international relations as underpinning the conceptual development of the term, then we can argue that there have been several changes and consequences for Europe. First and foremost at the supranational level, there are attempts being made to internationalize the problem of security. The term "globalization" has been used frequently to describe emerging patterns of security. States in an interdependent world have found it increasingly difficult to operate in terms of the idea of national security, and there are a number of indications that in defining new security agendas they are also attempting to elevate security to a supranational basis (e.g., in efforts to deal with drug problems, AIDS, crime, terrorism, immigration, pollution and the environment). These are problems that cut across state borders and several writers have suggested them as useful additions to broaden the concept of security.[44] Whereas security has traditionally been seen in the light of relationships between states involving alliances, sovereignty, and deterrence, it is now being extended to include other areas, including the domestic economy and society. In that sense security is "expanding" conceptually to deal with the new circumstances.

There is a widespread movement away from simply approaching security in terms of military issues, because other issues have been elevated in political salience and importance. In addition, other actors have increasingly come to play an important role in the provision and enactment of plans for these new versions of security (for instance the role of interior ministers in the Trevi forum, the Schengen agreements, and the ad hoc committee on immigration). In the next section I briefly examine the emergence of race and immigration on the new agenda in order to illustrate how security is being expanded.

European Security: The Dilemma of Immigration

With the demise of the Cold War, the breakdown of Communist regimes, and the disintegrative effects thereof, Europe and the community are faced with the problem of immigration on a massive scale. The period between 1989 to the present has really brought this issue home to the policymakers in the EC.

Postwar Immigration in Europe

After the Second World War, when Europe was in disarray and a virtual state of collapse, various regimes welcomed the vast influxes of immigrants from the Third World. They in effect provided employment for the displaced, and then when the Communist states were established they turned to southern Europe, North Africa, and the ex-colonies for a fresh supply of labor. By the middle of the 1970s one-tenth of the work force of France and West Germany were of foreign birth; Yugoslavia for instance had exported 10 percent of its workers. The immigrants in turn helped their host societies to develop and modernize their industrial infrastructures while receiving low wages and poor conditions for their efforts.

This period of immigration influxes came to an abrupt end with the 1973 oil shock, an event that changed many aspects of life in Europe. As inflation and unemployment rose in concert, so also did resentment against immigrant workers, even though many of the native workers would have been loath to fill the immigrants' shoes or status positions.

The relationship of race and immigration has become an important and highly problematic issue on the political agenda in Western Europe. This has occurred not only in terms of the domestic agenda but also at the level of supranational concern (i.e., the EC). Several questions are important here. What kinds of evidence do we have that this issue has become increasingly salient in political terms? How important is the comparative postwar immigration experience of France and Germany in this regard? And what kinds of theoretical explanations have been offered recently to provide a fuller understanding of this phenomenon, this apparent demographic and political crisis that Europe faces? Finally, it may be useful to consider the political implications of such relationships in the context of the "new" Europe of the 1990s.

There has been a great deal of discussion in the last few years—indeed, since the middle of the 1970s—on this topic, but only in this more recent period have these two related issues come to occupy such a dominant position in literature and in the media headlines. Several questions are interesting in this regard. First, it is necessary to provide some evidence to support this claim, that immigration has indeed become more salient. What evidence is there that indicates this? Second, what is the background to the immigrant problem, and how can we compare in this regard France and Germany, two of the central architects of the new Europe, and Germany certainly the most important economic power. And third, what kinds of explanations have been offered for aspects of this relationship, and what therefore are the political implications for the EC, for this so-called new Europe, and for the new context of race and immigration in the 1990s?

With the end of the Cold War in the late 1980s, it appears that the issues of race and immigration (though always on the agenda) have become more pressing and direct. The traditional concept of security rooted in East-West conflict is changing very rapidly to concern with other types of security. And in turn these types of security, or "threats" to European security, are more and more being defined in terms of immigration (legal and illegal), drugs, terrorism, and the environment. Again these are issues that have always been on the agenda but have hitherto been regarded as less important than the Cold War scenario. So the East-West conflict has apparently been displaced by a new enemy, or a new threat has been conjured up to replace the old one.

To some extent this movement is related to the broader aspect of the movement towards European union, EC 92, and the formulation of a common defense and security strategy. It can be seen, in other words, that while the European Community wants to eliminate internal borders and allow for the free flow of goods and services and European labor, at the same time it is also busy trying to erect external barriers to protect itself from what some regard as an unwelcome invasion, in part from the former Communist countries to the east and the ex–Soviet Union, and in part from the poor underdeveloped nations to the south, and specifically from what policymakers regard as the mahgrebin countries of North Africa (Algeria, Tunisia, Morocco, etc.).

Following on from that point, there are several indicators at the level of policy response to provide evidence that in fact the security agenda is changing.

The first type of response arose as early as 1976 in the wake of the oil shocks. It was prompted by the United Kingdom and consisted of a forum for interior ministers from EC countries to try to initiate policies relating to internal problems. This group set up liaison networks between the police forces and security systems of individual states, particularly to deal with questions of terrorism, political violence, and extremism. By the late 1980s, specifically by 1987, it had expanded its concerns to include the free movement across borders (including immigration, visas, asylum seekers, and border controls).

A second response was the Ad Hoc Group on Immigration set up in October 1986. Again it consisted of the interior ministers from each EC member, and again it was initiated at the U.K.'s suggestion. It sought to end the "abuses of the asylum process," and it passed a series of measures to deal with unwanted asylum seekers.

A third response was the **Schengen Agreement**, outside the overview of the EC. Initially this was a separate intergovernmental agreement signed in 1985 by Germany, France, Belgium, the Netherlands, and Luxembourg in an effort to harmonize policy on visas, coordinate crime prevention, and so on.

Inside the Schengen area, the principle of free movement applies to all EC nationals. There are also arrangements for tourists, asylum seekers, and legal immigrants from nonmember countries. The police within the area still operate according to national rules, but they adopt a different approach in that closer cooperation makes the external controls at the borders more effective.

In 1990, the second agreement, Schengen No. 2, was signed, and Italy, Portugal, and Spain were included. The group's purview was also expanded, becoming similar to that of the **Trevi Committee**, a cabinet-level EC board that formulates common policies to combat terrorism, drugs, and illegal immigration. Schengen provides for the exchange of information on new asylum seekers. Schengen countries have also agreed on a common list of about 115 countries whose nationals require visas to enter Schengen territories. And included in these are most of the refugee-producing countries of the Third World. The EC has argued that the Schengen measures constitute a laboratory of what the twelve (the EC) will have to implement by 1992. In other words the problems faced by Schengen are the same problems faced by the community.

Other major evidence that these issues of race and immigration have become highly politically salient may of course be drawn from the growth of political parties (particularly the Front National in France) who have a regular electorate across the board, maintain a dedicated following and support, and operate at all levels in national affairs and EC affairs. The Front National has managed a consistent 15 percent in French elections since the 1980s and did very well in the six by-elections at the parliamentary and municipal level in France in 1991.

Second, there have been major attacks on members of the immigrant community (the Turks) in the wake of the German reunification process and the revival of neo-Nazi groupings. These attacks have also, of course, occurred in France against Jews and North African immigrants. In other events, the Salman Rushdie affair in the United Kingdom, race riots, the shock results of the Belgium elections in 1991 in which an extreme right-wing party, the "Vlaams Bok" or "Flemish Bloc" obtained 10 percent of the votes in Flanders and 25 percent of the vote in Antwerp—all are indicators of the steady movement towards the politics of race and immigration. These issues appear to be coming to a head in the wake of EC 92, German reunification, and the end of the Cold War. The Pandora's Box of racism has apparently been opened up.

Before discussing the two cases of Germany and France, it is worth reflecting on why there was actually such large immigration in the postwar period. The reasons are fairly simple. After independence for the colonies in the Third World was achieved, there was a massive outpouring, a tremendous exit of people from the Third

World to the first. There was a real need for the industrialized countries to secure cheap labor to provide for the postwar reconstruction of Europe, and this labor came from the south, from the Third World. It is doubtful now whether countries like France could have developed modern economies without this cheap labor supply; in fact I would argue that French modernization was predicated upon the securing of this cheap labor. Note in this version of things that it is the actual labor, not the laborer, that is important.

The postwar social and economic developments in Western Europe coincided with one of the largest migratory waves in history between 1945 and 1974. Both France's and Germany's modernization and development were fueled and facilitated by cheap immigrant labor. Both seem in some ways to perceive the issue as a cultural problem; what they fear is Islamic fundamentalism to some extent. Both have been in the process of strengthening and tightening all immigration laws since, restricting and trying to get rid of the immigrants since 1974.

Explanations: Theoretical Views on Immigration

One of the most often cited and worked on views comes from political economy to explain the position of the modern immigrant in society. That is that cheap Third World labor was instrumental, indeed necessary, for the reconstruction of the economies of Europe in the post–Second World War period. By the early 1970s there were 11 million migrant workers in Europe who, in the words of *Fortune* magazine, were "indispensable to Europe's economy." As we see, they are of course seen as dispensable in times of economic recession and stagflation. The eighth French plan is quite clear on this, and I will quote it to illustrate how many felt about the role of the worker in industry:

> The new worker no longer needs to possess a specialist knowledge required by a long apprenticeship. Nor does he even need to have skills in writing or speaking French. He is required to perform duties of a repetitive nature fixed in advance and regulated by others. The ideal labour force is one that can be easily redeployed, needing only the barest training to be fully productive.[45]

And the view of the French government and European planners in general was that the immigrant was best suited to fill this role.

Europe in this view was divided into first-class and second-class citizens, or white and black, or indigenous workers and guest workers. In this sense the argument was made that class differences were being and are being overlaid and reinforced by racial and ethnic differences, a view that was first made clear by Freeman in his 1979 book on immigration and racial conflict.[46] In fact a two-tier work force has emerged in Europe, and it was completely reinforced in an institutional sense with the advent of EC 92, when citizens of member countries gained the right to travel across borders in search of work while guest workers were disallowed; this says much about the new freedom-of-labor movement in the new Europe.

In addition the policy responses (Trevi, Schengen, etc.) are clearly authoritarian in nature and may give us an insight into the new European state. As Maj. Gen. Clutterbuck has argued, "With so many immigrants in the EC, foreign terrorists can hide as easily as indigenous ones."[47] The next logical step for the right is, of course, to equate immigrants with terrorists in a manner similar to drug addicts. The trick would be to make each term synonymous with the other; then you have reduced different problems into one simple threat (and it all comes from the Third World anyway).

Another view following on from the first one and echoed on the left is that racism is not an internal phenomenon of individual states but is becoming a supranational issue. That is, Europe is moving from ethnocentric racism to Eurocentric racism, from the different racisms of different member states to a Common Market racism based on the notion of a white Europe. In this arrangement Spain, Portugal, and Greece, traditionally Europe's southern and poorer countries, are now receiving immigrants. Some predict that Spain will function as a southern European police force over the human mass from the mahgreb. These and some of the East European states are regarded in security terms as front-line states against an invasion of immigrants. Spain, France, Italy, and Portugal are attempting to establish a Conference for Security and Cooperation in the Mediterranean modeled on the European version. The fear of mass migration is certainly widespread: when the Albanians tried to land in southern Italy last year, the Italians' response was not to sympathetically receive people fleeing communism but to offer the Albanian government 62 billion lire in aid. This may of course have some unintended beneficial consequences for the Third World in terms of the transfer of resources from north to south in an effort to keep immigrants out.

All of these are factors in an increasing movement towards the politics of race and immigration and the emergence of these on the security agenda. In other words there is a move to Europeanize national and supranational issues traditionally seen as on the security agenda.[48] And these have implications for NATO, which handled traditional security concerns; the defense of European borders is, ironically, coming to mean something else.

These changing attitudes toward security started to find expression in the Paris charter in 1990, which was dominated by two assumptions. One has already been mentioned and is more of a fact than an assumption, that is, that the Cold War has ended and as a result the chance of East-West conflict has been significantly reduced. What Barry Buzan addressed as the East-West overlay has disappeared. A second assumption of the charter is that Europe needs to address the new "undercurrents" of conflict that had previously been ignored or suppressed by the East-West scenario—in other words, the "demands for prosperity and social justice and the rights of national minorities to democracy and freedom."[49]

The Fall of the Soviet Union: Implications for Europe

The end of the Cold War and the disintegration of the Soviet Union had enormous implications for Western Europe and its security arrangements—implications that will take several decades to work themselves out. Claims of a new "world order" were immediately heard in the days following the demise of the Soviet Union, but the fact remains that the complex chain of events on a global scale and their implications will be debated for decades to come. Clearly any new world order cannot arise overnight. The disappearance of two antagonistic military alliances at the end of the 1980s led to the end of a bipolar system, to be replaced by a multipolar arrangement. What would the new security arrangements be? The term "new security architecture" rapidly became the language in frequent use among politicians, the media, and security organizations. That there was a reconfiguration of power was not difficult to see, and much of the language of international-relations experts became redundant.

Three developments were of particular importance. First, the decline of the Soviet Union's power is of course probably the most important sea change in global politics because it paved the way for other major changes. Not only did the Soviets lose their sphere of influence and ability to control events in Eastern Europe, but also their multinational empire fell apart. When the U.S.S.R. collapsed on December 8, 1991, a monolithic bloc dissipated into fifteen different sections; the most striking feature of the new world map in 1992 was the establishment of fifteen independent national states that were internationally recognised. And these new states were in themselves by no means monolithic but subject to grave internal divisions and disputes. The formation of the Commonwealth of Independent States (CIS) was to replace the old Soviet Union as a revised arrangement, but already it had major problems. At the time the Soviet Union disintegrated, at least 164 ethno-territorial conflicts and claims had been identified within its boundaries (almost twice the number that had been identified only eight months earlier). Clearly the fall of the Soviet Union and its empire had created immense problems that allowed for political and social changes at other levels.

As a direct result of the decline of Soviet power, the second development, the reunification of West and East Germany, became possible. This second change saw the reemergence of the German "problem" or "question," which is concerned with the position of Germany in Europe. Can a powerful Germany be constrained peacefully by the remaining European powers? What exactly is Germany's role in Europe? And how can it be integrated within the European scenario? Between 1870 (the initial German unification) and 1990 (the second, present period of unification), no real solution to this dilemma was achieved. In the meantime, two world wars were waged, and after the second of these, in 1945, Germany was divided into ideological divisions, as in the wider sense was Europe.

When the Berlin wall (the symbol of that division) collapsed in 1989, the Soviets' influence in Eastern Europe also in turn disintegrated. The question still remains whether a powerful Germany can be firmly anchored within the "new" Europe.

The third development is the changing role of the United States as a major actor within Europe. Both the United States and the Soviet Union have lost their dominant positions as Germany has become more important, followed by France and the United Kingdom, and also perhaps by the reemergence of Russia. In other words the bipolar world of Europe between 1945 and 1990 has given way to the multipolar world of the various European powers (at least in the context of Europe) in the post–Cold War period—a return to the scenario but not the context of the pluralistic power configuration that dominated Europe before 1940. In fact, one expert has argued that the post–Cold War period has certain similarities with that of nineteenth century Europe in the sense that it represents "government without governance." In both of these periods there is a certain need for a new order in which cooperation between the great powers would be the central aspect within the broader framework of a "global community interest."[50]

The question remains of whether the Europeans can and will pursue some conception of collective security that will stabilize the multipolar system now forming. Certainly it is a possibility, given the "historic opportunity" to continue the peace which has prevailed since 1945. One would like to think that this could be organized on the basis of the European Community, but the EC's record in dealing with the Yugoslavian crisis appears to suggest that it has serious problems in organizing an effective collective security system. Institutions such as the EC, NATO, and the CSCE (the Conference on Security and Cooperation in Europe) already exhibit a high degree of institutionalization but appear to lack the political will to solve some of the most important security issues and to define their roles in a post–Cold War world of uncertainty.

Disintegration of Yugoslavia and the Role of the EC

The Balkans, which covers southern Hungary, Rumania, Bulgaria, Albania, and the former Yugoslavia, were clearly held together by a disciplined Communist state apparatus in the wake of the Second World War. The democratic revolutions that swept Eastern Europe and the Soviet Union in 1989 led to the disintegration of these regimes and in many ways the glue that held the diverse ethnic groups and peoples of this region together. Nowhere has the disintegration of communism been more disastrous than in the case of Yugoslavia. No one—intelligence agencies, academics, or journalists—predicted or even came close to predicting the decline of communism in the Soviet Union and the subsequent disintegration of its apparatus in the Soviet Union and Eastern Europe in 1989. Some Yugoslavians predicted violence after their longtime Communist leader, Joseph Tito, a man who had held the federation together, died in 1980. It is unlikely that any of them could have foreseen the extent and depth of the barbarity, however. The events took the Eastern bloc as much by surprise as they did the West. The dismemberment of the U.S.S.R. and Yugoslavia had far-reaching consequences that will take decades to unravel. Yugoslavia was a federation made up of six republics (Boznia-Herzegovina, Croatia, Macedonia, Montenegro, Serbia, and Slovenia) and two provinces (Kosovo and Vojvodina)—eight federal units in all. It consisted of 24 million people with twenty-four different ethnic affiliations and three major religions, encompassing the very diversity and in turn the fragility of Europe.

Since 1990, the disintegration of the Yugoslavian federation has been discussed in various new (and not-so-new) terms and concepts. It has been described as Balkanization—the process of larger states breaking up into several smaller ones, a process usually seen as negative, the idea being that smaller states are less viable than large ones. Other concepts discussed include retribalization of ethnic minorities and a crisis of nationalism and legitimacy. Perhaps the most famous new term to emerge is "ethnic cleansing," the attempt by one group to forcibly eradicate another through various means. One horrific method of this, for instance, is the rape of Muslim women in Bosnia by Serbian soldiers. The Yugoslavian ideal that groups and peoples that have historically been contentious could come together in peaceful cooperation has fallen apart, giving way to destructive nationalist and ethnic rivalries.

All of these concepts contain elements of the truth. The savagery and brutality that has been displayed in the period since the demise of communism at once prompts and yet defies most rational explanations. To understand the situation and the way in which it has an impact on Western Europe, it is necessary to understand some of its history—a history of conflict in many respects.

Historically the Balkans lie at the crossroads of European history and empires: the fourth-century division of the Roman Empire, the eleventh-century division of Christendom, and the seventeenth-century border between the Ottoman and Habsburg powers. And these fault lines have not gone unnoticed in modern times, as ancient feuds and myths are actively reengaged to foster nationalist aspirations. In fact there is continuity in terms of the conflict, an ongoing one. Discontinuities have clearly appeared in the types of regime and government in the region during the past few hundred years. But its history is replete with massacres, political violence, and internecine strife. In this sense it has always proved to be a difficult and problematic area. The First World War had its origins in events that took place in Sarajevo in 1914. In fact, Yugoslavia did not come into being until the end of World War I in 1918, when a Slavic union was formed consisting of Serbs, Croats, and Slovenes and including Montenegro and Bosnia-Herzegovina. Even then the name for this mixture did not appear until 1929, when King Alexander decreed the country to be Yugoslavia, "land of the South Slavs." Ethnic tensions in this "first" Yugoslavia were always apparent and surfaced intermittently through various forms of government during this period—relative pluralism in the 1920s and monarchical dictatorship in the 1930s. Between 1941 and 1944 a puppet Fascist government run by Croatia was established by the Axis powers; they waged a vicious racist campaign against the Serbs and the Jews, and a period of internecine strife and civil war among ethnic and national groups set in prior to the end of the war. Many of the memories, myths, and tragedies of this period helped to fuel the conflict after 1990. It was only the Croatian guerrilla leader, Josip Broz Tito, who emerged at the end of the war as Marshall Tito, who provided the region a unity hitherto unseen in its history. When he died in 1980, the federation, based on an ideology already in decline, began to fall apart. Tito may have been a progressive leader by Eastern bloc standards, breaking free of Soviet and Stalinist domination in 1948, but it was doubtful that the system could have long survived his demise. In January 1946 a republican federal constitution was initiated, and Yugoslavia was divided into six republics modeled on territorial units. The idea was to create a state with centralized Communist control but a significant degree of autonomy for each republic to give allowance for nationalist aspirations. This apparent paradox was a success in the following forty-five years until the collapse of Communism, when as the *Economist* has put it, the odds of history appeared stacked against it: "A geopolitical fault-zone. Religious and national rivalries. Lack of democracy. Ancient feuds. World War. Genocide."[51] It is a dark historical picture where death and tragedy are constant features of the landscape.

In these terms, then, Yugoslavia was an artifice, a product of external power rivalries and international conflict. With the end of strong leadership in 1980, and the end of any ideological glue in the form of communism, the revival of old historical scores seems in retrospect unavoidable.

The contemporary tragedy was initiated in June 1991 with a ten-day war in Slovenia, when nearly 3,000 federal soldiers from the Yugoslav army were sent in a futile attempt to prevent Slovenia from seceding from the federation. The operation was a failure. Thereafter, a seven-month war between Serbia and Croatia took place, with a January 1992 ceasefire organized by the United Nations bringing a partial halt to the conflict. Croatia lost a third of its territory; Yugoslavia by this time has almost shrunk to two republics, those of Serbia and Montenegro. In April 1992, a three-sided war started in Bosnia between Croats, Muslims, and Serbians. Clearly the media and world opinion have arraigned the Serbs, who appear to have committed many atrocities; the victims have been mainly Muslim, attacked by both Serb and Croat militia. By the end of April 1992, the Bosnian capital of Sarajevo, a place that has seen a surfeit of history this century pass before its eyes, was under siege by the Bosnian Serbian forces. Trade sanctions were enacted against the culprits, Serbia and Montenegro, in May 1992 by the United Nations, and a naval blockade was enforced in November of the same year. Full trade and diplomatic isolation was finally enacted in April 1993. This and various attempts at ceasefires, which have all failed, and various peace plans, which have also failed, were the efforts to persuade the parties involved to end the conflict.

The extent and scale of the killing in ex-Yugoslavia are less complicated than the causes and implications. Since the war began in 1991, thousands and maybe tens of thousands have died in the most savage civil strife to be seen on European soil since the end of the Second World War. Massacres, mass rapes, and ruthless shelling of towns have reached new levels of atrocity. Nearly 4 million Yugoslavian refugees have been created, according to UN estimates, and clearly the potential is far greater.

The Balkans in southern and eastern Europe have always evoked images of crisis, instability, and war to historians, geographers, and political scientists alike. It was Sarajevo in Yugoslavia that provided the decisive flashpoint for the beginning of the First World War (1914–18), and it is cities within the former Yugoslavia, like Sarajevo, that have seen the historic tragic events and new ones.

Yugoslavia and the EC

In one of its first and foremost major roles in the aftermath of the Cold War and then the gulf war of 1991, the community has failed to bring any acceptable sort of solution to the conflict. Indeed this may be hardly surprising, given the context and the complexity of the situation. One senior official from the European Commission in Brussels pointed out, "Europe has made a decision about Yugoslavia. . . . It has decided not to have its people killed there."[52]

But regardless of whether the EC decided not to have its own blood shed over Yugoslavia, it has tried through various diplomatic and physical efforts to end the conflict, mostly unsuccessful. The EC tried to mediate through Lord David Owen after the failure of NATO's Lord Carrington, along with the UN's Cyrus Vance. The intent was to divide the states even further as autonomous provinces based along ethnic lines. However the peace plans they devised in an effort to bring an end to the conflict have all been rejected by nationalists intent on pursuing their own plans.

In mid-1991, along with the United States, the EC prohibited the sale of arms to ex-Yugoslavia. In November 1991, it placed trade sanctions on Serbia and Montenegro. Several options were available to the West and the EC in this matter, but procuring agreement was a real obstacle. One option would have been to bomb Serbian targets in Bosnia directly in order to force a solution upon recalcitrant Serbs. Another indirect response was to provide the Bosnian Muslims with arms (a solution favored by Margaret Thatcher for instance), but the UN arms embargo applicable in all the states went against such a policy. Easing sanctions and the creation of safe havens for the civilians caught in the middle were the other type of option. Again the most marked thing about these different options was the degree of disagreement over their principle and implementation. Events in the

Balkans appear to be a paradox for all concerned, given the proximity to Western Europe and the trend towards integration in the European Community in the late 1980s and 1990s. The paradox concerns the twin processes of integration and disintegration taking place side by side. While nationalism was being perceived as a spent force, it was revived in the Balkans, driven by old and new ethnic nationalist claims.

However the problem of the Balkans did not simply originate with the end of the Cold War; it is several centuries old and driven by deep geopolitical premises.

And perhaps because of this, there appears widespread reluctance on the part of the United States and Western Europe under the EC to become more embroiled in the situation.

What is clear now is that the only force capable of acting against the Bosnian Serbs and the warring factions in the former Yugoslavia is NATO, and this means the concept of an "Atlantic Alliance" in which the United States plays a major part. This became increasingly clear in February 1994 when finally there was an ultimatum placed on the Serbs to remove their heavy weaponry from around the besieged city of Sarajevo and gradually lift the siege or face NATO air strikes. Without decision making at the top of the American military command, it would appear that Western Europe cannot pursue an independent policy in such scenarios.

The lesson that Europeans have drawn from history is that perhaps Bismarck was close to the target when he maintained that the Balkans are more trouble than they are worth. Still the region remains a historical problem that is likely to continue for a long time to come.

Conclusion

In the rapidly changing world of perceptions and reality of European security, it would be naive to provide any hard and fast tenets of the shape of security to come. In saying this, however, it is striking that new security concerns have emerged in the post–Cold War period. In part these still revolve around the idea of an "enemy"; previously it was convenient to use the Soviet Union. Now, however, threats appear less tangible, frontiers become symbolic, defining threats more difficult. Still the effort is being made; immigration, race, fundamentalism, identity, changing boundaries, among others, are becoming part of the package of "new" threats. Boundaries can also be used to delineate the poor Europeans from the rich ones.

The gulf and Yugoslavian crises have highlighted divisions between Europe and the United States and uncertainty within the EC and Europe itself over how to proceed. Confusion reigns over the role of European security institutions and their applicability in the post–Cold War era; consensus is difficult to find, prescriptions are endless.

Even the conceptual language of various proponents shares little. Some stress architectural metaphors such as "structure," "building blocks," or new "security architecture." Others (noticeably the British) prefer gardening examples, such as planting, growth, and fertilization.[53]

However, one thing is crystal clear: the challenges that confront European security are no longer based around one factor or one element such as the East-West scenario. Security has rapidly developed into a multifaceted concept; as one writer posits, "The biggest challenge which the people of Europe confront is how to think differently about security."[54] In this sense, research in political science should focus more and more on the many different faces of security and work to develop interdisciplinary notions rather than being confined to outmoded explanations provided by the field of international relations.

Conclusion

The European Community in recent years has been catapulted onto the world's stage as it strives for economic and political integration. Its drive toward integration has seen continuity in the postwar period, but this ideal is to a large extent a twentieth-century phenomenon. There have been historical efforts of Europeans to unify since early times; the crusaders in the twelfth century, for instance, mounted an early attempt to provide a common European foreign policy based on shared Western values against a common enemy of Muslims. However, it is only in the twentieth century and in the postwar period that we have seen a systematic attempt towards economic and political integration. The increased pooling of national sovereignty in an effort to develop federal union directly continues a train of thought and practice from Jean Monnet, Robert Schumann, and Konrad Adenauer in prewar and postwar Europe to the vision of Jacques Delors in the post–Cold War era.

Both Germany and France had good reasons to push for a united Europe in the post-1945 period. Europe was inherently weak, politically and economically. Internal dissension, two world wars, and the rise of two new superpowers had displaced the Continent as the center of the world's stage. The need to avoid any more military conflict and the accompanying devastation and bloodshed led politicians like Robert Schumann and Jean Monnet of France to devise plans promoting unification. There was, in the last analysis, a growing realization that a united Europe would be better served economically, politically, and in terms of security if united rather than divided. Furthermore, it seemed apparent that the advantages of pooling resources clearly outweighed the costs of maintaining divisions. After 1992, the European market of 320 million people will constitute the world's largest trading bloc, as opposed to twelve separate markets. Potentially there are enormous gains to be made from this simple fact. The changes of 1992 should add at least 5 percent to the community's GDP, perhaps creating 2 to 5 million new jobs in the process for a Europe that has suffered from high unemployment as a result of heavy costs, uncompetitive industries, and low productivity. A single integrated Europe will allow for economies of scale in manufacturing and allow the bloc to compete but not necessarily dominate within the international economy.

Despite the rapid pace of economic integration, there are of course some problems and discontinuities that threaten the integration process. We have examined the problems of the Common Agricultural Policy, the European Monetary Union, and other related difficulties, noting the divergence in members' views and the apparent inequalities in terms of benefits. The difficulties over the process of political integration, denoted by the debate over Margaret Thatcher's version of a Europe des Patries and Delors's federal arrangements pose a continuing dilemma, particularly in light of the Danish rejection of the cornerstone of European political integration in 1992, the Maastricht treaties. New dilemmas over what constitutes security and how to construct a meaningful defense in light of the collapse of the Soviet Union and Eastern Europe and the end of the Cold War also pose grave problems for a united Europe. Divisions over policy in the gulf war and the crisis in the former Yugoslavia indicate that we have somewhat less than a united Europe on many important issues. And we noted that European boundaries regarding immigration are hazy and in distinct need of redefinition, and the task for Euro-politicians is to devise solutions to such problems. Given that there is a degree of pessimism, one would do well to ponder just how far Europe has come in the years since 1985 and the acceptance of the single European Act. It has in effect made major strides.

When the European integrationist and French statesman Aristide Briand wrote his famous memorandum on May 17, 1930, arguing that economic union was unavoidably linked to security and security is a matter related to collective political decisions, it is unlikely that he foresaw the massive political changes that would occur sixty years later. However, he was politically astute enough to point out that the way forward was to develop common structures and institutions. Nowadays, the realization of that prescription in real economic and political terms seems inevitable, but clearly it has a long way to go given the recurrence of regional, national, and ethnic aspirations in the "new" Europe of the nineties.

Key Terms and Concepts

Each term appears in the text in boldface type.

Collective security
Common Agricultural Policy
   (CAP)
Common Market
Conference on Security and
   Cooperation in Europe
   (CSCE)
Council of Europe
Europe des Patries
European Coal and Steel
   Community (ECSC)
European Community (EC)
European Currency Units
   (ECU)
European Defense Community
   (EDC)
European Economic
   Community (EEC)

European Monetary Union
   (EMU)
European Political Community
   (EPC)
Exchange Rate Mechanism
   (ERM)
Federalism
Maastricht
North Atlantic Treaty
   Organization (NATO)
Schengen Agreement
Single European Act
Sovereignty
Subsidiarity
Supranationalism
Trevi Committee
United States of Europe
Western European Union (WEU)

7
Conclusion

In 1965, one author wrote that the "meaning of the word Europe has never changed," that "everyone knows what it is, and has the same notion of [Europe] as someone from the Middle Ages, or the enlightenment."[1] This is a clear misunderstanding of the context of European history, for as we have seen throughout the text, the meaning of Europe has changed enormously over the past few thousand years, often in dramatic and startling ways. Contemporary differences between political elites, policies, and public opinions show quite clearly that there are many different versions of what Europe constitutes and sharp divergences over the future of the European Community, a relatively new institution in the history of Europe.

At the beginning of this book I quoted an author who argued that the so-called new Europe was not really new at all, that it was in fact a curiously "old fashioned and American . . . concept." That is an interesting version of reality. It is startling that a continent that has experienced bloodshed and violence on a grand scale should reemerge in a new version sponsored by the EC as the consumer's dream, the world's largest single market. Europe since 1945 for most people has been a place of relative calm; the war that erupted in the Balkans in the 1990s illustrates that such peace and stability is a tenuous reality in a Europe that over the centuries has been drenched in blood.

In this sense, Europe and its various political systems, cultures, and peoples have had more than their fair share of discontinuities. The Balkans problem is not a new one; the region has been the scene of strife for at least several hundred years. The basic problems of identity, legitimacy, penetration, participation, and distribution have never been fully resolved here. They have been suppressed under the surface as religion, ethnicity, and age-old hatreds were under the Communist system after the Second World War. These discontinuities are not only apparent in the Balkans; one need look no further than Northern Ireland to see a violent and bizarre civil strife where religious and political loyalties are intermingled. For the uninitiated observer, the province must seem more akin in terms of political violence and its bitter effects to the Third World than to the advanced industrialized nation of which it is part, the United Kingdom. Terrorism, the Mafia in Italy, acts of violent anti-Semitism in France, neo-Nazis beating up poor Turkish immigrant workers in the newly re-unified Germany—hardly a scenario of an affluent paradise.

Discontinuities appeared to develop at a fast and furious pace at the close of the 1980s. Eastern Europe and the Soviet Union experienced various popular and elite revolutions in which the old Communist and hard-line orders collapsed and in many cases were replaced with fragmentation and the revival of ethnic strife. Czechoslovakia divided in two, the Yugoslavian federation fell apart, and everywhere, there were millions of refugees—people on the move, people leaving for political and economic reasons. German reunification, itself a major dislocation, saw a country coming together after more than forty years apart. Two societies that had experienced two separate political, social, and economic systems had little in common with each other. It was a traumatic experience, a marriage of reluctant partners with little chance of a honeymoon. It will take several decades before East Germany is fully constituted into the Federal Republic in terms of political and social integration.

These are not new agendas; they are old ones, they have been around for several centuries, and will continue to dominate the political menu for a long time to come. The dark undercurrents of Europe are visibly evident in the contemporary situation in Yugoslavia; they represent a problem for all parties concerned—individual nations, ethnic groups, and the larger institution of the European Community. Politics in this sense is rarely about continuity, not unless one can argue that the long line of discontinuities that we have seen in European politics actually "represents" continuity. As we have seen, to some extent there may be some merit in this argument.

It is clear in many of the cases that the idea of crises is a prominent feature in European politics, and that we can compare these crises across the board, cross-nationally in order to gain a better understanding and more useful perspective of the development of these different societies. We have seen, for instance, from a cross-national perspective that the issues of race, immigration, and ethnicity pose distinct problems for all societies. In some cases these problems are more apparent than in others (for instance presently in France and to a lesser extent Germany), but no European society seems immune to the dislocations of the modern world. Political violence is experienced across different nations in various forms; the United Kingdom, despite its history of political stability, sees acts of terrorism carried out on the British mainland and the periphery of Northern Ireland in a "war" that has been around for nearly 400 years by some accounts. Basque separatists in northern Spain continue to challenge central government; various Mafia groups in Italy constantly undermine the legitimacy of the state. And violence is perpetuated in France and Germany against various groups and institutions.

It is also clear that crucial questions of distribution and the allocation of wealth and resources have not been fully or even partially resolved in most of these so-called "advanced" industrialized nations. The gap between the haves and the have nots is likely to remain a permanent feature of the "new" Europe. Divisions between north and south are also important agendas for Western European countries and the EC. The gap between Italy's rich industrial North and the poor South (or mezzogiorno) is well known, but equally there is economic division between regions in the United Kingdom with a poor and mainly Celtic fringe and a core area of wealth and affluence, exacerbated by the "British disease." At the level of the EC such divisions are also seen between the northern EC countries and the poorer southern and Mediterranean societies, such as Greece, Spain, and Portugal. And as we noted in the section on the EC, Jacques Delors sees the task of political and economic integration to reduce these differences of inequality as highly important.

Europe has been the battleground for ideological cleavages throughout the last few hundred years, as witnessed by the Second World War. These cleavages will not disappear simply because communism has apparently disappeared. There will still be the great questions of social justice to be answered in the new Europe, because there will still be inequalities and uneven benefits. This is in the nature of capitalism, which is an imperfect system, and it is doubtful whether such issues can ever be fully resolved.

Continuity and discontinuity have been the broad themes of this book and the hope is that these can be assessed without imposing a completely rigid framework. We have seen that Europe and its nations have experienced large doses of both, some more than others but experienced nonetheless. At the beginning we posed the dilemma of the water levels in European societies, suggesting as Solzhenitsyn did that some may get lost in the river of history. Europe is not lost at this present stage; it is swimming to shore but at the same time dark undercurrents threaten to engulf it. In this sense the European Community may just be the life raft which ensures continuity and Europe's ability to overcome rather than be swamped by its problems.

Notes

Chapter 1: Introduction: Patterns and Trends in Western European Politics

1. Walter Russell Mead, "Dark Continent," *Harper's*, April 1991, pp. 45–53.

2. Hans Magnus Enzenberger, *Europe, Europe: Forays into a Continent* (New York: Random House/Pantheon, 1989).

3. Raymond Grew used the idea of five distinctive crises to explain the processes of political modernization in Western Europe from a comparative perspective. See Raymond Grew, et al., *Crises of Political Development in Europe and the United States* (Princeton, N.J.: Princeton Univ. Press, 1978).

4. Mattei Dogan and Dominique Pelassy, in *How to Compare Nations* (Chatham, N.J.: Chatham House, 1984), suggested this idea and many other excellent reasons for comparing different nations.

5. George Santayana, *The Life of Reason*, vol. 1, *Reason and Common Sense* (1905–6).

Chapter 2: The United Kingdom

1. For an excellent discussion of this period in more detail and the differences between Scottish and Welsh nationalism, see A. H. Birch, *Political Integration and Disintegration in the British Isles* (London: George Allen and Unwin, 1977).

2. The problem was that only 32.5 percent of the *total* electorate in Scotland said yes to these proposals, and while more voters voted yes than no, the vote was still not enough to secure devolution.

3. Richard Rose, *Politics in England*, 5th ed. (Glenview, Ill.: Scott Foresman/Little Brown, 1989), pp. 16–17.

4. Simon Lee, "Vague and Slippery Values," *The Listener*, Aug. 14, 1986, p. 6.

5. Philip Norton, *Constitution in Flux* (Oxford: Martin Robertson, 1982).

6. See Anthony Wright, "British Decline: Political or Economic?" *Parliamentary Affairs* 40, no. 1 (Jan. 1987): 41–55. This article provides a useful overview of some of the views that dominated the literature of British decline.

7. For useful overviews of John Major and the Conservative party leadership in general, see Edward Pearce, *The Quiet Rise of John Major* (London: Weidenfield and Nicholson, 1991), and Robert Shepherd, *The Power Brokers: The Tory Party and Its Leaders* (London: Hutchinson, 1991).

8. Gabriel A. Almond and G. Bingham Powell, *Comparative Politics: A Developmental Approach* (Boston: Little Brown, 1966), p. 50.

9. See Gabriel A. Almond and Sidney Verba, eds., *The Civic Culture: Political Attitudes and Democracy in Five Nations* (Princeton, N.J.: Princeton Univ. Press, 1963). This is the classic work on political culture in this period, reevaluated and rewritten in the light of events in *The Civic Culture Revisited* (Boston: Little Brown, 1980).

10. Almond and Verba, *The Civic Culture*, p. 8.

11. Alan Marsh, *Protest and Political Consciousness* (London: Sage, 1978).

12. Dennis Kavanagh, *Political Culture* (London: Macmillan, 1972), p. 14.

13. See Samuel Beer, *Britain Against Itself* (New York: Norton, 1982), p. 119. Beer devotes several chapters of his book to explaining his version of the collapse of deference.

14. A. King, *Why Is Britain Becoming Harder to Govern?* (London: BBC Publications, 1976).

15. Marsh, *Protest and Political Consciousness*.

16. If one asks, How militant is Britain? Marsh provides various thresholds of protest behavior. For instance, 43% of the sample population indicated that they would only sign a petition and nothing more; 35% said they would go further and take part in lawful demonstrations and even boycotts. Just over a fifth (22%) declared their willingness to enter a third threshold zone of illegal demonstration; half of this group would stop at unofficial strikes and withholding their dues from local authorities (i.e., rent or taxes).

17. Ronald Inglehart, *The Silent Revolution* (Princeton, N.J.: Princeton Univ. Press, 1977).

18. Marsh, *Protest and Political Consciousness*, p. 224. The model of postmaterialism is drawn from the comparative work of Ronald Inglehart, in particular *The Silent Revolution*. See also the survey evidence which supports these interpretations in S. Barnes and Max Kaase, eds., *Political Action: Mass Participation in Five Western Democracies* (London: Sage, 1979).

19. See Brian Wilson, "The 4,000 Pound Early Warning," *The Guard-*

ian, Sept. 21, 1987, for an analysis of just how difficult this tax would be to implement in Scotland. Wilson also points out that the extra cost of running the poll tax in Scotland in comparison to the previous domestic rates would be something in the region of £23 million.

20. *New York Times International*, May 18, 1992, p. 7.

21. John Dearlove and Peter Saunders, *Introduction to British Politics*, 2d ed. (Cambridge, England: Polity Press, 1991).

22. See "Scottish Councillors Burn Payment Books in Poll Tax Protest," *The Independent*, April 1, 1989.

23. In all, 170,000 Protestants were given land in Ulster; 150,000 were Scottish in origin, and the remaining 20,000 were English. Ulster represented the last part of Ireland to be dominated by the English authorities and obviously the most politically significant.

24. A. T. Q. Stewart, *The Narrow Ground: Aspects of Ulster 1609–1969* (London: Faber and Faber, 1977).

25. James Downey, *Them and Us* (Dublin: Ward River Press, 1983).

26. See Edmund Aunger, "Religion and Occupational Class in Northern Ireland," *Economic and Social Review*, 7, no. 1 (1975): 1–17; and Kenneth Christie, *Political Protest in Northern Ireland: Continuity and Change* (Reading, Berkshire, England: Link Press, 1992).

27. See the *Economist*, July 6, 1991.

28. *Economist*, Dec. 4, 1993.

29. *Economist*, Dec. 18, 1993.

30. Adrian Guelke, *Northern Ireland: The International Perspective* (Dublin: Gill and Macmillan, 1988).

31. In this sense I am following the definition of Van Den Berghe, who views *race* as a group that is socially defined on the basis of physical criteria. According to this view, then, the term *race* has no objective reality outside its social definition. See Pierre Van Den Berghe, *Race and Racism: A Comparative Perspective* (New York: Wiley, 1967).

32. V. S. Naipaul, *The Enigma of Arrival* (Harmondsworth, England: Penguin, 1987), p. 131.

33. Ibid., 145.

34. See *Commonwealth Immigration: Control of Immigration Statistics, 1963–74* (London: HMSO) for the figures.

35. Donley T. Studlar, "Political Culture and Racial Policy in Britain," in *Studies in British Politics*, 3d ed., edited by Richard Rose (London: Macmillan, 1976).

36. See A. Marwick, *British Society Since 1945* (Harmondsworth, England: Penguin, 1982) for the Gallup Poll figures and other aspects of British society. Also see V. Sivanandan, "From Resistance to Rebellion," *Race and Class*, 23 (Autumn 1981) for Thatcher's position.

37. See David Butler and Donald Stokes, *Political Change in Britain* (Harmondsworth, England: Penguin, 1971), p. 420, for breakdowns on opposition to immigration.

38. See the *Economist*, Dec. 7, 1991, p. 66.

39. One of the best and most authoritative works on the history of race relations in the United Kingdom is Dilip Hiro, *Black British, White British* (London: Grafton, 1990).

40. These figures are taken from Anthony H. Birch, *Nationalism and National Integration* (London, Allen and Unwin, 1989).

41. See Stuart Weir's argument in "Death Sentences," *New Statesman and Society*, Feb. 15, 1991, p. 16. Also, in the same article, Yasmin Alibhai offers a contrasting view arguing that the conflict is a local one between different communities within the United Kingdom.

42. See Tariq Modood, "British Asian Muslims and the Rushdie Affair," in *Political Quarterly*, 61, no. 2.

43. See Weir, "Death Sentences," p. 17.

44. See the *Independent Magazine*, June 12, 1993.

45. This definition appeared in an article by Michael Banton in *New Society*, Nov. 9, 1967. See also Michael Banton, *Race Relations* (London: Tavistock, 1967), p. 77b.

46. Sheila Patterson, *Dark Strangers* (Harmondsworth, England: Penguin, 1965).

47. See William Gwyn, "Jeremiahs and Pragmatists: Perceptions of British Decline," in *Britain: Progress and Decline*, edited by William Gwyn and Richard Rose (London: Macmillan, 1980).

48. See Anthony Wright, "British Decline: Political or Economic?" *Parliamentary Affairs*, 40, no. 1: 41–55.

49. See Tom Nairn, *The Breakup of Britain* (London: New Left Books, 1977).

Chapter 3: France

1. This quote is from Henry Ehrmann, *Politics in France* (Boston: Little, Brown, 1983), p. x. Ehrmann noted that Henry Kissinger had asked the Chinese leader this question during a conversation.

2. See David D. Bien and Raymond Grew, "France," in *Crises of Political Development in Europe and the United States*, edited by Raymond Grew (Princeton, N.J.: Princeton Univ. Press, 1978), p. 233.

3. This table was based on Dorothy Pickles, *The French Fifth Republic*, 3d ed. (New York: Praeger, 1965), pp. 3–5.

4. See Bela Belassa, "The French Economy under the Fifth Republic, 1958–1978," in *The Fifth Republic at Twenty*, edited by William Andrews and Stanley Hoffman (Albany: State Univ. of New York Press) for the comparative figures in the average growth rates in GNP for this period.

5. *Economist*, May 5, 1991.

6. *Economist*, May 11, 1991.

7. *Economist*, Nov. 23, 1991.

8. *The European*, Oct. 18, 1991.

9. Ibid.

10. "L'etat C'est L'Europe," *Economist*, Nov. 23, 1991, p. 3.

11. Alexis de Tocqueville, *The Old Regime and the French Revolu-

tion, trans. by Stuart Gilbert (Garden City, N.Y.: Doubleday, 1955), pp. 210–11.

12. Henry Ehrmann, *Politics in France* (Boston: Little, Brown, 1983), p. 12.

13. Charles Tilly has written a great deal about this. See, for instance, Charles Tilly, *The Contentious French* (Cambridge, Mass.: Harvard Univ. Press, 1986).

14. For a more detailed account of the May events, see Bernard Brown, *Protest in Paris: Anatomy of a Revolt* (Morristown, N.J.: General Learning Press). One author discusses the events as a last "moment of madness"; see Aristide Zolberg, "Moments of Madness," *Politics and Society* 2 (1972): 183–208.

15. See Maurice Duverger, *La Cohabitation des Français* (Paris: PUF, 1987).

16. According to James Shields, the electoral rise of the Front National is the most remarkable development in France since the left won its historic mandate in the presidential and parliamentary elections of 1981. See James Shields, "The Politics of Disaffection in France in the 1980s," in *Political Culture in France and Germany*, edited by John Gaffney and Eva Kolinsky (London: Routledge, 1991).

17. George Mosse, *Toward the Final Solution: A History of European Racism* (London: J. M. Dent and Sons, 1978), p. xv.

18. Ehrmann, *Politics in France*, p. 7.

19. Mosse, *Final Solution*, p. 110.

20. See *Le Monde*, May 15, 1990.

21. Geoffrey Harris, *The Dark Side of Europe* (Edinburgh, Scotland: Edinburgh Univ. Press, 1990), p. 20.

22. Ibid., p. 85.

23. *Le Monde*, July 6, 1992.

24. See George Ross et al., eds., *The Mitterand Experiment: Continuity and Change in Modern France* (Oxford: Oxford Univ. Press, 1987), pp. 136–39, and James Shields, "Campaigning from the Fringe: Jean-Marie Le Pen," in *The French Presidential Elections of 1988: Ideology and Leadership in Contemporary France*, edited by John Gaffney (Aldershot, England: Gower, 1987).

25. See Max Silverman, "Traveilleurs, Immigres, and International Relations," in *World Politics*, edited by Robert Aldrich and John Connell (London, 1989), and Michael Piore, *Birds of Passage: Migrant Labour and Industrial Societies* (Oxford: Oxford Univ. Press, 1980).

26. *Le Monde*, June 6, 1990.

27. Ibid.

28. See Georges Sorel, *Reflections on Violence* (London: Allen and Unwin, 1925). Sorel (1847–1922) was a revolutionary theorist who argued that the role of the "myth" was more important in political mobilization than rational principles. Therefore, logic and observation are unimportant in comparison to emotional triggers such as courage, enthusiasm, and sacrifice.

29. Edmond Alphandery, UDC, *Le Monde,* June 6, 1990.

30. See R. W. Johnson, "Wars of Religion," *The New Statesman and Society,* Dec. 15, 1989, for a useful account of this episode and the effect it had on electoral support for Le Pen.

31. *Le Monde,* June 6, 1990.

32. See Harris, *Dark Side of Europe.*

33. Yves Simon, *The Road to Vichy: 1918–28,* rev. ed. (New York: University Presses of America, 1988).

34. Le Pen argued that immigration had reached the status of a moral menace in France because the "evolution which is born of the divergence of demographic pressures in the world will, if it is not dyked, submerge our continent." See Peter Lennon, "Le Pen and the Kristallnacht of Carpentras," *Guardian Weekly,* May 27, 1990.

35. *Le Monde,* April 8, 1990.

36. Shields, "Politics of Disaffection," p. 142.

37. *Le Monde,* April 8, 1990.

38. Otto Kircheimer, "The Transformation of Western European Party Systems," in *Political Parties and Political Development,* edited by J. Palombara and M. Weiner (Princeton, N.J.: Princeton Univ. Press, 1966), pp. 192–93.

39. As Steven Wolinetz notes, the catch-all thesis ran into several problems in the 1970s as Western European party systems became more, not less, fragmented, belying the effectiveness of catch-all strategies. Moreover, the entrance of environmental parties formed around particular issues further undermined this view, which seemed rooted in the context of the 1960s. See Steven B. Wolinetz, "Party System Change: The Catch-All Thesis Revisited," *Western European Politics,* 14, no. 1 (1991). Also see Peter Mair, "Continuity, Change, and the Vulnerability of Party," *Western European Politics,* 12, no. 4 (1989), and Gordon Smith, "Core and Persistence: System Change and the 'People's Party,' " *Western European Politics,* 12, no. 4 (1989). Mair and Smith both defend Kircheimer's thesis in explaining party system change.

40. *New York Times,* March 24, 1985.

41. See Jacques Ellul, *Propaganda: The Formation of Men's Attitudes* (New York: Vintage, 1973).

42. Mort Rosenblum, *Mission to Civilize: The French Way* (New York: Harcourt Brace Jovanovich 1986), p. 4.

43. The populations for these overseas departments are as follows: Mayotte, 40,000; Reunion, 500,000 (includes St. Paul, New Amsterdam, Kerguelen, Crozet Islands, and Adelle Land); New Caledonia, 135,000 (includes Isle of Pines and Loyalty Islands); Wallis and Futuna, 9,500; French Polynesia, 138,000 (includes Society, Tahiti, Marquesas, Gambier, Leeward, and Tubual islands); St. Pierre and Miquelon, 5,000; Martinque, 325,000; Guadeloupe, 325,000 (includes Marie Galante, Ile des Saintes, Petite Terre, St. Barthelemy, and St. Martin); and French Guiana, 56,000 (includes St. Joseph, Ile Royal, Ile du Diable) (*Le Monde,* March 28, 1991).

44. Robert Aldrich, *The French Presence in the South Pacific 1842–1940* (London: Macmillan, 1990), p. 323. See also chapter 4 in this book for a useful overview of French economic interests in its Pacific colonies.

45. Phillipe Bernard, *Le Monde*, Nov. 11, 1991.

46. Vincent McHale, "France," in *Politics in Western Europe*, edited by G. Dorfman and P. Duignan (Stanford, Calif.: Hoover Institute, 1988).

47. *Economist*, July 6, 1991, p. 43.

48. Paul Webster, "France's Black Burden," *Guardian Weekly*, June 17, 1990.

49. "Interfering French," *New Statesman and Society*, July 3, 1992.

50. This quote was taken from an interview with Mitterand, *National Geographic*, 176, no. 1 (1989).

Chapter 4: Germany

1. A useful account of the inability of the Weimar Republic to deal with Germany's postwar problems can be found in David Abraham, *The Collapse of the Weimar Republic* (Princeton, N.J.: Princeton Univ. Press, 1981).

2. See Thomas Childers, *The Nazi Voter* (Chapel Hill: Univ. of North Carolina Press, 1983), p. 50.

3. See David Conradt, *The German Polity* (New York: Longman, 1989), pp. 6–9, for a useful summary of the various explanations of the failure of the Weimar Republic.

4. See Ken Smith, *Berlin: Coming in from the Cold* (London: Penguin, 1991), p. 4.

5. See Lewis Edinger, *Politics in West Germany* (Boston: Little, Brown, 1977), for a useful discussion of economic trends.

6. These figures are from Statistiches Bundesamt, *Statistisches Jahrbruch der Bundersrepublik Deutschland, 1979* (Wiesbaden, 1980), and cited in Baker, Dalton and Hildebrandt, *Germany Transformed* (Cambridge, Mass.: Harvard Univ. Press, 1981), p. 10.

7. The recession that the Weimar Republic faced allowed extremists like Hitler to eventually come to power. In 1929, roughly 1 million people were unemployed. By the winter of 1932–33, this number had passed 6 million, which coupled with falling industrial capacity and low wages to produce enormous discontent. Such miserable economic conditions paved the way for Hitler to take over. In the Germany that emerged after the 1945 period, these conditions never approached the same scale. For these and other figures on this, see Joseph Rovan, "Germany: The Great Banking Crash," *Le Monde*, July 22, 1991.

8. Roy C. Macridis, *Modern Political Systems: Europe*, 7th ed., (New York: Prentice Hall, 1990), p. 212.

9. See "Not as Grimm as It Looks," *Economist*, May 23, 1992, which argues that, like all good fairy tales, this one includes "not just a reunited family but monsters (the huge financial cost of unity), goblins (xenophobia and right-wing extremism), witches in gingerbread houses (the European

Community), strangers from dark woods (the lands to Germany's east), and ugly stepsisters (Germany's Western allies, ever fussing for it to take more responsibility, and then sulking when it does)."

10. Eva Kolinsky, "Socio-Economic Change and Political Culture in West Germany," in *Political Culture in France and Germany*, edited by John Gaffney and Eva Kolinsky (London Routledge, 1991), p. 34.

11. See Gabriel Almond and Sidney Verba, *The Civic Culture: Political Attitudes and Democracy in Five Nations* (Princeton, N.J.: Princeton Univ. Press, 1963). Almond and Verba found that only 7% of the West German public at the time were proud of their political system, while 33% were proud of their economic system.

12. See L. Edinger, *Germany* (Boston: Little, Brown, [1968] 1986), p. 81.

13. See David Conradt, "Changing German Political Culture," in *Civic Culture Revisited*, edited by Gabriel Almond and Sidney Verba (Boston: Little, Brown, 1980), pp. 212–72.

14. See Russell Dalton, *Politics in West Germany* (Boston: Little, Brown, 1989). Dalton notes the major social transformation and accompanying trends undergone by West German society in the postwar period. Between 1950 and 1975, for instance, university enrollments increased by more than 500% (p. 81). Conradt also notes that the number of people expressing an interest in politics increased from 27% in 1952 to 57% in 1983; see Conradt, *The German Polity*, 4th ed. (New York: Longman, 1989).

15. In the period between 1972 and 1976, political dissatisfaction with the regime increased from 8% to over 23%. See William Chandler and Alan Siaroff, "Postindustrial Politics in Germany and the Origins of the Greens," *Comparative Politics*, 18: 310–11.

16. See E.G. Frankland, "Parliamentary Politics and the Development of the Green Party in West Germany," *Review of Politics* 51, no. 3 (summer 1989); 386–91.

17. This quote is from Russell Dalton, *Politics in West Germany* (Boston: Little, Brown, 1989), p. 124.

18. Richard Gott, "A State of Anxiety," *Guardian Weekly*, Oct. 7, 1990. Gott quotes some of the few intellectuals in German society who were adamantly opposed to the process of reunification. The American historian Fritz Stern also argued in front of the German Bundestag on June 17, 1988, that "a united Germany has brought untold misery over the world," as reported by Ralf Dahrendorf in "On Your Marks," *Marxism Today*, March 1990.

19. Gunter Grass, *Two States—One Nation: The Case against German Reunification*, trans. by Krishna Winston with A. S. Wensinger (San Diego, Calif.: Harcourt Brace Jovanovich, 1990).

20. Hans Magnus Enzenberger, *Political Crumbs*, trans. by Martin Chalmers (London: Verso, 1990).

21. See Gunter Grass, "The West German Blitzkrieg," *Guardian*

Weekly, Nov. 11, 1990, pp. 22–23, for one skeptical intellectual's version of why the process of reunification was not a cause for jubilation. Also see Arthur Miller, "Anschlus, Angst, and a Great Enigma," *Guardian Weekly*, June 10, 1991, pp. 10–11, for an account of some of the German people's hopes and fears concerning unification.

22. See the *Guardian Weekly*, July 22, 1990, for details.

23. See the *Spectator*, July 1990.

24. See the special report on Germany in the *International Herald Tribune*, April 10, 1991, for some of the fears and prospects that conditioned France's relationship with Germany in the process of reunification.

25. From the Frank Sinatra recording "I'll Do It My Way."

26. *Economist*, Sept. 14, 1991.

27. Ibid.

28. *Guardian Weekly*, Feb. 2, 1992.

29. Ibid.

30. *Guardian Weekly*, Oct. 13, 1991.

31. *L'Evenement du Jeudi*, Aug. 27, 1992.

32. See Marc Fisher, "Germans Struggle with History," *Guardian Weekly*, July 11, 1993. Fisher was citing Norbert Gansel, a senior SPD legislator.

33. Peter Schneider, "Belated Marriage," *Time*, July 1, 1991.

34. An excellent study of the contemporary issue of immigrant labor in Germany from a historical perspective is to be found in Ulrich Herbert, *A History of Foreign Labour in Germany*, 1880–1980, trans. by William Templer (Ann Arbor: Univ. of Michigan Press, 1990).

35. See Conradt, *German Polity*, p. 65.

36. See Karl Deutsch and L. J. Edinger, *Germany Rejoins the Powers* (Stanford, Calif.: Stanford Univ. Press, 1959), pp. 40–42.

37. These figures are from a special report by James Ridgeway and Bettina Muller, "Wie Deutsch Ist Es?" *Village Voice*, Dec. 3, 1991, p. 40.

38. Smith, *Berlin*, p. 300.

39. See Daniel Vernet, "Germans Face Identity Crisis," *Le Monde*, Oct. 16, 1991.

40. See Andreas Juhnke, "The Hydra-Headed Monster of Germany," *New Statesman and Society*, April 12, 1993.

41. Ibid., p. 13.

42. See the article by Jonathan Eyal, written for the *Independent* and reprinted in the *Straits Times*, Aug. 2, 1993.

43. See "Attacks Renew Fears of German Racism," *Guardian Weekly*, Sept. 29, 1991.

44. See Laurent Carroue, "The Growing Strength of Germany—East and West," *Le Monde Diplomatique*, Aug. 1990, for an overview of the relative economic strength of Germany and its position in Europe.

45. See "Don't Mention the Wall," *Economist*, April 6, 1991, for these figures.

46. See "There She Blows," *Economist*, May 23, 1992, for these figures.
47. Ibid.
48. See *Newsweek*, May 1992. This analogy was suggested by Meinhard Eigel, director of the Institute for Economy and Society in Bonn.

Chapter 5: Italy

1. Joseph LaPalombara, *Democracy, Italian Style* (New Haven, Conn.: Yale Univ. Press, 1987), p. ix.

2. For an analysis of *risorgimento* as a form of European nationalism, see Peter Alter, *Nationalism* (London: Edward Arnold, 1989).

3. Salvadori has argued in this sense that "Italians are a nation but not a homogeneous race. Culture and tradition, not biological traits, give them unity." See Massimo Salvadori, *Italy* (Englewood Cliffs, N.J.: Prentice-Hall, 1965).

4. Ian Hamilton, *The Appeal of Fascism* (London: Anthony Blond, 1971).

5. Detailed historical material on Italian politics is provided in Dennis Mack Smith, *Italy: A Modern History* (Ann Arbor: Univ. of Michigan Press, 1969), and Martin Clark, *Modern Italy: 1871–1922* (New York: Longman, 1984). Various different views on the evolution of fascism in Italy can be found in *Italy from the Risorgimento to Fascism*, edited by A. William Salamone (New York: Doubleday, 1970). Alistair Hamilton, in *The Appeal of Fascism* (London: Anthony Blond, 1971), has also produced an interesting work, which deals with why famous writers and intellectuals were attracted to the doctrine of fascism in this period.

6. Frederic Spotts and Theodor A. Weiser, *Italy: A Difficult Democracy* (Cambridge: Cambridge Univ. Press, 1986), p. 217.

7. See Spotts and Weiser, *A Difficult Democracy*.

8. One author provides evidence that supports claims of political stability in Italy. He argues that the change "in the distribution of the vote in the Italian Republic has been minimal. . . . The Christian Democratic party (DC) varied in voting strength from 38.2% to 39.1% from 1963 until 1983, when it fell to 32.9%. The DC has dominated the governmental coalition since 1946, and it provided every prime minister until 1981. This remarkable electoral stability exists against a background of massive social and economic changes that have transformed Italy in a single generation." See Samual Barnes, "Secular Trends and Partisan Realignment in Italy," in *Electoral Change in Advanced Industrial Democracies* (Princeton, N.J.: Princeton Univ. Press, 1984), p. 205.

9. Spotts and Weiser, *Italy: A Difficult Democracy*, p. ix.

10. *Economist*, July 23, 1988.

11. Dante Germino and Stefano Passigli, *The Government and Politics of Contemporary Italy* (New York: Harper and Row, 1968).

12. Giacomo Sani, "The Political Culture of Italy: Continuity and Change," in *The Civic Culture Revisited*, edited by Gabriel Almond and Sidney Verba (Boston: Little, Brown, 1980).

13. The respective figures for France, the U.K., and West Germany in this period were 45%, 38%, and 22%, a startling difference between these and the Italian case. See Paul Ginsborg, *A History of Contemporary Italy, 1943–1988* (London: Penguin, 1990), statistical appendix, p. 443.

14. See Norman Kogan, *The Politics of Italian Foreign Policy* (New York: Praeger, 1963).

15. See Gabriel Almond and Sydney Verba, *The Civic Culture: Political Attitudes and Democracy in Five Nations* (Princeton, N.J.: Princeton Univ. Press, 1963), and Almond and Verba, eds., *Civic Culture Revisited.*

16. The question was asked in this way, "Speaking generally, what are the things about this country you are most proud of?" It was an open-ended question, meaning that the respondents came up with their own answers. For Italians, the largest category of answers was "Nothing" or "Don't know." After this, they cited the physical attributes of Italy but rarely mentioned politics or the political system as a reason to be proud. See Almond and Verba, *Civic Culture,* p. 102.

17. Ibid.

18. See Sani, "Political Culture of Italy."

19. Luigi Barzini, *The Italians* (London: Hamish Hamilton, 1966).

20. Almond and Verba, *Civic Culture,* pp. 135–36, 185, 267.

21. Sani, "Political Culture," p. 306.

22. On the other hand, it has been argued that Italian elections are not that important in a comparative sense. As the *Economist,* March 28, 1992, put it, "The world tends to ignore Italian elections. There is, after all, no obvious connection between them and the governments that come and go with such frequency (50 in 45 years)."

23. *Economist,* March 21, 1992.

24. See "Zuppa Milanese," *Economist,* May 16, 1992, p. 16.

25. See William Drodziak, "Decline and Fall in Italy," *Guardian Weekly,* March 7, 1993.

26. Ibid.

27. See Sani, "Political Culture," pp. 310–14. Compared to other European democracies there was relatively weak support for forms of direct action. Under 50% of the population approved of the act of signing a petition; only 4% of those interviewed claimed to have participated in a building sit-in, while most Italians strongly objected to any forms of violence against property and persons. This is hardly evidence of a "protest culture."

28. See "Italy's Earthquake," *Economist,* April 11, 1992.

29. See Raphael Zariski, *Italy—The Politics of Uneven Development* (Hinsdale, Ill.: Dryden Press, 1978), p. 126.

30. Spotts and Weiser, *Italy: A Difficult Democracy,* p. 185.

31. *Economist,* July 27, 1992, p. 39.

32. *Economist,* June 8, 1991.

33. *Economist,* April 3, 1993.

34. See Sian Griffiths, "Don among Dons," *Times Higher Education Supplement,* Oct. 15, 1993, for this quote.

35. *Economist*, Nov. 20, 1993.

36. Henry Tanner, "Red Brigade Intimidates Italians, But Fails in Efforts to Start Civil War," *New York Times*, May 17, 1978.

37. LaPalombara, *Democracy, Italian Style*, pp. 169–70.

38. Ibid., pp. 283–84.

39. See Robert B. Adolph, Jr., "Terrorism: The Causal Factors," *Military Intelligence*, July–Sept., 1982.

40. Bianfranco Pasquino and Donatella della Porta, "Interpretations of Italian Left-Wing Terrorism," in *Political Violence and Terror: Motifs and Motivations*, edited by Peter Merkl (Berkeley: Univ. of California Press, 1986). Another author, Pisano, also argues that terrorism derived from the "social inadequacies, political contradictions, and governmental weakness and permissiveness . . . in contemporary Italy." See Vittorfranco Pisano, "The Red Brigades: A Challenge to Italian Democracy," *Conflict Studies*, 120 (July 1980).

41. This question is posed in Robert Katz, *The Ordeal of Aldo Moro* (New York: Doubleday, 1980), p. 285. For other implications of the case, see Vittorfranco Pisano, *The Dynamics of Subversion and Violence in Contemporary Italy* (Stanford, Calif.: Hoover Institution Press).

42. Spotts and Weiser, *Italy: A Difficult Democracy*, p. 184.

43. For these figures, see Frank Wilson, *European Politics Today* (New York: Prentice Hall, 1990), p. 396.

44. Spotts and Weiser, *Italy: A Difficult Democracy*, p. 193.

45. Marco Martiniello and Paul Kazim, "Racism in Paradise?" *Race and Class* 32(3)(1991):80.

46. For this argument, see ibid., pp. 82–83.

47. For this report, see the *International Herald Tribune*, Aug. 19, 1991. Hundreds of refugees refused to budge from their position at Bari, however, citing economic and hunger reasons, "We are poor. We are fighting for our lives," one student argued. Another said (in Albania), "For supper, I eat only a tomato." *International Herald Tribune*, Aug. 13, 1991.

48. See the *Economist*, Aug. 17, 1991.

49. *Guardian Weekly*, Aug. 18, 1991.

50. As noted in the *International Herald Tribune*, Aug. 9, 1991, the problem was different for both sets of authorities involved: "It was clear that the exodus was an embarrassment to the Albanian government, slowly emerging from decades of Stalinist oppression, and also a serious headache for Italian authorities, who want the desperate migrants to stop regarding this as the promised land."

51. For this quote, see "Italy Confronts a Quandry: Albanian Refugees," *International Herald Tribune*, Sept. 19, 1991. In addition, see the *Guardian*, Aug. 16, 1991, for reports from the Spanish paper, *La Stampa*, on the plight of refugees.

52. *Fortune*, July 13, 1992.

53. See Massimo Roccas, "Italy," in *Integration and Unequal Development: The Experience of the EEC*, edited by Seers and Vaitso (London:

Macmillan, 1980), for the relevant indexes of regional differences in Italy over a twenty year period. Also, a very useful and stimulating analysis of the underdevelopment of the economic system of southern Italy is provided by Adrian Carello, *The Northern Question: Italy's Participation in the European Economic Community and the Mezzogiorno's Underdevelopment* (Newark: Univ. of Delaware Press, 1989).

54. Jacques Bethemont and Jean Pelletier, *Italy: A Geographical Introduction* (London: Longman, 1983).

55. Wilson, *European Politics Today.*

56. Carello, *The Northern Question*, p. 115.

57. See Bethemont and Pelletier, *Italy*, p. 105.

58. Wilson, *European Politics Today*, p. 330.

59. This quote is from E. Scalfari, "Un paese diviso tra le Alpi e le Piramidi," *La Repubblica*, Jan. 9, 1987. See Ginsborg, *A History of Contemporary Italy*, p. 530.

Chapter 6: The European Community: Beyond the Nation-State

1. Quoted in A. Sampson, *The New Europeans* (London: Hodder and Stoughton, 1986), p. 6.

2. There are many sources dealing with the initial and subsequent moves toward a European Union. The European Community has a series of documents that deal with this and other related topics. See, in particular, *European Unification: The Origins and Growth of the European Community* (1990). Other useful works are Roy Pryce, *The Dynamics of European Union* (London: Pinter, 1987), and Juliet Lodge, ed., *European Union: The European Community in Search of a Future* (London: Pinter, 1986). The field has become a real growth industry in publishing terms in the last few years, so there is no shortage of material on the subject.

3. Churchill had previously argued for such an idea in October 1942 when he wrote to his foreign secretary, "I look forward to a United States of Europe in which the barriers between the nations will be greatly minimized and unrestricted travel will be possible. I hope to see the economy of Europe studied as a whole." See Ernest Wistrich, *After 1992, The United States of Europe* (London: Routledge, 1989), p. 23, for this quote and, in general, for the federalist arguments for European unification.

4. H. L. Mason, *The European Coal and Steel Community: Experiment in Supranationalism* (The Hague: Martinus Nijhott, 1954), p. 4.

5. See Richard Isaak, *European Politics: Political Economy and Policy-Making in Western Democracies* (New York: St. Martins Press, 1980), on the initiation of these plans.

6. Michel Albert and James Ball, *Toward European Economic Recovery in the 1980s: Report for the European Parliament* (New York: Praeger, 1984).

7. Wistrich, *After 1992, The United States of Europe*, p. 5.

8. *International Herald Tribune*, Dec. 12, 1991, p. 3.

9. *Economist*, July 11, 1992.

10. Ibid.

11. The same writer pointed out that the essential point was not that CAP had "failed to concentrate help on poor farmers, but that it is incapable of doing so. Because most of its support is based on price per unit of output, it is inevitable that the larger farms (which are also the richest) will receive most support. We should therefore be quite unsurprised when we hear that 75 percent of EC support goes to the richest 25 percent." See Robin Simpson, "Feeding Poverty," *New Statesman and Society*, Dec. 8, 1989, p. 15.

12. William Nicoll and Trevor C. Salmon, *Understanding the New European Community* (Hemel Hempstead: Harvester Wheatsheaf, 1994), pp. 135–36.

13. *Economist*, Nov. 30, 1991.

14. *Economist*, Nov. 2, 1991.

15. Martin Feldstein, "The Case Against EMU," *Economist*, June 13, 1992.

16. *Economist*, Dec. 14, 1991.

17. There is a fairly large literature on the idea and practice of integration. One leading theorist describes it conceptually as the "process whereby political actors in several distinct national settings are persuaded to shift their loyalties, expectations, and political activities toward a new centre whose institutions possess or demand jurisdiction over the pre-existing national states." See Ernest Haas, *The Uniting of Europe* (Oxford: Oxford Univ. Press, 1958), p. 16. Also see Panayiotis Ifestos, *European Political Cooperation: Toward a Framework of Supranational Diplomacy?* (Brookfield, VT: Gower UK/Ashgate, 1987). For an overview of these theories and also for another perception, see C. Pentland, *International Theory and European Integration* (London: Faber and Faber, 1973).

18. L. Lindberg and S. Scheingold, *Europe's Would-Be Polity*, (New York: Prentice-Hall, 1970), p. 3.

19. Wistrich, *After 1992, The United States of Europe*, pp. 12–18. For additional excerpts from Thatcher's speeches, see Nicol and Salmon, *Understanding the New European Community*, p. 257.

20. See Dominic Lawson, "Saying the Unsayable about the Germans," *The Spectator*, Dec. 1, 1990, p. 8.

21. See "Crossed Channel Communications," *Guardian Weekly*, Dec. 22, 1991.

22. Klaus-Dieter Borchardt, *European Unification: The Origins and Growth of the European Community*, Jan. 1990, published by the EC.

23. For an exposition of a staunch federalist position, see David Marquand, "Now Is the Hour," *New Statesman and Society*, Jan. 26, 1990, pp. 12–13.

24. Borchardt, *European Unification*.

25. Jacques Delors interview, *Guardian Weekly*, April 5, 1992.

26. This quote was a response to the attempts of the European Commu-

nity to present a common stance against Iraq. See the *German Tribune*, Feb. 17, 1991, p. 2.

27. *The Straits Times*, Oct. 8, 1990.

28. This period started to see a convergence in the agendas of realists and idealists with interdependence and the concept of security. This was especially so with the changes in East-West relations after Gorbachev came to power in the Soviet Union and, of course, this process has continued to the present day.

29. Michael Howard, "Shooting at a Moving Target," *Times Literary Supplement*, March 13, 1992, pp. 7–8.

30. John Leech, *Halt! Who Goes Where?: The Future of NATO in the New Europe* (London: Brassey's 1990), p. 31.

31. See Joseph Joffe, "Collective Security and the Future of Europe: Failed Dreams and Dead Ends," who refers to CS as the *"idee clef"* in the post–Cold War security debate in Europe. As Joffe notes, in early 1992 the German Social Democrats included an "expanded NATO" in this classification, which would include Russia and the other former Soviet Republics.

32. Charles Maynes, "America Without the Cold War," *Foreign Policy*, no. 5 (Spring 1990).

33. International Security Council, *Nato and the Changing Geo-Political Environment* (Brussels: NATO, 1991), p. 9.

34. *Economist*, Feb. 15, 1992.

35. See the *International Herald Tribune*, Dec. 27, 1990, and the *Independent*, Jan. 30, 1991.

36. Quoted in Howard, "Shooting at a Moving Target." See Richard Ullman, *Securing Europe* (London: Adamtine, 1992), and Adrian Hyde-Price, *European Security Beyond the Cold War* (London: Sage, 1991). See also "Why NATO?" *Economist*, May 23, 1992, for support for the continued existence of NATO and the value of the American security contribution.

37. Jan Zielonka, "Europe's Security: A Great Confusion," *International Affairs*, 17, no. 1 (1991).

38. Lothar Brock and Hans Henrik-Holm, "European Security in Transition: Overlay and Undercurrents," paper delivered at the 1991 International Political Science Assoc. World Congress, Buenos Aires, Argentina, July 21–25, 1991.

39. Stuart Hall, "Europe's Other Self," *Marxism Today*, Aug. 1991, pp. 18–19. Hall argues that the "two favourite markers in this discourse are 'refugees' and 'fundamentalism.' "

40. Ian Davidson, "The Search for a New Order in Europe," *International Affairs*, 66, no. 2 (1990): 275–83.

41. Barry Buzan, *People, States, and Fear*, 2nd ed., (Boulder, Colo.: Lynne Rienner, 1991), p. 447.

42. Hall, "Europe's Other Self," p. 18.

43. International Security Council, *NATO and the Changing Geo-Political Environment*, p. 10.

44. See Barry Buzan et al., *The European Security Order Recast: Sce-*

narios for the Post–Cold War Era (London: Pinter, 1990); N. Brown, *The Future Global Challenge: A Predictive Study of World Security, 1977–1990* (London: RUSI, 1977); and Jessica T. Mathews, "Redefining Security," *Foreign Affairs*, 68, no. 2.

45. A. Perotti, "L'Immigration en France depuis 1900," *Projet*, no. 171–72:17.

46. Gary Freeman, *Immigrant Labour and Racial Conflict in Industrial Societies: The French and British Experience, 1945–1975* (Princeton, N.J.: Princeton Univ. Press, 1979).

47. Richard Clutterbuck, *Terrorism, Drugs, and Crime in Europe after 1992* (London, 1990), p. 153.

48. See Brock and Henrik-Holm; "European Security in Transition," p. 5.

49. "Charter of Paris for a New Europe," Nov. 1990, Paris, Mimeo. Cited in Brock and Henrik-Holm, "European Security in Transition."

50. See K. J. Holsti, "Governance Without Government: Polyarchy in Nineteenth-Century European Politics," in James N. Rosenau and Ernst-Otto Czeimpel, eds., *Governance Without Government: Order and Change in World Politics* (Cambridge: Cambridge Univ. Press, 1992), p. 56.

51. *Economist*, Aug. 22, 1992.

52. "Annus Horribilis for Europe as the War Clouds Gather," *Guardian Weekly*, Dec. 6, 1992.

53. Howard, "Shooting at a Moving Target, p. 8.

54. Michael C. Pugh, ed., *European Security Towards 2000*, (Manchester, U.K.: Manchester Univ. Press, 1992).

Chapter 7: Conclusion

1. See Mia Rodriguez-Salagado, "Europe and 1992," *History Today*, 42 (1992):11–16. She quotes Yan Brekilien on this matter.

Index